THE 50 GREATEST ATHLETES IN BOSTON SPORTS HISTORY

THE 50 GREATEST ATHLETES IN BOSTON SPORTS HISTORY

MARTIN GITLIN

Essex, Connecticut

An imprint of The Globe Pequot Publishing Group, Inc.
64 South Main Street
Essex, CT 06426
www.globepequot.com

Distributed by NATIONAL BOOK NETWORK

British Library Cataloguing in Publication Information available

Library of Congress Cataloging-in-Publication Data
Names: Gitlin, Marty, author.
Title: The 50 greatest athletes in Boston sports history / Martin Gitlin.
Other titles: Fifty greatest athletes in Boston sports history
Description: Essex, Connecticut : Lyons Press, [2025]
Identifiers: LCCN 2024052411 (print) | LCCN 2024052412 (ebook) |
    ISBN 9781493084944 (paperback) | ISBN 9781493084951 (ebook)
Subjects: LCSH: Athletes—Massachusetts—Boston—Biography. | Athletes—Ratings of—
    Massachusetts—Boston. | Sports—Massachusetts—Boston—History.
Classification: LCC GV697.A1 G58 2025 (print) | LCC GV697.A1 (ebook) |
    DDC 796.092/274461 [B]—dc23/eng/20250210
LC record available at https://lccn.loc.gov/2024052411
LC ebook record available at https://lccn.loc.gov/2024052412

♾️™ The paper used in this publication meets the minimum requirements of American National Standard for Information Sciences—Permanence of Paper for Printed Library Materials, ANSI/NISO Z39.48-1992.

Contents

INTRODUCTION

Lively discussions often ascending (or descending depending on the point of view) into heated debates have raged for generations. The topic? Who are the greatest athletes in American sports history? And who belongs atop the list of every individual sport?

Names of the all-time greats are spoken with passion and reverence. But it can be legitimately claimed that only one city has boasted the best—those who top the list—in every major sport. And that is Boston. The greatest need not be mentioned in this introduction but sports fans anywhere and everywhere know who they are. Their identities are obvious.

The task here, however, was painstaking. Questions abound when choosing the top 50 athletes to have ever graced a Boston uniform. After all, contrasting baseball players to football players to hockey players to basketball players is far more complicated than comparing apples to oranges. The athletic requirements for each sport differ greatly. Statistics in one have no similarity to that of another. And how does one judge, for instance, a baseball star of the 1940s to a gridiron great of the 2010s?

The answer to the latter question? You don't. One must rank athletes based on dominance during the era in which they competed. Modern athletes are indeed bigger, stronger, faster. That does not mean they are better. Their clear advantages in more sophisticated, year-round training and coaching methods, in-depth statistical analyses that break down opponent tendencies, and financial motivations make any other comparison approaches unfair.

My motivation was to spur fun discussion. Surely most will disagree with at least a few of my selections and rankings. That is unavoidable and even welcome. But what nobody should question is ranker objectivity.

Among the other aspects of these rankings to consider includes the number of players from each team that earned a spot on this list. The Red Sox have the most not only because of the number of tremendous athletes who played for them but also because they have been around the longest—since the American League was born in 1901. Sprinkle in a couple who played baseball for other Boston teams and the explanation becomes obvious. The Patriots have the fewest among those ranked not only because they were born in 1960 but because until Tom Brady ushered in a dynasty, the club had not employed an abundance of players worthy of a ranking among the top 50 Boston athletes of all time.

So read about what made the greatest great with a bonus ranking of the finest athletes ever born in or near Boston. Learn about how their upbringing and the honing of their skills at lower levels affected their careers. Gain knowledge of the critical moments during which the athletes of old rose to the occasion or remember when those in your lifetimes shined and made you happy to be a fan of theirs and their teams.

Don't forget . . . just like the sports themselves, ranking is only a game.

CHAPTER 1

Bill Russell

"The Secretary of Defense"

Bill Russell. Wikimedia Commons, photographer unknown

ESSENTIALS
Sport: Basketball

Born: February 12, 1934

Died: July 31, 2022

Years Active: 1956–1969

Years with Boston: 1956–1969

Position: Center

KNOW THE CAREER NUMBERS
15.1 Points per game

22.5 Rebounds per game

133.6 Defensive WAR

11 NBA championships

5 Most Valuable Player awards

12 All-Star selections

WHY RUSSELL IS NO. 1
Mere statistics cannot do justice to the impact Russell made on the Celtics, the NBA, and basketball. He was simply the most powerful defensive force in league history and perhaps ever in the annals of American team sports. Russell proved the significance of the less glamorous aspect of the game, defending with ferocity, switching onto ballhandlers with athleticism previously unfathomable among centers, blocking shots, and rebounding better than any of his contemporaries. He was the ultimate winner as those annual Celtics championships attest. Only Montreal Canadiens Hall of Famer Henri (The Rocket) Richard matches his 11 titles among all four major team sport athletes.

Russell did not compile the best numbers among those listed here, because those that traditionally shine the brightest in all sports are offensive. He could have scored more, but he recognized the talents of teammates such as Bob Cousy, Bill Sharman, Tom Heinsohn, Sam Jones, and John Havlicek throughout his career. Russell was the man in the middle, a tremendous passer who understood the value of finding open teammates in an offense of constant motion. His selflessness was a key component to team success, particularly in the postseason against the individual brilliance of archrival Wilt Chamberlain.

ALL ABOUT RUSSELL BEFORE BOSTON

The power of William Felton Russell extended far beyond the basketball court. His parents instilled in him that strength while growing up in West Monroe, Louisiana, where he was born. The most bigoted and violent representatives of the Jim Crow South who frightened millions of African Americans into subservience—4,673 were lynched from 1882 to 1936—could not prevent his folks from earning advanced degrees and standing up to terror. His father was attacked by a gun-wielding assailant who refused to wait behind white customers at a gas station. Russell's mother was called a racial slur by a local sheriff for wearing a dress deemed too elegant for a Black woman. Such incidents filled the young Russell with indignation and a strong racial consciousness that spurred action into the civil rights movement and battle for Black power in the late 1950s and 1960s.

The family escaped the oppressive environment of the racist South for Oakland, which resulted in Russell playing basketball for McClymond High School. He performed clumsily and ineffectively, but his size earned him a scholarship to the University of San Francisco. He sprouted to six feet nine inches while gaining coordination, mobility, and skills that transformed him into the most dominant player in the college game. He paired with guard and future Celtics teammate K. C. Jones to transform the Dons into a national power. They won 56 consecutive games and successive NCAA titles. Russell averaged 20.7 points and 20.3 rebounds per game in three seasons, piquing the interest of Boston coach and general manager Red Auerbach. His teams had for six seasons proven to be playoff quality but not championship caliber. Auerbach felt the missing piece was a dominating big man to team with the Hall of Fame backcourt duo of Cousy and Sharman.

NBA history would have changed dramatically had the Rochester Royals, who owned the first pick in the 1956 draft, not already employed star center Maurice Stokes. They provided a path to Auerbach, whose team was selecting too low to snag Russell. So did the Hawks, who had the second choice and was willing to talk trade. The Celtics swapped undersized All-Star center and local St. Louis hero Ed Macauley and even tossed in talented Cliff Hagan for the rights to draft Russell. The deal resulted in the 1958 title for St. Louis and a dynasty for Boston. The Celtics snagged K. C. Jones and Heinsohn in perhaps the greatest draft haul ever for any franchise.

Russell bounced no basketball for Boston until 16 games into the regular season. He remained obligated to the US Olympic team in the process of winning the gold medal in Melbourne.

In a Celtics Uniform and Beyond

Russell adapted to the NBA immediately. The greatest defensive force in basketball history was about to turn the Celtics into a machine. He led the league with 19.6 rebounds a game as a rookie. His impact proved all-pervasive on both ends of the court. His intimidation as a shot-blocker limited opponents offensively, and his rebounding and passing launched the fast-break for which Auerbach and his team became legendary. It allowed nearly eight points fewer per 100 possessions than it had the year before. Teammates even began funneling those they guarded toward Russell, who boasted an unparalleled ability to slide over and cover guards and forwards from the center position. The half-court attack also revolved around Russell and his passing to cutters from the post.

That the Celtics won their first championship after drafting Russell is unsurprising. His 32 rebounds in a double-overtime Game 7 showdown in the finals against Macauley, Hagan, and the Hawks helped clinch the 1957 crown in what many claim to be the greatest battle in NBA history.

Russell's playing career was highlighted by brilliant playoff series and single-game performances, particularly one-on-one against the offensive juggernaut Chamberlain in arguably the most storied individual rivalry ever in American sport. Some argue it was no rivalry despite Wilt the Stilt stuffing stat sheets because Russell perennially emerged victorious. Others assert the Celtics won because they had a better team and system. No matter the viewpoint their fabled on-court battles continue to spark debates six decades later. The greatness of Chamberlain can be affirmed through numbers. That of Russell was unrelated to statistics. Rather, it was his defensive domination, intimidation, ability to make his team-mates better, and overall effect on the game that could never be cited in a box score.

The result was the annual achievement of the ultimate goal. Russell was the most important cog on teams that captured 11 championships in 13 seasons. His brilliance played an integral role in clinching those crowns. He saved his best for last every year. Even Chamberlain recognized his superiority when asked who was better.

"I pick him as the No. 1 center of all time because he was a complete, complete basketball player," Chamberlain said. "I'll pick Bill over me because he also helped his team a lot more than maybe I could have helped my team to win. Sometimes the pure power of you makes you more individualistic. I have said this before, Wilt Chamberlain on the Boston Celtics would not have been the same. Sometimes, less is better, that's how I view it. . . . You can't ask for more from that position."[1]

So educated and tuned had Russell become with the Celtics' style and so inspirational had he grown as a leader that Auerbach installed him as his coaching successor in 1966. It would be another nine years before a major American sports franchise (the 1975 Cleveland Indians when they named Frank Robinson as manager) hired another African American to head a team. Russell guided the Celtics to successive championships, including an upset of Chamberlain, West, Baylor, and the heavily favored Lakers in 1969 in his last series as a player, after which he also retired as a coach.

Most athletes, including superstars, fade from memory when they hang up their sneakers. Russell's impact grew. His status as a role model gained greater strength through his words and deeds. He continued to speak out on civil rights, having participated in 1967 in a famous summit along with other prominent Black athletes to further Black entrepreneurship. He spent decades as an NBA analyst on game telecasts. Most importantly he established himself as the personification of grace, good nature, and humility.

HIS GREATEST GAME

Russell's most epic performance was Game 7 of the 1962 NBA Finals against all-time greats Jerry West, Elgin Baylor, and the Los Angeles Lakers. He scored 30 points and a mind-numbing 40 rebounds in a 110–107 overtime victory. His 19 rebounds in the fourth quarter remain a league record that might never be broken.

SIDE STORY

Russell was heavily involved in the civil rights movement in the early 1960s. When a hotel restaurant in Louisville refused to serve the Black players before an exhibition game in 1961, Russell led a strike of the game. His white teammates did play. Bob Cousy later admitted shame for participating. Russell attended the March on Washington in 1963 and turned down an invitation to sit onstage with Martin Luther King.[2]

WHAT RUSSELL SAID

"The most important measure of how good a game I played was how much better I'd made my teammates play."[3]

WHAT WAS SAID ABOUT RUSSELL

"Bill Russell, the man, is someone who stood up for the rights and dignity of all men. He marched with (Dr. Martin Luther) King; he stood by (Muhammed) Ali. When a restaurant refused to serve the black Celtics, he refused to play in the scheduled game. He endured insults and vandalism, but he kept on focusing on making the teammates who he loved better players and made possible the success of so many who would follow." —President Barack Obama[4]

Chapter 2

Tom Brady

"The GOAT"

Tom Brady in 2019. Wikimedia Commons, All Pro Reels

ESSENTIALS
Sport: Football

Born: August 3, 1977

Years Active: 2000–2022

Years with New England: 2000–2019

Position: Quarterback

KNOW THE CAREER NUMBERS
89,214 Yards passing

649 Passing touchdowns

212 Interceptions

7 Super Bowl championships

5 Super Bowl Most Valuable Player awards

3 Most Valuable Player awards

15 Pro Bowl selections

WHY BRADY IS NO. 2
The debate is over. Lively discussions featuring opinions about the greatest quarterback in NFL history once filled living rooms and bars across America. Was it Johnny Unitas? Joe Montana? But no more. By the third decade of the 21st century it had been greatly acknowledged that it was Tom Brady. He had become the accepted GOAT—greatest of all time.

The reasoning was all-encompassing. It was his accuracy, that rare ability to consistently hit receivers between the numbers and in stride, resulting in critical yards after catch. It was his penchant for rising to the occasion. Teams that gave Brady one minute to drive downfield for the winning score regretted it. It was his leadership. The respect he earned from coaches and teammates was unmatched among quarterbacks in his generation. It was his talent for making his receivers better. Those who might have forged decent careers on other teams gained superstardom with the Patriots. Does anyone truly believe Julian Edelman would have averaged 1,000 yards receiving over five full seasons with anyone else throwing him the ball?

So why is the greatest quarterback ever in the most popular American sport not No. 1? Because Russell not only revolutionized basketball but played his position with far greater athleticism. But take nothing away from Brady. He ended the debate.

All about Brady before New England

Unsurprisingly given his future fiery demeanor on the football field, Brady came from a highly driven family. He was born and raised in San Mateo, California, the youngest of four siblings. His three sisters were passionate athletes who infused in him a competitive spirit and pushed him to maximize his talents. His interest in the NFL emerged early in his youth for good reason. He rooted for the perennial Super Bowl champion San Francisco 49ers in their heyday behind the quarterbacking brilliance of Joe Montana and Steve Young and the GOAT of their own—wide receiver Jerry Rice. Brady attended every home game.

When he wasn't watching football he was playing it at recess and after school. Brady was an altar boy at St. Gregory's Elementary School but did not play quarterback like one. He gained a keen appreciation for the mental, emotional, and physical toughness required to excel. Rather than shy away from such challenges he embraced them. They made him love playing football even more.

Brady was no can't miss prospect. He did not earn the starting job at all-boys, all-Catholic Junipero Serra High School until his junior year. He compiled impressive but not overwhelming statistics, completing 53 percent of his passes for 3,702 yards and 31 touchdowns in two seasons. However his skills motivated the University of Michigan to offer him a scholarship. He accepted it despite having been recruited by the Montreal Expos after he had proven himself as a talented catcher on the baseball team.

Brady spoke often about overcoming the odds throughout his career as an underdog. His college career proved it. He was again forced to wait until his junior year to become a starter (future NFL standout Brian Griese owned that role his sophomore year). When he did take the reins neither his athleticism nor numbers inspired scouts to turn cartwheels over his potential. He averaged 15 touchdowns and eight interceptions as the Wolverines twice fell short of national champion-ship contention.

Those who expressed shock and indignation over the 2000 NFL draft snubs were likely not surprised then. The report released after the scouting combine read as follows: "Poor build, skinny, lacks great physi-cal stature and strength, and gets knocked down easily."[1]

That analysis motivated Brady throughout his career. He spoke often about being more motivated by criticism than praise. He seethed as one player after another slid off the board while he waited. And waited. Six quarterbacks were among the 198 players taken before him. The Patriots finally snagged Brady in the sixth round. He soon made the critics eat their words.

IN A PATRIOTS UNIFORM AND BEYOND

Brady talked about relegation after landing and keeping the starting quarterback job for the Patriots in 2001. He lamented the role of the backup, holding a clipboard on the sidelines, feeling distant from team-mates, and having no role in the outcome of games. He spoke from experience. Brady played backup for two years at Michigan and again as a rookie with New England.

That status proved temporary. Something was happening with the Patriots. It revolved around veteran starter Drew Bledsoe. His starting job seemed tenuous heading into 2001. He had not performed as well the previous two years as he had as a three-time Pro Bowler in the mid-1990s. His touchdown totals were falling. His interception numbers were rising. And the team was losing. Their 5–11 record in 2000 was their worst since 1992.

So Bledsoe was on thin ice before Jets linebacker Mo Lewis caused an ankle injury and severely damaged his lung on a hard hit in Game 2 of the 2001 season. But there is an unwritten rule in team sports. That is, you don't lose your job due to injury. The addendum? You don't lose it unless your backup is Tom Brady. Second-year coach Bill Belichick handed him the reins. And he never let go. Soon Bledsoe was slinging the pigskin for Buffalo.

The 24-year-old Brady was a game manager. He had yet to blossom into the prolific passing machine of his heyday. But he won. He guided the Patriots to enough scoring drives to allow their stifling defense to clinch victories. They won 11 of 14 behind Brady as Belichick refused to reinstate Bledsoe upon his return to health, emphasizing that owner Robert Kraft was paying him to do what was best for the team. The formula resulted in the first Super Bowl triumph in franchise history. Brady tossed just one touchdown pass in the postseason but had established one trait that remained throughout his career. He was a winner. And a Pro Bowler selection. It would become an annual achievement.

So would title contention. Brady led the Patriots to the playoffs every year but one from 2003 to 2019. His regular-season quarterback record during that stretch was an absurd 199–54. His run of eight Super Bowl appearances in 17 years was unprecedented. Though his greatness could never be defined by sheer numbers, it seemed his statistics became more startling every season. He became the first NFL quarterback to throw 50 touchdown passes in 2007. He exceeded 5,000 yards passing in 2011. He emerged that year as the first quarterback to lead a team to a 16–0 record and won both MVP and Player of the Year honors.

He saved his best for last. There was his five-completion drive culminating in a game-winning field goal to beat Carolina in Super Bowl XXXVIII. And his four-touchdown performance to overcome Seattle in Super Bowl XLIX. And his outrageous comeback from a 28–3 deficit to stun Atlanta in Super Bowl LI. One cannot cite such longstanding brilliance and claim a pinnacle. But if there was one that was it. His teammates expressed wonderment over the leadership and unflagging confidence Brady displayed during that harrowing defeat of the Falcons.

"He's laser-focused, and the entire time, there wasn't a time where we looked at Tom like he knew this thing was over," marveled Patriots receiver Chris Hogan after the game. "There wasn't a doubt in my mind. We have one of the best quarterbacks that ever played the game."[2]

One of the best? By that time the argument was over. That Brady was the greatest quarterback in NFL history was widely accepted by then. Some debated who was more responsible for the team's unparalleled success—Brady or Belichick. But it did not matter. The problem was not between Brady and his coach. A fractured relationship with the organization, which refused to commit to keeping him until he reached his goal of playing until age 45, caused his departure to Tampa Bay. That refusal backfired when he won his seventh Super Bowl in 2021 while the Patriots continued to search for their franchise quarterback and had begun to collapse.

Brady finally retired after the 2022 season. Though he ended his career with the Buccaneers he would always be remembered wearing a Patriots uniform.

HIS GREATEST GAME

Brady kicked off the playoffs in style after his outrageous 2011 regular season. He threw for 363 yards and six touchdown passes in a 45–10 pounding of Denver. Included were three scoring strikes to tight end and new favorite target Rob Gronkowski. His 137.6 quarterback rating in the game was the second best of his playoff career, exceeded only by the 141.4 he achieved when he completed 26 of 28 passes with three touchdowns and no interceptions in beating Jacksonville three years earlier. OK, let's call it a toss-up.

SIDE STORY

Brady was far more than a football player. He was a pop culture icon, perhaps the most well-known athlete of his generation. He hosted *Saturday Night Live* in 2005 and voiced himself in an episode of *The Simpsons* that same year. He also appeared in an episode of *Entourage* in 2009 and in the *Entourage* movie in 2015.

WHAT BRADY SAID

"A lot of times I find that people who are blessed with the most talent don't ever develop that attitude, and the ones who aren't blessed in that way are the most competitive and have the biggest heart."[3]

What Was Said about Brady

"It's different when you play him. It's not just that you put him on a pedestal and say, '*This is the greatest of all time,*' it's that this guy is a competitor who can beat you in so many different ways and understands the game at a totally different level. I caught myself rewatching some of the stuff he's done over the years, and it's remarkable how he knows how to find the vulnerable spots, how he knows how to find the perfect play." —Pittsburgh Steelers defensive end Cam Heyward[4]

CHAPTER 3

Bobby Orr

"The Godfather"

Bobby Orr scoring during the 1970 Stanley Cup finals. Wikimedia Commons, Djcz

ESSENTIALS
Sport: Hockey

Born: March 20, 1948

Years Active: 1966–1979

Years with Boston: 1966–1976

Position: Defenseman

KNOW THE CAREER NUMBERS
888 Points

264 Goals

624 Assists

574 Plus/minus

125.1 Offensive WAR

3 Hart Memorial Trophies (MVP)

8 Norris Trophies (Top Defender)

2 Stanley Cup championships

9 All-Star selections

WHY ORR IS NO. 3
Just as Bill Russell revolutionized the center position in basketball, Bobby Orr revolutionized the defenseman position in hockey. Russell did it with defense. Orr did it with offense. Defensemen before Orr focused almost solely on defending. Their forays into offensive playmakers or goal scorers were often the result of fluky puck slides and fortunate positioning. Their mindset was to clear the puck and allow their offensive teammates to take over. Orr rushed up the ice to join the attack. He assisted and scored by design. He did so brilliantly, even leading the NHL twice in points during an amazing six-year run of 100 or more. And he still managed to skate back into position to defend effectively enough to win the Norris Trophy every season from 1968 to 1975.

An athlete of Orr's credentials might have landed atop a list of the greatest in other cities but the best of Boston outclasses most. That he ranks higher than Williams and Bird speaks volumes of his impact. It is rare when the arrival of any athlete spurs an epic franchise turnaround but that of Orr transformed the Bruins from perennial patsies to title contenders, though the May 1967 acquisitions of Phil Esposito and Ken Hodge in a steal of a deal with Chicago certainly helped. They had been the worst team in hockey for nearly a decade before Orr arrived. Within five years the Bruins were two-time Stanley Cup champions.

All about Orr before Boston

Orr would never have graced the ice with his greatness had he not survived sickness at birth. He recovered to display his talent at an early age and soon made his mark. He grew up in the hockey hotbed of Ontario, where his fast-skating, prolific-scoring father Doug had made the Orr name a local legend. Bobby was small as a youth, but his dad groomed him to play forward to take advantage of his speed and puck-handling abilities. Former NHL defenseman Bucko McDonald, who coached Orr in the late 1950s, foresaw his potential in that position. McDonald was a hockey prophet. He envisioned Orr combining offense and defense and encouraged him in that pursuit.

Despite a lack of size—just 5-foot-6, 135 pounds at age 14—Orr began receiving attention from NHL teams even before he hit his teenage years. Taking the lead was Boston, which arranged for him to play with its Junior A hockey affiliate in Oshawa while living at home. He attended no practices but performed well enough in games against much older competition to earn second-team all-league honors. He had become a wunderkind. Despite playing defense with Oshawa he had emerged as a scoring machine. He averaged more than a point per game in his first two full seasons and finished his last year with a ridiculous 38 goals and 56 assists for an average of two points per game.

Orr was still just 18. That was the minimum legal age to play at the highest level. His first professional contract was also the first negotiated by an agent. He immediately became the highest-paid player in NHL history. He was worth it. The Bruins believed he was ready. And he was. The league would never be the same.

IN A BRUINS UNIFORM AND BEYOND

It was the debut of dreams. Orr played his first NHL games at the Boston Garden against the Red Wings and legend Gordie Howe. His impressive performance already had fans and the media talking Calder Trophy as the rookie of the year. He blocked shots, checked with authority, and moved opposing players away from the net. Orr even assisted on a goal in a 6–2 victory. And though such triumphs remained rare for a Bruins team that had still not awakened from its decade-long doldrums, the seeds had been planted for a swift and complete turnaround.

Orr indeed won top rookie honors and even made the all-NHL second team. He placed second in defenseman scoring and displayed an amazing combination of skating creativity and physicality. The ice was his canvas. Critics were unused to an aggressive offensive mindset, and that play style from a defenseman was called reckless. They considered him too daring and claimed his full-speed forays beyond the blue line would eventually wear him down and weaken his defensive effectiveness. They believed his body could not sustain the regular-season grind. They felt vindicated when Orr injured his knee on a mad rush to the offensive end as a rookie. Knee problems did eventually shorten his career. In those 10 seasons with Boston, he established himself as arguably the greatest all-around player in NHL history.

That declaration had been widely spoken before Orr hit his mid-20s. It was no wonder he had already signed the league's first million-dollar contract. Among those who echoed his praises was Bruins coach Tom Johnson. "Bobby has all the tricky moves, the fakes and blocks that excite the experts," he told *Sports Illustrated*, which selected Orr its Sportsman of the Year in 1970. "He does things that no other hockey player can do, and a lot of people just take it for granted. But he also does the things that excite the newcomer: the rink-long rushes, the hard body checks and that whistling slap shot of his. He has the quality of directing the attention to himself. He runs things. The puck is on his stick half the time. If you're looking at your first hockey game—and lots of people are nowadays—all you do is watch Orr and you catch on fast."[1]

The numbers became absurd. Orr led the league in assists in five of six years from 1970 to 1975 missing out only in 1973 after losing six weeks after knee surgery. He topped the list in plus/minus six times, including a plus-124 in 1971 that remains an NHL record. He played arguably the most critical role in transforming the Bruins from doormat to champion.

Orr performed brilliantly in 1970 to lead the team to its first Stanley Cup crown since 1941. He scored nine goals and added 11 assists in just 14 playoff games. His dominance keyed that of his team. Boston swept both the semifinals against Chicago and finals against St. Louis. Orr scored five points in the championship round. Included was the Cup clincher—his legendary "flying goal" 40 seconds into overtime in Game 4. His defense helped the Bruins hold the Blues to just seven total goals in the series. Two years later Orr tallied eight points in a finals defeat of the Rangers, tying Esposito and Hodge for team honors. No other Boston defenseman scored more than one. Orr copped the Conn Smythe Trophy for top Stanley Cup performer in both those seasons.

Knee problems indeed cut his career short. Orr signed with Chicago as a free agent in 1976 and quickly faded away. He played just 36 games over his last three years.

Orr struggled financially post-retirement. He was drowning in debt and was forced to sell off much of what he owned. He returned to Boston and rebuilt his life. He worked as a scout for several teams before becoming a player agent and eventually president of the Orr Hockey Group agency, which was acquired by the Wasserman Media Group in 2018. Always one to support charitable endeavors and work with youth, Orr coached a group of junior Canadian Hockey League players in an annual game featuring its premier prospects.

HIS GREATEST GAME

Orr took four shots on goal at the Garden against the Rangers on November 15, 1973. He scored on three of them. He added four assists for a career-high seven points in a 10–2 victory. That was the sixth of nine hat tricks Orr registered during his career. That is the most for any defenseman in NHL history.

Side Story

The only major world competition in which Orr suited up was the 1976 Canada Cup. He performed to his standards, winning MVP of the event and helping the team to the championship. He tied Denis Potvin as the highest point scorer for Canada.[2]

What Orr Said

"The love and passion I had for the game was my key. I never had that taken out of me by my parents or a silly coach."[3]

What Was Said about Orr

"If Bobby has a problem, it's just that he has no fear. No fear whatever. If nothing else will do, I swear he'll use his head to block a shot. He's already been hurt bad and he'll keep on getting hurt. But that's his style. He won't change. He won't play it safe." —Bruins goaltender Gerry Cheevers[4]

CHAPTER 4

Ted Williams

"The Splendid Splinter"

Ted Williams baseball card from 1954. Heritage Auctions, Bowman Gum

ESSENTIALS
Sport: Baseball

Born: August 30, 1918

Died: July 5, 2002

Years Active: 1939–1942, 1946–1960

Years with Boston: 1939–1942, 1946–1960

Position: Left field

KNOW THE CAREER NUMBERS
.344 Batting average

521 Home runs

.482 On-base percentage

2,021 Walks

.634 Slugging percentage

1.116 OPS

125.1 Offensive WAR

0 World Series championships

1 American League pennant

2 Most Valuable Player awards

19 All-Star selections

WHY WILLIAMS IS NO. 4
Is the player generally acknowledged as the finest pure hitter in baseball history a mere fourth on this list? Several factors weigh into the equation.

One is athleticism. The sport simply does not require the same consistent and continuous level of athleticism required for those competing in football, basketball, and hockey.

A second is that greatly due to the Yankees dynasty that lasted from 1923 to 1964, Williams never won a World Series championship. When he faced his lone opportunity in 1946, he was stifled by the St. Louis shift and batted a mere .200.

Yet another was the competition. Bill Russell remains the most dominant defensive force to ever lace up a pair of sneakers in the NBA and a champion of champions. Tom Brady is generally in the modern era as the greatest quarterback ever with more Super Bowl rings than any other. Bobby Orr revolutionized the defenseman position with his offensive brilliance.

Adding to the reasoning for what some might consider a surprising placement of fourth among all-time Boston athletes was that Williams was neither a premier fielder nor a baserunner. Though the Gold Glove Award honoring defensive excellence was not rewarded in Major League Baseball until 1957—three years before he retired—modern analytics indicate he remained a poor defender throughout his career. He compiled a negative Defensive WAR (wins above replacement) in each of his 17 full years (he missed complete or partial campaigns to fight in World War II and the Korean War). He stole a mere 24 bases in those seasons combined. Yet none of these shortcomings should significantly detract from his legacy.

Williams felt a passion for hitting unmatched in baseball history. His unrivaled diligence to maximize his already incredible hitting talent led to legendary practice sessions that ended with limp arms and bloody hands. Though all claims about athletes are subjective, one cannot go wrong contending that Williams was the greatest pure hitter the sport had ever produced.

The numbers bear it out. Though icons such as Ty Cobb and Rogers Hornsby finished their careers with higher batting averages, both played at least some of their careers in the dead-ball era, one far more conducive to slapping base hits around the diamond. The .344 average compiled by Williams remains the best among those who played their entire careers in the live-ball era. He might have even broken Babe Ruth's career record of 715 home runs had he not lost five seasons to World War II and the Korean War.

ALL ABOUT WILLIAMS BEFORE BOSTON

Born in San Diego as the son of a photographer and former US Cavalry soldier and Mexican American mother, Williams received little parental supervision. He spent much of his time playing baseball with his younger brother Danny at the North Park Playground. His talent caught the attention of playground manager Rod Luscomb, who groomed his talent and helped transform him into a wunderkind.

What many don't know is that Williams proved equally effective on the mound as at the plate at Hoover High School. He struck out 21 in one particularly dominant performance against Redondo Beach, which attracted scouts from such clubs as the Yankees and Cardinals who showed interest in both of his baseball skills.

One problem remained. His mother perceived major league ballplayers as drunks and bums and had no intention of signing a consent form that would allow her son to launch his career. She did what she considered the next best thing. She inked a deal that landed Ted with the minor league San Diego Padres. That forced him to remain close to her so she could keep an eye on him.

Unlike Ruth a generation previous, Williams quickly dropped his ambitions as a pitcher. He hit .271 in his first year—not too shabby for a kid yet to graduate from high school. Though he failed to homer that season, his raw talent impressed all, including *San Diego Evening Tribune* sportswriter Earl Keller, who offered the following before the 1937 season:

> *If you want to make a little extra money to put in the old sock, bet it on young Teddy Williams to be taken as the outstanding Major League prospect after this year's Pacific Coast League baseball race is finished. . . . Williams will be heavier and in better condition than ever when the 1937 season rolls around. From his mother, we learn he has put on more than five pounds since the 1936 season ended.*[1]

That crystal ball had not been foggy. Williams raised his batting average to .291 that year while finally showing his power potential with 23 home runs. He was the only left-handed batter to slam a baseball over every right-field fence in the Pacific Coast League. He had already begun to earn comparisons to fast-rising Yankees superstar Joe DiMaggio, thereby forging a rivalry that would last until Joltin' Joe retired after the

1951 season. Williams would eventually play second fiddle in the hearts and minds of awards judges, even placing second in Most Valuable Player voting to DiMaggio in 1942 and 1947 despite winning the Triple Crown in both of those seasons.

IN A RED SOX UNIFORM AND BEYOND

The big-league organization with whom he would stay until he retired in 1960 had been eyeing him since he turned pro. Red Sox scout Eddie Collins, who later also signed future Hall of Fame second baseman Bobby Doerr, asked San Diego teammates about Williams. Their reviews were glowing. They raved about his quick bat that could pull the fastest of fastballs over the fence. His obsession with hitting had also become evident.

The Red Sox had yet to promote Williams. His contract obligations insisted upon by his mother prevented him from moving away from San Diego for two years. But in 1938 the bird was ready to fly—and he flew to Minneapolis to play for the Millers of the American Association. Williams had matured as a person as well as a player. The gawky kid who would irritate fellow patrons at the movie theater with loud laughter and pretend to swing a bat while jumping up and down on his bed at six in the morning had grown. The result was one of the greatest seasons in the history of minor league baseball. The 19-year-old Williams won the Triple Crown with the Millers that year, batting .366 with 46 home runs and 142 RBI. He even paced the circuit with 130 runs scored. Such numbers were remarkable given that it was the first time in his life he had been removed from his comfort zone in Southern California.

That achievement paled in comparison to what he accomplished as a Red Sox rookie the following season. The Boston media had embarked on a Williams frenzy as it approached. The pressure on Williams was enormous. Though the Pesky Pole and Green Monster in Fenway Park were inviting, the spacious major league ballparks that beckoned were far more challenging for home-run hitters than the bandbox in Minneapolis.

Well, for mortal hitters, anyway. Not Ted Williams. He established his career path by ravaging pitchers in 1939, starting his career with a nine-game hitting streak that included a two-homer game against Detroit. He continued to rake as he became more familiar with American League hurlers, raising his average to over .300 by July 5 and maintaining it the rest of the season. He embarked on a .468 blitz late that sent it soaring to .327 and finished the year there with 31 home runs and a league-best 145 RBI. He placed fourth in the AL Most Valuable Player balloting behind DiMaggio, super slugger Jimmie Foxx, and Cleveland Indians ace right-hander Bob Feller despite playing in 29 more games and besting the Yankees superstar in nearly every major statistical category.

Williams didn't send many baseballs beyond the Pesky Pole or over the Green Monster early in 1940. He was batting just .179 through eight games and, though his average soared, peaking at .382 in early June, he had just four home runs, and his mistakes on defense, which was never a priority, were glaring. The local sportswriters and fans began to disparage his performance. Always sensitive to criticism, he reasoned that he was a perfectionist who was simply trying too hard, and what right did media members who couldn't hit a baseball over a fence if they were standing in center field and it was tossed underhanded have to tell him how to hit? And when he heard boos cascading from the Fenway stands, he vowed never to acknowledge the fans as long as he remained in a Boston uniform. "That's it, I'm never going to tip my hat again," he said. And he didn't—not even when the thought crossed his mind as he rounded the bases after homering in his last major league at-bat 20 years later. Indeed, his epic feud with the Boston media was launched in 1940.[2]

Neither Boston fans nor Williams expressed much frustration in 1941. Part of his greatness as a thinking man's hitter was developing a daily routine. He had settled into one by that year that started with a 6 a.m. fishing trip at Sunset Lake along with teammate Charlie Wagner, followed by the swinging of a bat or broomstick in the clubhouse around noon as he began preparation for 3 p.m. games (Fenway did not host a night game until 1947). Williams spent hours daily mimicking his swing, sometimes with a hairbrush in front of a mirror. He even took extra batting practice after games.

While other major leaguers were out drinking and carousing, Williams ate a quick dinner and took in a Western at the theater. He believed that boozing weakened his body and mind, as well as his focus on hitting. Over the past two years, he had memorized tendencies and repertoires of American League pitchers, pored over box scores, and made friends with umpires to gain information with them about AL hurlers.

Williams was driven to greatness and it all came to fruition in 1941, a season many consider the finest ever achieved by a major league hitter. Nobody had broken the .400 barrier since Rogers Hornsby in 1925. It seemed that batting averages that high were part of the last vestiges of a bygone era. Williams reached .400 on May 25 during a 23-game hitting streak in which he hit an even more ridiculous .489 and continued to flirt with the magic number the rest of the year. He appeared destined for immortality when he reached .413 in mid-September, but a mini-slump lowered his mark to .400 with a season-ending doubleheader looming against the Athletics in Philadelphia. With the Red Sox playing for nothing but pride, Williams was offered the option by manager Joe Cronin of sitting out to ensure he would make history, but his pride would not allow it.

He had much to think about on the evening of September 27, the night before his date with destiny at Shibe Park. He felt antsy sitting in the Ben Franklin Hotel, so he took a three-hour walk around the City of Brotherly Love with clubhouse man Johnny Orlando, who stopped occasionally for a hard drink while Williams drank a soft one outside. "I kept thinking about the thousands of swings I had taken to prepare myself," Williams said years later. "I had practiced and practiced. I kept saying to myself, 'You are ready.' I went to the ballpark the next day more eager to hit than I had ever been."[3]

Williams was certainly ready physically, mentally, and emotionally. In the opener, he singled to start the second inning, homered to open in the fifth, singled in the sixth, and singled in the seventh. He added a single and double in his first two at-bats in the nightcap and finished the season at .406, a mark that would forever remain a symbol of incredible achievement. The greatest hitters in baseball history, including such sweet swingers as Rod Carew and George Brett, flirted with .400, but could not maintain the pace.

Despite the historic season, Williams finished behind DiMaggio in the MVP balloting. The unfairness of the balloting that has always been tilted toward those who played for pennant winners in a most individual sport reared its ugly head. Willians owned an on-base percentage more than 100 points ahead of DiMaggio, batted 51 points higher, accrued 71 more walks, scored 13 more runs, and hit seven more homers. But DiMaggio captured the attention of the baseball world with his epic 56-game hitting streak, was more popular with the media, and performed yet again for the American League champion.

Meanwhile, an event thousands of miles away from Boston and New York rocked baseball, America, and the world. The Japanese bombing of Pearl Harbor on December 7 sent many men packing to fight overseas. Williams had an out—he was a sole supporter of his divorced mother—and he indeed played ball in 1942. He was criticized by some as a coward for not joining the battle as he captured the first of his two Triple Crowns while also leading the league in every major statistical category.

Williams soon proved his patriotism. Though he never fought in combat, he spent the next three years training to be a Navy and Marine Corps pilot, eventually teaching others as a flight and gunnery instructor. The Red Sox languished in mediocrity as stars such as Williams, Bobby Doerr, and emerging infielder Johnny Pesky fulfilled their military duties. Fenway would certainly be rocking when they returned in 1946.

The penchant for the media to honor players on pennant winners with awards swung in his direction that year when he earned his first MVP despite not leading the league in any of the Triple Crown categories. He won it again in 1949 when the Sox finished second to DiMaggio and the Yankees. He was simply the most productive hitter in the sport. Williams led the AL in on-base percentage and slugging percentage every season in which he played from 1941 to 1949, then again in 1951, 1954, and 1957 at the age of 39. Pitchers were downright frightened of him—he paced the American League in walks eight times.

Williams had a stormy relationship with the fans and media. He only once led the Sox into the World Series. In a sport driven by individual achievement more so than teamwork, he could certainly not be blamed. The Sox failed like every other team to overcome the Yankees in a dynasty that lasted throughout his career and beyond.

Nobody displayed a more devastating combination of consistent line-drive hitting and power than Williams. Few argue the assertion that Ted Williams was the greatest hitter in baseball history. Others earned their way into the conversation and a few have been established as better all-around players. But the best pure hitter ever? Williams rightfully tops most rankings.

HIS GREATEST GAME

July 14, 1946. Fenway Park. Cleveland in town. Williams lined out in his first at-bat. His next four plate appearances: grand slam, solo home run, single, three-run homer to win the game. He finished with eight RBI. Williams played in his only World Series that season.

SIDE STORY

Williams served one stint as a major league manager with mixed results. Eccentric Washington Senators owner Bob Short hired him to manage the typically woebegone team in 1969 and he transformed them into a winner—for one season. He even won Manager of the Year honors. But the Senators collapsed under the weight of weak talent and dissension as Williams became unpopular with many of the players. He managed the team to a 100-loss season in its first year in Texas in 1972 before quitting.

WHAT WILLIAMS SAID

"A man has to have goals—for a day, for a lifetime—and that was mine, to have people say, 'There goes Ted Williams, the greatest hitter who ever lived.'"[4]

What Was Said about Williams

"They can talk about Babe Ruth and Ty Cobb and Rogers Hornsby and Lou Gehrig and Joe DiMaggio and Stan Musial and all the rest, but I'm sure not one of them could hold cards and spades to Williams in his sheer knowledge of hitting. He studied hitting the way a broker studies the stock market and could spot at a glance mistakes that others couldn't see in a week." —Carl Yastrzemski

CHAPTER 5

Larry Bird

"The Hick from French Lick"

Larry Bird at a post-game press conference. Wikimedia Commons, photographer unknown

ESSENTIALS
Sport: Basketball

Born: December 7, 1956

Years Active: 1979–1992

Years with Boston: 1979–1992

Positions: Small forward, power forward

KNOW THE CAREER NUMBERS
24.3 Points per game

10.0 Rebounds per game

6.3 Assists per game

.496 Field goal percentage

145.8 Win shares

3 NBA championships

3 Most Valuable Player awards

12 All-Star selections

WHY BIRD IS NO. 5
One can argue that the four athletes ranked above Larry Bird are the best to ever play their sports. Nobody claims Bird is the premier basketball player in NBA history. He was certainly second-tier and the best of the rest on this list.

His impact on what was a foundering league upon his arrival is undeniable. Known cynically at the Great White Hope, his rivalry with fellow league freshman Magic Johnson, which started in college and continued as the Celtics battled the Los Angeles Lakers for championships, helped save the NBA from itself. No longer were finals being shown on tape delay, an unimaginable circumstance in the modern era. Attendance skyrocketed. So did TV ratings. That rejuvenation would have been impossible had Bird not realized the potential predicted of him as a dominant force at Indiana State.

Bird was a killer. He did everything well. He nailed feathery smooth jump shots from anywhere on the floor. He battled against bigger and stronger power forwards and centers for rebounds and putbacks. His passing was unrivaled for a big man. He was an elite ballhandler for his size. He was a passionate defender who made up for a lack of quickness with intensity and fine footwork. Fans will always recall with relish his vast offensive talents, but few know he led the NBA in defensive win shares four times, including his rookie season.

Most of all he was a champion. He performed brilliantly in the playoffs and with NBA crowns on the line. It's no wonder he won two Finals MVPs. His title-round battles against Magic were showdowns of legend. He was, after all, nicknamed "Larry Legend."

ALL ABOUT BIRD BEFORE BOSTON

Few NBA players since at least the 1970s were geographically less likely to blossom into superstardom than Bird. The poor Indiana corn country town of French Lick with its population of 2,059 was quite distant from the big-city playgrounds or major suburban-area gymnasiums where thousands honed their skills. His learning space was the dirt driveway next to his modest home and his rusty hoop and wood backboard stuck to a ramshackle barn behind it.

Bird practiced tirelessly on all aspects of his game. In the Hoosier State, where high school basketball is embraced, he emerged as a whiz kid by his junior season at Springs Valley High School. He was the star attraction. Attendance skyrocketed. The blond sharpshooter often drew nearly 2,000 fans to packed arenas. His Blackhawks went 19–2 that season. Bird broke the all-time school scoring record as a senior. His final home game drew 4,000 fans.

But not all was well. At age 18 his alcoholic father committed suicide. The impact of that tragedy and inability to adjust to college life as a University of Indiana freshman playing under taskmaster Bobby Knight caused him to transfer to local junior college Northwood Institute State. He quit school after three weeks, after which he worked as a garbage man, a job he later claimed to have loved because it gave him a sense of accomplishment. He had broken up with his wife of less than one year and needed money to support their daughter, who was born after their split.

Bird was wasting his talent. He enrolled at Indiana State and proved he had lost none of his skills or passion for basketball. He transformed a Sycamores team that had previously struggled to play .500 ball into a national championship contender. He averaged more than 30 points and 10 rebounds a game in his first season. Season ticket sales tripled. By his senior year he had become a superstar. He led his team to an undefeated season and an NCAA finals showdown against Johnson and Michigan State. It remains the most-watched title clash in history. Though Indiana State lost, Bird was named College Player of the Year. He had only begun to scratch the surface of his enormous talent.

In a Celtics Uniform and Beyond
Heading into the 1979 season only two rookies had turned NBA doormats into contenders. They were dominant centers Lew Alcindor (later Kareem Abdul-Jabbar) and Wilt Chamberlain. Then came Bird. The Celtics had won just 29 games the previous season. They finished 61-21 the following year and reached the Eastern Conference finals. He led the team in scoring, rebounding, and steals while establishing himself as one of the premier three-point shooters in the league.

Bird and fellow forward Cedric Maxwell were beacons of youth potential in an aging club that featured fading stars such as Tiny Archibald, Dave Cowens, and Pete Maravich. Then it happened. June 9, 1980. Red Auerbach pulled off one of the greatest heists in NBA history. He swapped two first-round picks to Golden State for superstar center Robert Parish and the rights to select Kevin McHale. An all-Hall of Famer frontcourt was in place.

Parish and McHale were All-Stars who gained deserved stardom. Bird emerged as a superstar, a trash-talking killer without whose brilliance three championships could not have been achieved. He hit the game-winning bank shot in a taut Game 7 of the 1981 Eastern Conference finals to avenge the defeat to Philadelphia the previous year. He led the Celtics with 27 points and 13 rebounds in Game 6 against Houston to clinch his first NBA crown two weeks later.

Proclaiming Bird as confident would qualify for the Understatement of the Year Award. His belief in his abilities extended beyond cockiness.

He did not keep it to himself. He was known as Larry Legend and that legend included trash-talking on the court and backing it up. Stories from his peers abound. Included was one from journeyman Mike Gminski.

"I was with the 76ers at the time," Gminski recalled. "We go up by one with about four seconds to go. They call timeout, get the ball at half court. (Charles) Barkley is guarding Larry. Bird comes up to him and says, 'You know who's getting the ball, don't you?' Charles kind of nodded his head. Larry said, 'I tell you what I'm going to do: I'm going to get the ball, take two dribbles down the baseline and shoot a fadeaway jump shot.' I'm on the weak side. I've got McHale. Bird takes two dribbles down to the baseline, fadeaway jump shot, and the ball was halfway to the net and I just started walking to our locker room. I knew it was good."[1]

Then there was teammate Joe Kleine.

"It was late in the game, and Hubie Brown was on the bench, motivating, flames coming out of his neck," said Kleine. "Larry is taking the ball right out in front of him late, and he looks over at Hubie and goes, 'Kevin is going to post up right there, I'm going to throw him the perfect pass, he's going to throw it back to me and I'm going to make a three.' And he did."[2]

That unshakable belief helped Bird shine with crowns on the line. His production amazed all despite the immense contributions from Hall of Fame teammates McHale, Parish, and guard Dennis Johnson. He scored at least 35 points in 10 double-double playoff performances. He even achieved a 30-point triple-double in a series-clinching blowout of the Knicks in the 1984 Eastern Conference semifinals. He often refused to come off the court. Bird played minutes unthinkable in the modern game, including 56 in overtime defeats of Chicago and Milwaukee in successive postseasons.

Bird never led the NBA in a significant regular-season statistic. But his consistent all-around brilliance in playing his entire career with the Celtics (he averaged a double-double in each of his first six years) resulted in three league championships. Nothing is more important to a player's legacy.

Back problems forced Bird to retire in 1992 despite a continued competitive drive. He did not leave the Celtics. He remained as a front office assistant before landing a job as head coach of the Indiana Pacers. Bird brought the same level of intensity and work ethic to that gig, guiding the team to a 58–24 record in his first season, earning NBA Coach of the Year honors, and pushing Michael Jordan and the Bulls to seven games in the conference finals. Two years later he led the Pacers into the NBA Finals before resigning, making good on his promise to coach only three seasons and earning a promotion to President of Basketball Operations. He remained with that organization into 2024.

His Greatest Game
Blowouts limit numbers. That is one ironic truth about sports and athletes. This is especially true in the NBA. Bird likely would have achieved the rare quadruple-double against Utah on February 18, 1985. He had 30 points, 12 rebounds, 10 assists, and a ridiculous nine steals heading through three quarters. The Celtics led 90–66. His participation thereafter was deemed unnecessary. Though his playoff brilliance was more important, Bird never played a more complete game.

Side Story
Bird was a trash-talker extraordinaire. Examples abound from on-court competition, but perhaps the best occurred before the three-point contest in 1986 during the All-Star festivities in Dallas. Bird walked into the Eastern Conference locker room and announced, "Who's coming in second?" Recalled Bird years later, "They're all sitting there, and they sort of put their heads down, and I said, 'Hey, I'm just looking to see who's coming in second.' I just did it for a joke, but they didn't like that very well."[3]

What Bird Said
"I wasn't real quick, and I wasn't real strong. Some guys will just take off and it's like, whoa. So I beat them with my mind and my fundamentals."

What Was Said about Bird
"Looking into Larry Bird's eyes is like looking into the eyes of an assassin." —Atlanta Hawks superstar Dominique Wilkins

CHAPTER 6

Ray Bourque

"The Offensive Defenseman"

Ray Bourque, right, controls the puck in a 1979 game against the
Washington Capitals. Wikimedia, Dave Stanley photo

ESSENTIALS
Sport: Hockey

Born: December 28, 1960

Years Active: 1979–2001

Years with Boston: 1979–2000

Position: Defenseman

KNOW THE CAREER NUMBERS
395 Goals

1111 Assists

1506 Points

493 Plus/minus

229.1 Point shares

19 All-Star selections

5 Norris Trophies

3 Most Valuable Player awards

12 All-Star selections

WHY BOURQUE IS NO. 6
The Top 5 seems obvious though the order certainly deserves debate. This is where it gets tough. Red Sox superstar Carl Yastrzemski? Celtics legends John Havlicek and Bob Cousy? Patriots Hall of Fame guard John Hannah?

No coin flip is needed. It's Bourque for many reasons. One is longevity. Bourque played 21 of his 23 seasons with Boston. His achievements take a backseat to no other contender. He won Rookie of the Year and earned 17 consecutive All-Star appearances. He tallied more goals, assists, and points than any defenseman in league history.

Bourque exuded a rugged style most effective for a defenseman yet proved deadly on the offensive end with hard, accurate passes and shots. He could score from anywhere. He brought steady leadership to the Bruins throughout his career. Bobby Orr blazed a new trail for the position and Bourque followed it, establishing himself as the second-best Bruin of all time.

ALL ABOUT BOURQUE BEFORE BOSTON

Bourque was born three days before New Year's Eve in 1960 in Saint-Laurent, Quebec. He was inspired as a youth by the success and style of the Montreal Canadiens and quickly emerged as a premier talent. He had already risen to the ranks of pro prospect at age 12 when his mother died of cancer.

Within three years he was a junior hockey standout. He was drafted that year into the Quebec Major Junior Hockey League. Despite his tender age he totaled 12 goals and 36 assists with two different teams. Yet he had just begun to tap into his potential. The 17-year-old Bourque recorded 94 points, which included 71 assists, the following season.

He was blossoming in an era of individual offensive juggernauts, even among defensemen. NHL teams considered him a strong prospect but were not salivating over his future. Bourque waited as other defensemen such as Rob Ramage, Craig Hartsburg, and Keith Brown were selected ahead of him in what was considered a bountiful draft class. The Bruins understood his value. They traded goalie Ron Grahame to the Kings for the eighth overall pick, which they used to snag him.

Bourque finished his career ranked ahead of all defensemen taken ahead of him in games played and points. The only other draftee who outshone him in those categories was Oilers and Rangers legend Mark Messier.

IN A BRUINS UNIFORM AND BEYOND

Bourque wasted no time making teams who passed on him in the 1979 draft regret it. He had all but clinched the Calder Cup for top rookie by midseason. He established an NHL rookie record for a defenseman with 65 points and earned the first All-Star nod for a rookie nongoalie in league history. He scored 27 goals in his second year and even attracted some Hart Memorial Trophy votes for Most Valuable Player.

Bourque was neither a classic physical defenseman nor a bully. He spent little time in the penalty box. He was not a particularly brutal checker. But he could throw his body around effectively. He had already blossomed into a complete player and was still improving. Not bad considering Bourque had yet to celebrate his 20th birthday.

One issue persisted. Bourque had yet to gain the respect as a defenseman of the Professional Hockey Writers Association, which selects postseason award winners. Even a breakout 1983–84 season during which he scored 96 points only landed him third place behind more traditional defensemen Rod Langway and fellow offensive juggernaut Paul Coffey in the Norris Trophy voting. Yet they placed him among the top five for the Hart Trophy.

Recognition finally arrived in 1987 when he nearly won the Norris Trophy unanimously and finished behind only scoring machine Wayne Gretzky for the Hart Trophy. He soon began to play a critical role in transforming the Bruins from a consistent playoff qualifier into a Stanley Cup contender. He helped them reach the championship round in 1988 and 1990. Unfortunately that was during the height of Edmonton's dominance and Boston managed just one victory in two Stanley Cup series. Bourque contributed eight points in nine games but the Bruins were overwhelmed.

A narrative emerged. Would Bourque ever win the big one? The question begs the obvious answer for athletes in all sports and of all generations: He could not do it alone. The Bruins simply did not boast the talent to beat a steamroller such as the Oilers. All Bourque could do was plug away. He scored 94 points in 1990 and came within one vote of becoming the first NHL defenseman since Orr to win the Hart Trophy. Quite commendable given that Gretzky and Mario Lemieux were both at the peak of their games.

"He sneaks up on us and always gets off six or seven shots," said Buffalo forward Mike Foligno. "Afterward we look at each other and say 'How'd he get so many?' . . . Bourque controls so much of the game that he draws all the attention. He causes opponents to react [to him], and in the course of that reaction his teammates are left open."[1]

Team records started to fall. He became its leading career scorer among defensemen during the 1990–91 season. Then he overtook Phil Esposito and Johnny Bucyk to amass the top point total in franchise history. Yet his annual salary of $600,000 fell far short of those in the NHL earning $2 million or more.

Bourque continued to pepper away at goaltenders. He finished his career with 6,209 shots on goal, the most of any NHL defenseman ever. His 360 consecutive games with at least one shot on goal is also a league record. But none of that was enough for him. He wanted to win the Stanley Cup. As the Bruins slipped into mediocrity and he approached age 40 he was traded to Colorado. His Avalanche captured the Cup in 2001. Bourque had achieved his final goal. He retired after that season.

The Bruins retired his jersey on October 4, 2001. Bourque remained a staple of the Boston community. He opened an Italian restaurant in the North End neighborhood and showed his charitable side by launching the Bourque Family Foundation.

His Greatest Game

It was all for naught but Borque scored two goals in the third period to force overtime in Game 1 of the 1990 Stanley Cup finals against Edmonton. The second tied the score at 2–2 with just 1:29 remaining in regulation. Bourque slammed nine shots on goal at goaltender Bill Ranford. The Oilers needed three overtimes to win.

Side Story

Bourque wore No. 7 early in his career with the Bruins. But in 1987 he gave it back after the team retired it to honor Phil Esposito. Bourque was permitted to continue to wear it as long as he played but decided instead to use the occasion to honor Esposito in a unique way. He put on two No. 7 jerseys, then skated over to Esposito during a ceremony honoring the legend, handed the jersey to Esposito, and revealed his new No. 77 for the crowd to see. He wore that number for the rest of his career in Boston and Colorado. Both teams retired that number even though he played less than two years with the Avalanche.

What Bourque Said

"I'm not Bobby Orr, that's for sure. Nobody playing defense will ever control the game as well as he did. I'd be happy just to be half the player he was."[2]

What Was Said about Bourque

"You can [scout] Bourque all you want. But what good is it going to get you? He just reacts to what he sees. The great players are all like that."
—Minnesota North Stars general manager Lou Nanne[3]

CHAPTER 7

Carl Yastrzemski

"Yaz"

Carl Yastrzemski at bat at Fenway in the 1970s. Wikimedia Commons,
Steve Carter photo

ESSENTIALS
Sport: Baseball

Born: August 22, 1939

Years Active: 1961–1983

Years with Boston: 1961–1983

Positions: Left field, first base

KNOW THE CAREER NUMBERS
.285 Batting average

452 Home runs

1,844 RBI

.379 On-base percentage

78.3 Offensive WAR

18 All-Star selections

3 Batting titles

1 Most Valuable Player award

2 American League pennants

WHY YASTRZEMSKI IS NO. 7
The man affectionately known as "Yaz" played his entire career during a pitching-rich era in major league baseball. He performed at a time of National League dominance. But he continued to crank out line drives as a hitting machine who wore out the Green Monster, led the AL in doubles three times in four years, slammed enough home runs, and even impacted the game on the bases to become a first-ballot Hall of Famer. He took over for the retired Ted Williams his rookie year as the Sox's super slugger and face of the organization.

Longevity, production, and consistency earned him the seven spot. Average overall defense (though iconic manager Billy Martin praised his work in left and he played the Green Monster expertly) that resulted in just a 1.0 career defensive WAR and the greatness of competition prevented him from landing higher.

Yastrzemski launched his Boston career in a rare era of losing. Owner Tom Yawkey's refusal to integrate in the 1950s set the franchise back and eventually resulted in annual struggles. After Frank Malzone faded, Yaz provided the team's only consistent combination of average and power into the mid-1960s. He was arguably the best player in the American League into the next decade, thrice belting 40 or more home runs, winning the Triple Crown in the Impossible Dream season of 1967, earning two batting titles, and pacing the AL in on-base percentage four times from 1965 to 1970. It's no wonder he made the All-Star team 15 years in a row.

ALL ABOUT YASTRZEMSKI BEFORE BOSTON

Carl Michael Yastrzemski seemed destined from his infancy in Southampton, New York, to play baseball. His father competed in semi-pro ball and might have forged his professional career had he and his uncle not inherited a 70-acre potato farm during the Depression. The financial benefits of playing the sport and the probability of years in the minors and no time in the majors altered many a career path decades before the advent of free agency.

Dad presented his 18-month-old son with a tiny baseball bat that he dragged around inside and outside the home. He used it at the age of six to hit tennis balls his father tossed his way after supper. The two played imaginary games between the Red Sox and Yankees. Little Yaz had no preference—he loved both teams.

Baseball was a family affair. His father formed a semipro team that included four brothers, two brothers-in-law, and three cousins. Carl served as the batboy before joining as a player at age 14. His father channeled his passion for the sport on him. Some believe Dad lived vicariously through his son before and after he gained stardom with the Sox. But he did not serve as his batting instructor for long.

"He taught me the fundamentals," Yastrzemski explained during his rookie season in Boston. "He told me only to swing at good pitches. But about the time I became a sophomore in high school he stopped. And that probably helped me more than anything. Sometimes you have to work things out for yourself."[1]

That talent brought attention. The kid performed well as a pitcher and hitter while playing semipro ball during high school. His father took the lead in trumpeting his skills, promoting him more for his bat than his arm. Soon his favorite teams showed interest. The Yankees sent to their home scout Ray Garland, who offered a $60,000 bonus. Playing the role of agent before athletes hired them, his father demanded $100,000. A stunned and angered Garland tossed a pencil to the ceiling. That was all his dad needed to see. He threw Garland out of the house. The Yankees were still enjoying their dynasty but they certainly regretted not signing Yastrzemski after their mid-1960s collapse.

The Red Sox also failed to meet the asking price, so Yastrzemski sifted through many college offers and chose Notre Dame to play baseball and basketball. Soon offers exceeding $100,000 flooded in. The Sox did not make the biggest pitch but a family desire for him to play on the East Coast near his home motivated him to sign with them. He was not the most impressive physical specimen at 5-foot-11, 160 pounds—Boston general manager Joe Cronin was taken aback by his lack of size—and he struggled at first at Class B Raleigh. Manager Ken Deal suggested he move closer to the plate. That simple adjustment transformed Yastrzemski into a stud. He batted .400 for the rest of the 1959 season to earn an invitation to Fenway Park to meet the legendary Ted Williams.

Yaz might have skyrocketed right to the majors in 1960. But he was playing second base, and the Red Sox already had eventual batting champion Pete Runnels there. So they trained Yaz as a left fielder in the minors to take over for Williams. He batted .339 and even recorded 18 assists in the outfield. Teddy Ballgame retired after that season as expected. Yastrzemski filled his shoes from the start quite admirably.

IN A RED SOX UNIFORM AND BEYOND

Six players received votes for 1961 American League Rookie of the Year, including winner and Boston pitcher Don Schwall, who immediately thereafter faded into obscurity, and fellow Sox hitter Chuck Schilling. Yastrzemski outproduced Schilling in every major offensive category yet garnered no votes.

By his second season he could no longer be ignored. He established a statistical pattern he maintained nearly his entire career—among the league leaders in doubles, dangerous but not overwhelming power (aside from his mid-1960s surge), batting champion contender, great eye at the plate that led to consistently high walk totals, and on-base percentage. He also emerged as one of the premier clutch hitters in the sport.

His ability to rise to the occasion grew most pronounced in 1967, though one could rightly claim the lowly Sox created no such opportunities previously. Boston embarked that season on a pennant quest in the most heated race in baseball history. Four teams, including Chicago, Detroit, and Minnesota, remained alive for the crown heading into the final weekend. The Twins, Red Sox, and Tigers were all tied for the top after the latter won the first game of the Sunday doubleheader. Fenway Park was packed for a Boston-Minnesota showdown. Yaz, who had batted .500 in his previous nine games, slammed four hits in a victory that resulted in a pennant after the Tigers lost Game 2 to the Angels.

Yastrzemski had achieved one of the greatest seasons in baseball history. He won the American League Triple Crown (it was not accomplished again until Miguel Cabrera in 2012) by batting .326 with 44 home runs and 121 RBI. Teammates marveled at his penchant for clutch hitting. "Yaz hit 44 homers that year and 43 of them meant something big for the team," said fellow Sox slugger George "Boomer" Scott. "It seemed like every time we needed a big play, the man stepped up and got it done."[2]

The man who did not step up was Minnesota baseball writer Max Nichols, who inexplicably prevented Yastrzemski from winning AL MVP unanimously by voting instead for Twins versatile infielder and outfielder Cesar Tovar, whom he offered lamely was more valuable to his team. Yastrzemski kept slugging in the World Series with three home runs in a seven-game defeat dominated by St. Louis superstar right-hander Bob Gibson.

The Year of the Pitcher was still the Year of Yaz. He led the AL with a .301 batting average in 1968 and remained a force during an amazingly consistent stretch of six Sox seasons in which they won between 84–89 games. Proclaimed by many to be fading away in his mid-30s after the

Sox overcame his mediocre 1975 to win the pennant, he rebounded to twice exceed 100 RBI and continued to contribute into his 40s.

By that time the franchise records had begun to fall. He passed Ted Williams, to whom he hated to be compared, on the all-time hit list (though it must be cited that Williams lost five years to the military) in 1977 with 2,665, then reached 400 home runs, 1,000 extra-base hits, and 3,000 total hits in 1979. The fans and organization grew more appreciative every year. A pregame ceremony before his second-last game with the Sox on October 1, 1983, drew a sellout crowd. He broke down and cried upon stepping to the microphone and concluded his speech with the simple words, "New England, I love you."

The feeling was mutual. The inevitable became reality in 1989 when Yastrzemski was elected into the Baseball Hall of Fame.

HIS GREATEST GAME

Yaz batted .369 with four home runs in 17 postseason games. The best of the best was Game 2 of the 1967 World Series. That is when he slugged two home runs and drove in five in a 5–0 defeat of St. Louis that knotted the series. Included was a three-run shot in the seventh inning that all but clinched victory.

SIDE STORY

Yastrzemski was not always the most popular player. He was sometimes criticized for a lack of hustle. A spotlight on that complaint was offered in *Ball Four*, the controversial 1970 bestseller authored by former Yankees pitcher Jim Bouton, which chronicled the 1969 season. Bouton wrote the following:

> *Carl Yastrzemski was recently fined $500 for loafing and I've been keeping an eye on him. Sure enough, he hit a ball to second base today and loafed all the way to first. I'm afraid Yastrzemski has a bit of dog in him. Always did, and people around baseball knew it all the time. When things are going good Yastrzemski will go all out. When things aren't going so well he'll give a half-ass effort. But he's got so much ability that the only thing you can do is put up with him. I asked a*

few of the Red Sox if they thought he deserved the fine and thought they would defend him. But they said, "He deserved it all the way."[3]

What Yastrzemski Said

"I think about baseball when I wake up in the morning. I think about it all day and I dream about it at night. The only time I don't think about is when I'm playing it."[4]

What Was Said about Yastrzemski

"He reminded me of myself. He's wound up like a clock. He's ready to go." —Ted Williams[5]

CHAPTER 8

Bob Cousy

"Houdini of the Hardwood"

Bob Cousy hustles for the ball in a 1960 game against the
New York Knicks. Library of Congress

ESSENTIALS
Sport: Basketball

Born: August 9, 1928

Years Active: 1950–1963, 1969–1970

Years with Boston: 1950–1963

Position: Point guard

KNOW THE CAREER NUMBERS
18.4 Points per game

7.5 Assists per game

5.2 Rebounds per game

40.6 Offensive WAR

50.5 Defensive WAR

13 All-Star selections

8 Assist titles

6 NBA championships

WHY COUSY IS NO. 8
Celtics coach Red Auerbach launched a revolution. Cousy was his general. It was a bloodless coup. The Celtics took over the NBA with a new fast-break style that produced layups, open jumpers, and plenty of points before opposing players could establish defensive positioning. Cousy was the point guard who spearheaded the break.

But he was more than that. He was a showman. He was Pete Maravich before Pete Maravich. His no-look and behind-the-back passes thrilled fans and helped popularize a sport that had received more attention at the college level. His court awareness remains many decades later among the best in league history.

As is true in most sports, basketball players from far older generations cannot be compared statistically with those of the modern day. Cousy only shot .375 from the field for his career, but it must be noted that many of his shots were long jumpers and his percentage of makes was typical for the era. His greatness was as a playmaker. Cousy was also an excellent on-ball defender. He elevated the performance and production of his teammates with his ballhandling and passing.

The game has changed. Skill levels have increased. Cousy has not for many years been considered in debates about who is the greatest player of all time as he once was. But he certainly ranks among the all-time best. That claim can be made about only a few players from the 1950s.

ALL ABOUT COUSY BEFORE BOSTON

Cousy grew up too poor to be a gym rat. He was a ghetto rat. The son of French immigrants on Manhattan's East Side, his activities of choice were stickball and stealing hubcaps. His moonlighting father finally saved enough money driving cabs to put a downpayment on a house in Queens. That is when Cousy began playing basketball.

Not that he played it well. He was twice cut from the Andrew Jackson High School junior varsity team. It seemed his future as a hoopster had taken a hit when he fell out of a tree at age 13 and broke his right arm. The injury was a blessing in disguise. He learned to dribble and shoot with his left hand. Cousy emerged in neighborhood leagues as an ambidextrous playmaking guard. He landed a spot on the varsity and captured the city scoring championship as a senior by tallying 26 points in the final game of the season.

His life in New England was about to begin. He accepted a scholarship at Holy Cross in Worcester. But coach Alvin Julian did not embrace what he perceived as his showboating style. The sport was simply not ready for such slick ballhandling and passing. Cousy came off the bench for a team that won the national championship. His playing time remained limited as a sophomore starter. Cousy considered returning to New York and transferring to St. John's.

Holy Cross fans played a role in stopping it. With five minutes remaining in a game against Loyola of Chicago at Boston Garden, they began chanting "We want Cousy!" Julian relented. Cousy clinched victory by ditching a defender with a behind-the-back dribble, which he popularized, and nailing a left-handed hook shot at the buzzer.

Those who credit Celtics coach Red Auerbach for his talent evaluation and insight in scouting Cousy after the NBA was formed should understand that he drafted 6-foot-11 Chuck Share instead. He even tossed a backhanded insult at Cousy. "We need a big man," Auerbach said. "Little men are a dime a dozen. I'm supposed to win, not go after local yokels."[1]

The comments drew sharp rebukes in the media. Cousy was taken by the Tri-Cities Blackhawks, traded to the Chicago Stags, who soon folded, then landed with the Celtics only after the names of their players were placed in a hat. Auerbach wanted one-time league-leading scorer Max Zaslofsky. He was disappointed when he had to settle for Cousy. That sentiment did not last long. While Zaslofsky faded, Cousy blossomed into the greatest guard in the NBA.

Just one major detail remained. Cousy was more than a local yokel. He was a local hero. Fans clamored for Auerbach to sign him. But Cousy had opened a driving school for women in New England. He wanted more financial stability. He had asked the Stags for $10,000 a year before they bit the dust. Cousy was offered $6,000. So he staged a holdout. He finally signed with Boston for $9,000.

In a Celtics Uniform and Beyond

The stunning immediacy of the Celtic turnaround from patsy to powerhouse cannot be attributed solely to Cousy. His ballhandling and passing wizardry proved an ideal fit for the new fast-break style employed by Auerbach. The additions of sharpshooters Ed Macauley and Bill Sharman transformed Boston into a power. Auerbach still thirsted for the linchpin center to anchor the defense. The drafting of Russell in 1956 turned the Celtics into a perennial champion.

Auerbach did not appreciate the flair Cousy exhibited on the court but he certainly embraced the results. He was tearing up the league by his second year. His averages of 21.7 points and 6.7 assists both nearly led the NBA. He led the league at 7.7 assists per game the next season. It was a remarkable statistic in the era before the 24-second clock. But it was no anomaly. Cousy dished out between 7.1 and 9.5 assists per game for eight consecutive years to pace the NBA in all of them. His peripheral vision dribbling full speed downcourt and ability to hit the open man in stride with behind-the-back or no-look passes for easy baskets thrilled fans and endeared him to his teammates.

"Cooz was the absolute offensive master," said former teammate and future Celtics coach Tom Heinsohn. "What Russell was on defense, that's what Cousy was on offense—a magician. Once that ball reached his hands, the rest of us just took off, never bothering to look back. We didn't have to. He'd find us. When you got into a position to score, the ball would be there."[2]

Included was the 1956–57 season as Cousy, who snagged outlet passes from the rookie Russell to unleash the most devastating fast break ever seen in the league, helped Boston to its first NBA championship, and won Most Valuable Player honors. He spearheaded the offensive attack that led to six consecutive crowns from 1958 until he retired in 1963. The Celtics dominated despite a wealth of talented opponents, including superstars Dolph Schayes (Nationals), Oscar Roberston (Royals), Bob Pettit and Cliff Hagan (Hawks), Elgin Baylor and Jerry West (Lakers), and Wilt Chamberlain (Warriors). Boston won because it was a better *team*. Cousy and Russell were its glue.

Cousy retired at age 35 with great fanfare. What became known as the "Boston Tear Party" was a reciprocal love affair. He was rendered speechless for periods of what was intended to be a seven-minute farewell to the fans that lasted 20 minutes before his last regular season game at the sold-out Garden.

He hung up his sneakers but was far from done with basketball. He coached Boston College to a 117–38 record over six seasons, transforming that team into a national power. His hatred for playing the cutthroat recruiting game motivated him to accept the head coaching position with the Royals, which moved to Kansas City as the Kings. He even returned to play seven games for Cincinnati during the 1969–70 season to spark his players. Among his proteges was slick superstar point guard Nate "Tiny" Archibald, who boasted the same style as Cousy had a decade earlier.

Cousy remained a Boston icon. He moved to the broadcast booth to provide commentary on television Celtics games from 1974 to 1989 before accepting an offer to serve as president of the Basketball Hall of Fame, authoring a book on basketball strategy and promoting the sport in Europe and Asia.

His Greatest Game

It was March 21, 1953. The Celtics sought to eliminate Syracuse in the first round of the playoffs. Cousy fought through a leg injury. He tied the game with a last-second free throw to send it into overtime. He scored six points in that extra session to force a second one. He remained on a roll. His 25-foot jumper tied the game in the third overtime. The Celtics trailed 104–99 in the fourth overtime before Cousy embarked on another blitz. He finished with 50 points in a game that lasted three hours and 11 minutes and resulted in 10 players fouling out. Cousy made 30 of 32 free throws in the victory.

Side Story

Cousy's retirement in 1963 motivated praise from a VIP—President John F. Kennedy. He wired Cousy, "The game bears an indelible stamp of your rare skills and competitive daring."[3]

What Cousy Said

"In whatever sport of field of endeavor you are interested, you should do whatever is necessary to compliment your God-given talent with proper mental preparation so as to do 'the best you can.' The criterion should be to fully exploit your potential rather than to win at any cost. What more could anyone ever ask of you than to be the best you possibly can?"[4]

What Was Said about Cousy

"He always shows you something new, something you've never seen before. Any mistake against him and you pay the full price. One step and he's past the defense. He's quick, he's smart, he's tireless, he has spirit and he is probably the best finisher in sports today." —Knicks coach Joe Lapchick[5]

CHAPTER 9

John Hannah

"Hog"

ESSENTIALS
Sport: Football
Born: April 4, 1951
Years Active: 1973–1985
Years with New England: 1973–1985
Position: Guard

KNOW THE CAREER NUMBERS
183 Games played
183 Games started
9 Pro Bowls
7 All-Pro selections

WHY HANNAH IS NO. 9
Offensive linemen are the most anonymous athletes in major American sports. That is especially true with guards, who do not even receive recognition for protecting quarterbacks from onrushing defensive ends. The position does not attract the spotlight. Perhaps one in a generation becomes a household name. From the early 1970s to the mid-1980s it was John Hannah.

His notoriety certainly extended beyond his palindromic last name. The first Patriot enshrined into the Pro Football Hall of Fame blocked his way onto the NFL All-Decade team. He used his bruising style and strength to simply push linemen and linebackers to the ground and open huge holes for a New England running game that blossomed into the best in football. He played perhaps the most important role in the 1978 team setting a league record with 3,165 rushing yards. His talents allowed Steve Grogan to emerge as one of the premier running quarterbacks in the sport.

The power and mobility required of a pulling guard in the ground game helped place Hannah high on this list. So did his durability, longevity, and consistent excellence. Other athletes received more appreciation because of the position they played. But few were better at their jobs than Hannah.

ALL ABOUT HANNAH BEFORE NEW ENGLAND

College recruiters streamed to Chattanooga, Tennessee, in the late 1960s to scout a Baylor School for Boys offensive lineman who was driving lineman five yards off the line of scrimmage with his footwork and power. That was hefty John Hannah, who weighed 11 pounds at birth and 150 in fifth grade. He honed his skills under the tutelage of coach Major Luke Worsham, who taught him to focus on a target, aim for the numbers with his helmet, keep his eyes open, and use leverage to blast through. Worsham placed Hannah against four offensive linemen in a drill he despised. But it taught him well.

Hannah also excelled in wrestling and track and field in high school His shot toss exceeding 61 feet was a school record. Not bad considering he put little effort into that sport.

"He didn't even work at track," said younger brother Charley, a standout offensive tackle for Tampa Bay and Oakland. "He'd just show up for the meets. There were so many things he could do. At that time he might have been the greatest large athlete in the world."[1]

Despite weighing 305 as a junior—40 pounds heavier than his NFL playing weight—he ran a 4.85 in the 40-yard-dash for a combine scout. His reputation spread. Among those who zeroed in on Hannah was

Raiders coach and future Hall of Famer John Madden, who stunned many by announcing that he was best player he'd seen at a Hula Bowl workout. Madden never regretted what amounted to a prediction of pro potential. He claimed years later that he would pick Hannah first if starting an NFL team.

Patriots scout Dick Steinberg was particularly impressed with his raw power. He pulled Hannah aside in a hotel lobby between Hula Bowl practices and peppered him with quiz questions he gave all prospects. Steinberg marveled at his intelligence. The team targeted Hannah in the draft and snagged him fourth overall. Taken second by Philadelphia was fellow offensive lineman Jerry Sisemore, who performed well in the NFL but was no Hannah.

In a Patriots Uniform and Beyond

Boston had suffered through six consecutive losing seasons when Hannah arrived in 1973. Two more followed. But as he blossomed into a perennial Pro Bowler the team began to win. It was no coincidence. One statistic that spotlights his impact was averaging rushing yards per attempt. The Patriots led the NFL in that category in 1976, 1978, and 1983. They finished among the top 10 six times during his career.

Such success appeared unlikely in his rookie year. He recalled one confrontation with huge Chiefs lineman Buck Buchanan. "He said, 'Home Boy, I'm gonna welcome you to the NFL,'" Hannah recalled. "One time he actually picked me up and threw me. No one had ever done that before. Then I started trying to cut him and he just stepped over me—or on me."[2]

Hannah felt he only had himself to blame. He had grown cocky under the weight of his achievements. New England proved to be a culture shock for the boy from Alabama. He credited religion with finding tranquility and a positive mindset. Hannah began studying the techniques of other offensive linemen and the weaknesses of defenders. His strength and quickness did the rest.

Even when the Patriots struggled to run the ball effectively Hannah remained a stalwart. The NFL Players Association named him Offensive Lineman of the Year every season from 1978 to 1981. He might have won it in 1977 had he not missed three games with a contract dispute. Statistics and awards can only prove part of an offensive lineman's greatness. The eye test tells the rest, particularly when judged by peers. Among them was the always appreciative Madden.

"The thing I always liked about Hannah is that he has that defensive player's attitude, that same aggression," he said. "There's no rule that says an offensive player has to have that milder kind of personality, although most of them seem to. I've heard that when you tend to go after people aggressively, like Hannah does, it hurts your pass blocking, and I looked for that weakness in Hannah. But I never saw it, except maybe in his first year or so."[3]

The blossoming of Hannah contributed greatly to transforming New England from patsy to contender. His blocking helped the Patriots turn a 180, going from 3–11 to 11–3 in 1976, his first All-Pro season. They paced the NFL in average yards per rush that season.

Hannah continued to improve. He became a mainstay in the Pro Bowl, earning spots in 10 consecutive years. He even finished seventh in the Offensive Player of the Year balloting in 1979, quite the feat for a guard.

But the ultimate goal for any player eluded him. That was playing in the Super Bowl. He finally reached in 1986 to cap his final season. Though the Patriots were destroyed by the steamrolling Bears, their appearance in that grand finale remains a testament to Hannah's impact on the franchise.

Hannah dabbled in coaching high school football for several years but settled into cattle farming in his home state of Alabama. He spoke passionately about trying to survive in that struggling industry in 2023.

His Greatest Game

It's impossible to statistically judge the finest performance for a guard but the 1985 AFC Championship against Miami was certainly a highlight. In the second-last game of his career, he bullied defensive linemen as Boston rushed for 255 yards in earning its first Super Bowl berth. The Patriots depended on Hannah, rushing on an amazing 59 of 71 offensive plays.

SIDE STORY

Hannah won the National Prep Wrestling championship as a heavyweight and continued to compete at the University of Alabama before quitting to concentrate on football.

WHAT HANNAH SAID

"[Alabama coach Bear] Bryant taught me some lessons when I was at Alabama. The biggest lesson he taught me at Alabama was that it's not always the guy with the talent that wins. It's the guy with the most guts. He'll stick it out and play hard all the way through the game. A lot of guys with talent will play tough for a quarter or two but take some breaks. When he takes those breaks, that's the time to take care of him. And that was a huge lesson, and that's what really kind of got me over the hump. I always figured there were a lot of guys more talented than me in the NFL, but I would outwork most of them."[4]

WHAT WAS SAID ABOUT HANNAH

"His IQ was very high. If you look at the great offensive linemen in history you'll find that they were all smart people." —Patriots scout Dick Steinberg[5]

CHAPTER 10

John Havlicek

"Hondo"

John Havlicek. Wikimedia Commos, The Sporting News

ESSENTIALS
Sport: Basketball

Born: April 8, 1940

Died: April 25, 2019

Years Active: 1962–1978

Years with Boston: 1962–1978

Position: Swingman

KNOW THE CAREER NUMBERS
20.8 Points per game

6.3 Rebounds per game

4.8 Assists per game

.439 Shooting percentage

57.7 Offensive win shares

74.1 Defensive win shares

11 All-NBA

8 All-Defensive team

13 All-Star appearances

WHY HAVLICEK IS NO. 10
That John Havlicek spent the first half of his NBA career as perhaps the greatest reserve in major American sports history adds strength to a top 10 ranking among all Boston athletes. He didn't even become a starter until the 1969–70 season, after Bill Russell retired. But he was on the court with games and championships on the line, including taut Game 7 of the Eastern Conference finals against Philadelphia, when his heroics inspired iconic Celtics radio announcer Johnny Most to utter his most famous on-air proclamation: "Havlicek stole the ball!"

Havlicek did everything well. Though the departure of Russell as a player and coach marked the end of the Celtics dynasty, he remained their best player into the mid-1970s and helped them win NBA titles in 1974 and 1976. He achieved a WAR between 9.7 and 12.5 in six consecutive years. That is a testament to both his offensive and defensive effectiveness.

Havlicek was never the dominant force like others among Boston's best but he was a superb athlete. His talent and mindset fit ideally into the team-first, fast-break system and he proved himself one of the stingiest defenders in the league. Havlicek worked tirelessly on all aspects of his game and used his amazing stamina to stay in constant motion on the court. Mere statistics, no matter how strong and consistent, do not do his impact justice.

ALL ABOUT HAVLICEK BEFORE BOSTON

Havlicek was the son of a Czechoslovakian immigrant father and second-generation Croatian mother. He was born in the mining town of Martins Ferry, Ohio, which borders Pennsylvania and West Virginia. His parents ran a general store and lived above it.

His mom and dad refused to allow their son to own a bike for fear of heavy car traffic. So Havlicek sprinted to keep up with friends (among them Hall of Fame knuckleball pitcher Phil Niekro). He speculated in his 1977 autobiography that the constant running and exceptional lung power was how he developed his legendary fortitude.

Havlicek did not focus on one sport. He emerged as one of the premier three-sport athletes in the country at Bridgeport High School, earning all-state honors in football, basketball, and baseball. He used his powerful arm to throw long touchdown passes. He played every position but catcher on the diamond. And he dominated on the hardwood.

The latter was his focus at Ohio State. He did not play football for Woody Hayes. He hung up his baseball spikes after playing first base for one season despite having batted over .400 in high school and starring in American Legion ball. Havlicek instead played a pivotal role along with fellow NBA Hall of Famer Jerry Lucas and future Celtics teammate Larry Siegfried transforming the Buckeye basketball team into a national power and 1960 NCAA champion (their last through 2024) during his sophomore season.

His steadiness and all-around talents were already pronounced. He improved statistically every year at Ohio State, averaging 17 points and

9.7 rebounds per game as a senior and shooting better than 50 percent from the floor in his last two years, a rarity in that era of college or pro basketball.

Never mind that Havlicek played only basketball for the Buckeyes his last three years. Major League Baseball and NFL organizations drooled over his athleticism. The Tigers, Pirates, and Yankees all sought to sign him. Cleveland even drafted Havlicek to play wide receiver. He was beaten out by future All-Pro Gary Collins and cut in camp.

It would not have mattered. He had decided to play for the Celtics, which had selected him ninth overall. The 1962 draft proved to be a gold rush. Among those taken were Dave DeBusschere, Lucas, Zelmo Beaty, and Chet "The Jet" Walker. All enjoyed fine careers. But the best of all was Havlicek.

IN A CELTICS UNIFORM AND BEYOND

Havlicek joined a juggernaut. Boston had won the last four NBA championships. They already boasted such stars as Bill Russell, Sam Jones, Tom Heinsohn, and Bob Cousy. Logic dictated that Havlicek would be forced to watch and learn from the bench. Veteran contributors Frank Ramsey, Tom Sanders, and K. C. Jones were also established contributors. But Havlicek defied logic.

Havlicek had to prove he was ready to compete for playing time with teammates and effectively against opponents. His discipline, ability to learn the NBA game, preparation for every game, tireless movement without the ball, and pure talent earned him the sixth-man role in which he thrived immediately. He played 27.5 minutes per game as a mere rookie on yet another title-bound team and averaged 14.3 points and 6.7 rebounds.

His production coming off the bench was remarkable. In an era when top starters remained on the court for 40-plus minutes every night and were sometimes never removed, the Celtics' fast-break style demanded more rest. That allowed Havlicek to thrive. He averaged 30–38 minutes per game until Heinsohn installed him as a starter in 1969, after which he led the NBA for two seasons at more than 45 minutes per game. His point and assist totals rose steadily throughout. He averaged 21.4 points in 31 minutes per game during the 1966–67 season. His passing and court awareness resulted in his assist totals doubling over the next three years.

Havlicek never tired. The result was increased effectiveness after landing a starting role. The added playing time as a starter did not limit his numbers. He peaked statistically in 1970–71 with averages of 28.9 points, 7.5 assists, and 9 rebounds per game. When evaluating his greatness, one must consider all the playoff and championship games Havlicek and his teammates played.

That is when Havlicek was at his best on both ends of the floor. Though he sometimes struggled to shoot well from the field in the postseason early and late in his career, he attacked the basket persistently, leading to a parade to the foul line. He reached double figures in free throws 28 times. His positive 19.3 combined offensive and defensive win share in the playoffs speaks volumes about his impact. He often played hurt. Among the most notable instances was the 1973 Eastern Conference finals against New York. He played the last three games with a separated shoulder that forced him to dribble and shoot left-handed.

He was the "quintessential Celtic—unselfish and loyal," said Knicks standout and future US senator Bill Bradley. "For 10 years, John Havlicek was my toughest opponent in one of the biggest rivalries in the league. Night after night, he was the epitome of constant motion. He only needed a half a step to beat me, which he usually did."[1]

Unlike Russell, whose affability and brilliance as an analyst proved a perfect fit for the broadcast booth, Havlicek quietly stepped away from the sport upon retirement, opting instead for the golf course and the business world. He admitted to not following the modern NBA. He lambasted those who asserted its superiority.

"I certainly think we could compete and given the same latitude" as modern players—"wraparound dribbles, three or four steps to the rim—we would be even better," he said. "For every dunk they'd get on us, we'd probably get two backdoor layups on them."[2]

The Celtics dynasty ended after Havlicek joined the starting lineup. Expansion and inevitability made it impossible to maintain. It must be cited that Boston had just one losing year during his career. Two terrible seasons followed his retirement and preceded the arrival of Larry Bird.

HIS GREATEST GAME

Tough choice. Havlicek scored 54 points and hit 16 of 24 shots in Game 1 of a first-round playoffs series against Atlanta in 1973. Given the urgency of Game 6 in the NBA Finals against Jerry West, Elgin Baylor, and the Lakers in 1968, his 40-point, 10-rebound, 7-assist explosion stands on top. The Celtics battered Los Angeles on the road to clinch the crown.

SIDE STORY

The NBA redesigned its Sixth Man of the Year trophy in December 2022 and renamed it the "John Havlicek Trophy" in his honor. Its first recipient in 2023 was Celtics guard Malcolm Brogdon. The award had been given before the name change in 1983. Among its first winners were Celtics centers Kevin McHale and Bill Walton.

WHAT HAVLICEK SAID

"One of the things I'm constantly aware of is that we have to keep moving. If we keep moving, something is bound to happen."[3]

WHAT WAS SAID ABOUT HAVLICEK

"He's right on your shirt whether you're five feet from the basket or 20. He's harder to get shots on than anybody." —Milwaukee Bucks guard Jon McGlocklin[4]

CHAPTER 11

Phil Esposito

"Flipper"

ESSENTIALS
Sport: Hockey
Born: February 20, 1942
Years Active: 1963–1981
Years with Boston: 1967–1976
Position: Center

KNOW THE CAREER NUMBERS
459 Goals

553 Assists

1,012 Points

36 Hat tricks

101.1 Offensive point shares

5 Art Ross Trophies

1 Hart Trophy

8 All-Star appearances

2 Stanley Cup championships

WHY ESPOSITO IS NO. 11

Granted, Esposito played his first four seasons with the Black Hawks. Yes, he completed his career with the Rangers. But he wore a Boston uniform exclusively throughout his peak seasons. The statistical achievements in comparison were vast. He only led the NHL in goals and points with the Bruins. He competed in each of his All-Star games for Boston. He earned all his awards there.

Esposito's prolific scoring and Bobby Orr's all-around brilliance helped the team turn a 180 in remarkably short order to transform itself from perennial patsy to Stanley Cup champion. Esposito led the league in goals every year from 1969 to 1975. He topped everyone in points five times. He recorded nearly two points a game during a historically prolific 1970–71 season in which he averaged eight shots on goal.

Esposito was incredibly skilled for a 200-pounder who was not a premier skater. He never rushed his shot. He had an innate sense of when to shoot and did so with deadly accuracy. His knack for scoring within a few feet of the net frustrated defensemen and goalkeepers, as did his ability to maintain possession of the puck despite the best efforts of quicker and more mobile opponents. Esposito played eight full seasons with Boston. That's enough to grant him a primo spot on this list. Others ranked lower were more athletic. His productivity earns him No. 11.

ALL ABOUT ESPOSITO BEFORE BOSTON

Esposito was born in an Italian community of hockey hotbed Sault Ste. Marie, Ontario. Brother and fellow future Hall of Famer Tony, who stopped many of his sibling's shots as a Black Hawks goalkeeper, arrived on earth a year later.

They practiced hockey at 5 a.m. before school. They skated again every day after classes and following supper. Their roles were already clearly defined as kids. Phil shot the puck at Tony. It served as healthy competition that continued for decades. When they weren't playing ice hockey, they strapped pads to their knees and slapped a rolled-up wooden sock down the basement floor with their hands. They even played table hockey. "I'd pull the lever and slap that steel marble all over the place," Phil recalled, "and even then Tony used to make some terrific saves."[1]

Their competitiveness intensified. They joined a neighborhood team. Phil recalled one game in which Tony allowed the winning goals to score. Rather than console his crying brother he chastised him in front of their teammates. Phil admitted to being the meanest kid on the squad. That was not indicative of his later personality. He grew into a happy-go-lucky sort while Tony became the more serious type.

The younger Esposito proved his offensive talent immediately at the organized youth level. Signed by the Black Hawks at age 18, he averaged an absurd 1.5 points and 1.8 assists per game for the Sarnia Legionnaires Junior B team during the 1960–61 season. He racked up 12 points in a playoff game. Soon he was blasting pucks past goaltenders for Chicago's minor league affiliate in St. Louis, with whom he scored 90 points in his first year and 80 in just 46 games in 1964 before his promotion to the NHL. He proved his worthiness to goal-machine teammates Stan Mikita and Bobby Hull before the league experienced a scoring explosion.

Chicago general manager Tommy Ivan did not accurately read his potential. He believed Esposito was too slow and soft around the net. So he sent him to Boston in 1967 in one of the most lopsided swaps in league history. His arrival and that of Orr were about to turn the Bruins around.

In a Bruins Uniform and Beyond

What Ivan misread was not only Esposito's scoring capacity. The Black Hawks GM also failed to understand his potential leadership. Neither did Orr until Esposito joined the Bruins. But it did not take long for the super offensive defenseman to realize it.

"The minute Phil was traded to us from Chicago four years ago he changed this whole team," Orr said in 1971. "We were a last-place club. Now we're the champions. Give the credit to Esposito. He went around training camp bringing us together. He'd say, 'Come on, guys, I know we can make the playoffs, but we got to stick together.' We did, and we still do. We're like a team of brothers. I know Phil has scored a lot of points, but to my mind he's even more important off the ice. He's the main force that holds us together."[2]

He also helped hold them together on the ice with a unique style of play that resulted in goals. Esposito used patience and timing to deliver passes and shots on target and at the ideal moment. He was mistaken by some as slow and even lazy but his long strides covered long stretches of ice quickly. He placed himself 10–15 feet in front of the goal mouth and peppered away with a quick stick. Longtime linemates Ken Hodge (with whom he was traded from the Black Hawks) and Wayne Cashman benefited from his passing and threat as a scorer that demanded defensive attention. It emerged as the highest-scoring line in NHL history, breaking the mark set by Esposito, Hodge, and Ron Murphy in 1969.

Esposito often exploded in the playoffs. There was his four-goal, two-assist performance in the opener of a 1969 sweep of Toronto. And the five-point effort to temporarily save the Bruins against the Montreal machine in Game 2 of the semifinals that same year. And the hat tricks against the Rangers and Black Hawks in a 1970 postseason run that resulted in Boston's first Stanley Cup crown since 1941. Esposito scored eight points in a four-game dismantling of St. Louis in the finals. He finished his Boston career with 102 goals in 71 playoff games. That remained a Bruins record for decades.

The 33-year-old Esposito was sent to the Rangers in 1975 in a swap of future Hall of Famers that brought high-scoring defenseman Brad Park to Boston. Esposito remained productive on the downside of his career but certainly not at the level he achieved with the Bruins. He retired at age 39 but remained involved in hockey as a trade-happy general manager of the Rangers and cofounder along with brother Tony of the expansion Tampa Bay Lightning. He served as their first president and GM. Esposito considered his work placing an NHL team in Florida as his greatest achievement in hockey. He also manned the broadcast booth for many years as an analyst.

HIS GREATEST GAME

It was the second round of the 1969 playoffs. Boston desperately needed a victory at home against the powerful Canadiens, who had won the first two in Montreal. The Bruins did not just win. They dominated. That was because of Esposito. He scored the first goal of the game, assisted on the second, scored the third, and assisted on two more. He was involved in every goal in a 5–0 victory. It was not one of his four playoff hat tricks—he had scored six points two weeks earlier in a postseason opener against Toronto—but given the pressure of the moment it, tops the list.

SIDE STORY

In 1992 Esposito became the first NHL general manager to sign a female player. That was goaltender Manon Rheaume, who was placed in goal for part of one period in an exhibition game against St. Louis. She saved seven shots but allowed goals to Jeff Brown and Brendan Shanahan.

WHAT ESPOSITO SAID

"Play with passion and heart. If you don't carry passion into sport—or into any job for that matter—you won't succeed."

WHAT WAS SAID ABOUT ESPOSITO

"He gets the puck and fires it into the goal while you're still trying to figure out how he got the puck in the first place. He's so strong that he can fend off the other guy with one arm and skate right around him. The only way I know to stop him is to put somebody on him and shadow him constantly, but then you're opening things up for his two linemates." —Bruins teammate Ed Johnston

CHAPTER 12

David Ortiz

"Big Papi"

David Ortiz at bat against the White Sox in 2006. Wikimedia Commons

ESSENTIALS
Sport: Baseball
Born: November 18, 1975
Years Active: 1997–2016
Years with Boston: 2003–2016
Positions: First base, designated hitter

KNOW THE CAREER NUMBERS
.286 Batting average
541 Home runs
1,768 RBI
.380 On-base percentage
56.7 Offensive WAR
10 All-Star selections
3 RBI titles
3 American League pennants
3 World Series championships

WHY ORTIZ IS NO. 12
David Ortiz was slow. His weak defense made him the ultimate designated hitter. He could do everything with the bat. He hit for average. He hit for power. He twice led the league in walks. He was among the greatest clutch hitters in baseball history. He was also perhaps the most inspirational ever to wear a Red Sox uniform.

It could be argued that Ortiz played the most significant role in ending the 86-year Curse of the Bambino and helping Boston win an MLB-best four World Series titles in the first two decades of the 21st century. His power bat, penchant for rising to the occasion with playoff and World Series games on the line, and motivating respect from teammates made him a Sox legend even before he retired after the 2016 season.

Ortiz was not *athletic*. But one cannot dispute his production. Advanced analytics often take a backseat to traditional numbers. Ortiz managed 10 100-plus RBI seasons. Like fine wine, he got better with age. He finished his career with a flourish. He averaged 110.5 RBI in his last four years and led the American League in that category with 127, slugging percentage (.620), and doubles (48) in 2016 before bowing out on top at age 40.

ALL ABOUT ORTIZ BEFORE BOSTON

Everyone in the Red Sox organization should have been required to send thank-you notes to Minnesota General Manager Terry Ryan at least once a week. He decided that David Ortiz could not hit left-handed pitching and was destined to be a full-time DH. On December 16, 2002, they waived Ortiz to avoid paying him more upon his arbitration eligibility and make room for prospect Matt LeCroy. Five weeks later he was signed by the Red Sox.

Thank you, Terry Ryan. "Obviously it's a situation that I watch and I've observed and I see what he's done and I see what he's meant to the Boston Red Sox," Ryan said in 2016. "OK, I screwed it up. It was a very bad baseball decision. We thought we had better options. We were wrong in a big way."

Ortiz's journey began in a tough area of Santo Domingo, Dominican Republic. He was raised in an atmosphere of crime and drugs. His father, Enrique, a car mechanic, and his mother Angela Rosa, who worked for the Department of Agriculture, protected him from the most harmful aspects of the environment. They provided the financial essentials for survival and a moral compass that allowed him to avoid the pitfalls of crime into which many fell. They instilled into David the value of hard work. His interest in sports also kept him safe and on a positive path.

Baseball became his passion. His father encouraged that love. Ortiz excelled in baseball and basketball at Estudio Espaillat High School. Soon he was attracting the attention of scouts. Like many Latin American players he grabbed the opportunity at a young age. He signed with Seattle at age 17. The Mariners too spent years kicking themselves over underestimating Ortiz. He improved every year as a mere teenager, batting .332 in rookie ball in 1995 and .322 with 18 home runs and 93

RBI in Class A at age 20 the following year. They traded him in 1996 to the Twins.

Ortiz soared through the Minnesota organization. He advanced from Class A-Advanced to the big-league club in 1997 to earn 51 at-bats. The moment was not too big for him. He did what he had done since arriving in professional baseball—batted over .300 and showed glimpses of power. Yet the Twins never showed faith in him. They bounced him from Triple-A to the majors until finally settling him on the Twins as a platoon player in 2001. His performance in 2002 should have convinced them of his potential. He slammed 32 doubles and 20 homers in just 412 at-bats. Soon he was sent to Boston in one of the most regrettable departures in baseball history.

IN A RED SOX UNIFORM AND BEYOND

His Red Sox career is not defined by statistics. It must be placed into context. The club had not won a World Series in 85 years when he arrived. They were perennial playoff contenders in the toughest division in baseball. Boston managed six winning seasons in the last seven with three postseason runs. The Curse continued. Even the least superstitious fans in Red Sox nation had believed in it for years, particularly after the 1986 World Series debacle against the Mets.

The Sox required more than his booming bat. They needed an inspiring presence. One was tied to the other. Teammates, coaches, front office personnel—everyone—loved his unifying and genuine personality. They also marveled at his mental and emotional approach to hitting. "David is so smart," said David Ross, a teammate and future Cubs manager. "We were talking hitting in the back of the plane once, and I'm thinking 'I don't think like this, no wonder I'm a (lousy) hitter.' His words were 'be your nature.' If you're a fastball hitter, don't miss the fastball; if you hit breaking balls, crush the breaking ball. Get in the box and know who you are and don't lose sight of that."[1]

Ortiz led both by words and deeds, particularly in the biggest moments on the biggest stage. There was his two-run double in Game 4 of the 2003 ALDS against Oakland that snatched victory from the jaws of defeat and became the turning point of the series. He completed a three-game sweep of Anaheim in the first round of the 2004 playoffs with a home run. His blast to win Game 4 of the ALCS that year against New York launched the comeback of the ages as Boston became the first team in baseball history to rebound from a 3–0 deficit to win a playoff series. Ortiz's two-run homer in Game 7 helped finish off the stunned Yankees.

The clutch hits just kept coming. With the Sox fighting to return to the playoffs in 2005 he hit one walk-off homer, a game-winning 11th-inning homer, a go-ahead eighth-inning homer, and a walk-off single during an epic 23-game September stretch that prevented his otherwise slumping team from spiraling into the abyss.

The 2013 World Series, during which he batted a staggering .688 with four multi-hit games and a .760 on-base percentage, was another example of his greatness with championships on the line. Ortiz went 3-for-3 in Game 4 to reverse the course of the series. He opened the fifth with a double and scored the tying run. He then organized a spontaneous team meeting in the dugout. "We don't get here every day," he said. "Let's relax and play the game the way we know how. We're better than this right here. Let's loosen up and play the game the way we do. Let's go." The Sox did not lose another game in capturing their third championship in 10 years.

Ortiz had already proven his capacity to inspire not only with his bat but with his words and emotions. Following the Boston Marathon bomber attack in 2013, he addressed the Fenway crowd that included a group of police and first responders, heroes on that tragic day. They would never forget his message. "This jersey that we're wearing today it doesn't say 'Red Sox.' It says, 'Boston.' We want to thank you for you, Mayor Menino, Governor Patrick, the whole police department, for the great job that they did this past week," Ortiz said. "This is our fucking city. And nobody is going to dictate our freedom. Stay strong."[2]

Ortiz concluded his career after a loss to Cleveland in the 2016 ALDS with a .289 career postseason batting average, 17 home runs, 22 doubles, and 61 RBI. Most satisfying is that he tortured the hated Yankees in 2003 and 2004 with five home runs and 17 RBI in 14 games, including the four that ended the Curse of the Bambino and helped launch the greatest run of baseball titles in the twenty-first century. Though he participated in only three of them, Ortiz was the most important Red Sox player during that stretch.

Ortiz continued his charity work postcareer. He launched the David Ortiz Children's Fund in 2007 to help kids from Boston to the Dominican Republic and beyond. His life could have ended on June 9, 2019, when he was the victim of a shooting at a bar in the Dominican. The bullet forced surgeons to remove parts of his intestines, colon, and gall bladder but he survived. So have the memories of his greatness in a Red Sox uniform.

HIS GREATEST GAME

The Sox would not have earned a shot at the Yankees in the 2004 ALCS had they not dispatched the Angels the previous round. Ortiz made sure of it in Game 3 with two doubles and a home run, including the series-clinching two-run blast in the 10th inning.

SIDE STORY

Ortiz played most of his career in Boston but was not a Patriots fan. He became a lifelong Green Bay Packers fan after he met his future wife Tiffany while playing minor league ball with the Wisconsin Timber Rattlers in the Seattle organization.[3]

WHAT ORTIZ SAID

"Sometimes you just don't feel the same every day, it doesn't matter what you do, but when you have people looking forward to seeing you perform for them, that puts you in the mood, and that's natural in Boston. That's why it's such a special place to play."

WHAT WAS SAID ABOUT ORTIZ

"I played with David the longest of anyone. I was amazed at this: His ability to slow the game down in a big moment was second to nobody. From day one, in a big moment, everything was in slow motion. He found a way to come through in moments where you dream of as a kid. He did it every single time. There is no one in the game that has done that." —Dustin Pedroia

CHAPTER 13

Paul Pierce

"The Truth"

Paul Pierce in 2008. Wikimedia Commons, Keith Allison photo

Essentials

Sport: Basketball

Born: October 13, 1977

Years Active: 1998–2017

Years with Boston: 1998–2013

Position: Swingman

Know the Career Numbers

19.7 Points per game

4.8 Rebounds per game

3.5 Assists per game

.445 Shooting percentage

.368 3-point percentage

86.9 Offensive win shares

63.1 Defensive win shares

4 All-NBA

10 All-Star appearances

Why Pierce Is No. 13

Consistent. Durable. Dependable. Passionate. Clutch. These are all words that describe Pierce and his contributions as one of the premier athletes in Boston sports history. He excelled as a beacon of light during a rare period of Celtics mediocrity and maintained his greatness as part of the Big Three after the arrival of Kevin Garnett and Ray Allen.

Pierce averaged between 18.6 and 26.8 points per game for 14 consecutive seasons. He shot at least 44 percent from the field and 35 percent from beyond the arc nine years in a row during his prime. He rebounded well for a comparatively short swingman at 6-foot-5 and worked hard to raise the level of performance of teammates with his passing.

He never led the NBA in any statistical category and was generally considered a second-tier standout rather than a superstar. He performed his best with victory or defeat hanging in the balance and the stakes were highest. Pierce finished his career among the top 15 scorers in league history. His Hall of Fame induction was never in doubt.

ALL ABOUT PIERCE BEFORE BOSTON

Pierce was born and raised in the Los Angeles suburb of Inglewood, which suffered from one of the highest crime rates of any community in the country. Gangs and drugs were a lure but Pierce felt a far healthier attraction to basketball as a young child. He had the Celtics–Lakers showdowns to thank for that. He watched Larry Bird, Magic Johnson, and all the other stars on his uncle's tiny television. He was hooked.

Another positive influence was Scott Collins, a local police detective who coached youth basketball and helped low-income children learn the sport. He even snuck kids into Laker games at the Forum when he worked security there. Pierce also became a prolific bowler.

Not that he appeared destined for the NBA when he arrived at Inglewood High School. Pierce was merely average. He was cut from the varsity as a freshman but stayed persistent, practicing at 5 a.m. before school and earning a spot on the squad as a sophomore. He remained on the bench until one tournament game in which Inglewood fell far behind. Pierce went on a tear to lead a huge comeback. A star was born. He emerged as the premier prospect in the state. Scouts converged. He decided on powerhouse Kansas.

Pierce excelled from the start, winning Big Eight Freshman of the Year honors and successive conference tournament MVPs. Most intriguing was his penchant for performing his best in the biggest games. Eight other college players were selected before him in the 1998 draft and none outperformed him in the NBA—only Vince Carter came close. Pierce wasted no time making a huge impact on the Celtics.

IN A CELTICS UNIFORM AND BEYOND

Only three players had drained more clutch shots than Pierce when he retired in 2017. They were Dirk Nowitzki (who was picked before him in the 1998 draft), LeBron James, and Kobe Bryant. Distinguished company. Clutch shots are defined as go-ahead field goals with five or fewer seconds remaining in a game.

That statistic would come as little surprise to Boston fans. They watched Pierce outshine his basic statistics in the most critical moments. He and Bryant topped the list in buzzer-beaters—shots made as the clock wound down to zero—with 10 during that period. Even blanketed defenses could not prevent him from nailing game-winners.

That included critical playoff moments. There was the go-ahead three-pointer in Game 1 of the 2003 first round against Indiana that preceded his four put-away foul shots. There was the game-winning shot in overtime to beat Chicago in the momentum-swinging Game 5 of the 2009 playoffs. He did the same in the postseason against Miami the following year to all but complete a sweep. Pierce appeared to have buried James and the Heat in the 2012 Eastern Conference finals with a critical three-pointer.

None of it would have been possible had he not survived being stabbed in the face, neck, and back during an altercation at a nightclub in 2000. The incident gave Pierce a perspective on his life and career. "I'm fortunate to be here," he said. "I feel a lot older from the simple fact that I had a brush with death and saw my life flash before my eyes. You grow up 10 times as fast."[1]

His confidence level extended beyond cockiness. Pierce was a trash-talker who backed up the bravado. Among those who learned that was Pacers forward Al Harrington, who famously engaged in a verbal exchange with Pierce with the clock winding down in the third quarter of Game 3 in the 2003 playoffs. Pierce dribbled, stared at his defender in the eye, repeated "Here I come, here I come," then buried a bomb in his face.[2]

Most impressive is that Pierce played his first nine seasons as one of only a few offensive threats. Defenses focused on him yet he maintained strong scoring averages and shooting percentages every season. When Allen and Garnett arrived to form "The Big Three," he worked selflessly to create a seamless transition. He took significantly fewer shots but remained efficient. Pierce saved his best for last, scoring 50 points in the first two games of the NBA Finals against the Lakers and earning series MVP as Boston captured its first championship in 22 years.

Pierce continued his remarkable consistency until leaving for Brooklyn in a blockbuster trade in 2013 that eventually netted Jaylen Brown. The Celtics unloaded him just as he was fading. But he would never fade in the memory of their fans.

His postcareer became memorable as well. Among his achievements was the success of his Truth Fund, which provided funds for underserved youth, and his 2021 induction into the Hall of Fame.

His Greatest Game

The Celtics could not have won the 2008 title without his heroics, particularly in Game 7 of the Eastern Conference semifinals against his archrival James and the Cavaliers. His 41 points on 13-of-23 shooting told only part of the story. He outwrestled James for a loose ball with a minute remaining to help cement the victory. Pierce added five assists in the victory. Boston outscored Cleveland by 10 points with him on the floor.

Side Story

Pierce lost his ESPN gig in 2021 for posting an Instagram video of himself at a poker game seemingly drunk with twerking strippers. He had been an analyst on *The Jump* and *NBA Countdown*.

What Pierce Said

"I'm not a guy who goes into the neighborhood, gets beat up by the bully's gang, and then now I want to join their gang. That's just not me. I wanna fight—let's go! I mean, I'm gonna stand up for myself. That's just the competitive nature of where I come from, the era I grew up in."[3]

What Was Said about Pierce

"One of the best tempo scorers I've ever seen. He just puts the defender on a string all night. They're dropping, off-balance . . . but he's always balanced." —Celtics coach Doc Rivers[4]

CHAPTER 14

Bobby Doerr

"The Silent Captain"

ESSENTIALS
Sport: Baseball
Born: April 7, 1918
Died: November 13, 1917
Years Active: 1937–1951
Years with Boston: 1937–1951
Position: Second base

KNOW THE CAREER NUMBERS
.288 Batting average
223 Home runs
1,247 RBI
.362 On-base percentage
46.5 Offensive WAR
9 All-Star selections
3 RBI titles
3 American League pennants
3 World Series championships

WHY DOERR IS NO. 14

Doerr earned his induction in Cooperstown. He deserves this spot ahead of other prominent Red Sox despite missing the 1944 pennant race and the 1945 season to World War II. His numbers were not tainted by steroid accusations like Roger Clemens and Manny Ramirez. He played his entire career in Boston unlike those two, as well as Jim Rice and Carlton Fisk. His achievements are worthy of this ranking.

He was overshadowed throughout his career by Ted Williams. But Doerr gained his admiration as a quiet leader and tremendous hitter with line-drive power. Doerr exceeded 100 RBI six times. While the three-man shift befuddled Williams in the 1946 World Series, perhaps costing Boston the crown, Doerr rose to the occasion by batting .409 and compiling a .458 on-base percentage. He proved his worth defensively that season, leading the league in defensive WAR while placing third in the American League MVP voting. His .980 career fielding percentage was the best all-time among second basemen when he retired.

ALL ABOUT DOERR BEFORE BOSTON

The most populous state in the country ranked only eighth in 1920. California was growing in numbers—including the future heart of the Red Sox. Doerr was one of three from the Golden State along with Ted Williams and Dom DiMaggio. Johnny Pesky was also from the West Coast (Portland, Oregon).

Doerr was born in Los Angeles and spent much of his youth in the Great Depression. His father strained to provide for his three kids toiling for the local telephone company after the hard economic times limited him to part-time work. Bobby practiced ceaselessly on the playground baseball diamonds near his home. His American Legion team featured several future major leaguers, including shortstop and Brooklyn Dodgers All-Star Mickey Owen.

While brother Hal was reaching the brink of the major leagues as a catcher before falling short, Bobby was honing his skills and gaining valuable experience competing in semipro ball against professional players. His talents were noticed by the Pacific Coast League Hollywood Sheiks, who signed him at age 16 to a contract with the express guarantee to his father that they would allow him to attend high school during the winter and earn his diploma.

Doerr had yet to develop power. He was merely a singles hitter but did raise his average to .317 in 1935. Soon thereafter he signed with the Red Sox. By 1936 he had proven himself one of the finest prospects in the sport. Though he still lacked a home run stroke he led the PCL with 238 hits and slammed 37 doubles. Doerr was still a teenager when he arrived for spring training the following year. He was on the verge of breaking through in Boston.

IN A RED SOX UNIFORM AND BEYOND

One obstacle stood in the way as Doerr prepared for 1937. That was incumbent starting second baseman Eric McNair, who was coming off a strong season after arriving in a trade from the Athletics. Yet Doerr usurped him for the starting job and went 3-for-5 batting leadoff on opening day having just turned 19 two weeks earlier. But McNair regained the starting spot after Doerr was beaned in the head and heated up at the plate. Doerr remained the backup until September.

It wouldn't happen again. Doerr sent McNair back to the bench in 1938 and motivated Boston to trade him to the White Sox after that season. Doerr took the job and ran with it offensively and defensively. Though it remained secure until back issues forced him to retire at age 33 and he never played winter ball, Doerr played as if someone was ready to beat him out.

"I think it was good for me to get away after a full season," he said. "In those days, I don't think anyone ever got too complacent. Even after I played ten years of ball, I still felt like I had to play well or somebody might take my place. They had plenty of players in the minor leagues who were good enough to come up and take your job, and I think that kept us going all of the time. I hustled and put that extra effort in all of the time."[1]

Doerr added power without sacrificing average to blossom into a Hall of Famer. He increased his home run total from 5 to 12 to 22 from 1938 to 1940 and slammed at least 13 home runs every season for the rest of his career. He reached double figures in doubles, triples, and homers in 1940, 1944, 1947, and 1950. His .528 slugging percentage led the American League in 1944. Doerr managed arguably his best season in 1946 after losing part of 1944 and all of 1945 to the war. He drove in 116 runs to help the Sox run away with their first pennant since 1918 and finished third in the MVP vote behind Williams and Detroit ace Hal Newhouser.

Doerr would have continued to play and likely been inducted sooner into the Hall of Fame had he not sustained a back injury in 1951 that ended his career. Rather than risk a more serious injury, he retired to his farm in Oregon, where he raised cattle before accepting work with the Red Sox as a roving minor league coach and scout. He served as first base coach under new manager Dick Williams during the Impossible Dream season of 1967 and remained on the staff for three years. Doerr earned the admiration of the players, including second baseman Mike Andrews, to whom he taught the nuances of the position.

"Bobby Doerr was my mentor," Andrews said. "When I was in the minors, I always seemed to improve when he came along. I had so much faith in him that if he told me I'd be a better hitter if I changed my shoelaces, I'd have done it."[2]

Doerr later worked as a hitting coach for the expansion Toronto Blue Jays before the veteran's committee finally voted him into the Hall of Fame in 1986. Two years later the Red Sox retired his uniform No. 1. It was about time. While playing stellar defense, Doerr had finished his career 35 years earlier with more RBI per game than did contemporary and later superstars Stan Musial, Mickey Mantle, Willie Mays, Ernie Banks, and Mike Schmidt.

HIS GREATEST GAME

The Battle of the Sox on May 13, 1947, at Fenway Park could have been renamed Bobby Doerr Day. Doerr hit for his second career cycle that afternoon—almost three years to the day he accomplished his first one. Such heroics appeared unlikely after he grounded out in his first at-bat and again in his third. But Doerr, who had homered in the fourth inning, tripled in the seventh, then doubled and singled in a nine-run eighth to complete the cycle. Williams contributed two homers in the 19–6 blow-out of Chicago.

SIDE STORY

Superstar Cleveland pitcher Bob Feller concluded his brilliant career with three no-hitters. He would have had five if not for Doerr, who managed the only hit in two of his one-hitters. Doerr blooped a hit over second base to ruin one in 1939 and smashed a liner over shortstop in 1946 to wreck the other.[3]

WHAT DOERR SAID

"People ask, 'Don't you wish you played now?' No. I know the money is better, but I just feel fortunate to have played then. I think we had more fun. We played the game hard, but there is so much pressure on these guys."[4]

WHAT WAS SAID ABOUT DOERR

"Doerr was easily the most popular player of the Red Sox and possibly the most popular baseball player of his era. He was so modest and his disposition so gentle that his colleagues often described him as 'sweet.' He was the kind of man other men might have envied had they not liked him so much." —Author David Halberstam in *Summer of '49*[5]

CHAPTER 15

Andre Tippett
"Martial Arts Master"

ESSENTIALS
Sport: Football
Born: December 27, 1959
Years Active: 1982–1993
Years with New England: 1982–1993
Position: Outside linebacker

KNOW THE CAREER NUMBERS
151 Games played
139 Games started
100 Sacks
5 Pro Bowls
2 All-Pro selections

WHY TIPPETT IS NO. 15
Tippett enjoyed a shorter peak period than most other star Boston athletes. He lost the last five games in 1986 to an injured knee, faded a bit as a pass rusher in 1988, and was slowed by shoulder surgery that cost his 1989 season. He dominated for several years before that and remained a strong force for the rest of his career.

No Patriots defensive player was ever as dominant at his best. Tippett used his black belt in karate to shed blockers and terrorize opposing quarterbacks after destroying running backs who tried in vain to protect them. He averaged nearly a sack per game from 1983 to 1988 and played a critical role in the team's Super Bowl run in 1985 with 16.5 sacks. Quite impressive given he played strong-side linebacker against better quarterback protection. Tippett earned a Pro Bowl spot in the last five of those seasons.

A lack of longevity prevents Tippett from ranking higher. Others excelled far longer. Others won more awards. Few were better in their prime than Tippett.

ALL ABOUT TIPPETT BEFORE NEW ENGLAND

Tippett was born in Birmingham, Alabama, but the family hightailed out of the city known as "Bombingham" for its Ku Klux Klan terrorism when he was seven years old and moved to Newark. That city was also unsafe but the fatherless child escaped the crime-ridden streets and gang activity through martial arts. He began studying at age 12 and emerged as a passionate practitioner.

"We grew up poor," he said. "My mom raised six of us. I was the oldest, so I somewhat became the [family's] protector. . . . I was a big guy, too, so people tested me. You're thrown into [fighting]. Many times, I had to fend off people or take off running because I was outnumbered."[1]

Tippett embraced the Bruce Lee movie *Five Fingers of Death* and saved up enough money to buy new issues of *Black Belt* magazine. He studied a defensive martial art called Bando at the local YMCA before branching out. Karate played a significant role in his success on the football field.

Not at first. Tippett was cut from the high school squad as a skinny freshman but eventually performed well enough to land a scholarship at the University of Iowa, where he earned All-American status and helped the Hawkeyes to their first Rose Bowl in 22 years in 1981 and back again the following year. He led the Big Ten while setting a school record in tackles for loss yardage in 1980.

That success did not motivate NFL teams to consider Tippett a premier prospect. Pick after pick dropped off the draft board as he awaited a call. Included were six linebackers. The Patriots finally snagged him No. 41 overall. He would prove to be the only player not selected in the first round who reached the Pro Football Hall of Fame. A stellar NFL career was about to begin.

IN A PATRIOTS UNIFORM AND BEYOND

Though Tippett played every game during his strike-shortened 1982 season, he only started one. He emerged in 1983 with 8.5 sacks but did not blossom into a quarterback's worst nightmare until Raymond Berry was hired as Patriots coach midway through the following year. Berry and his assistants, particularly defensive coordinator Rod Rust, sought to maximize his talent. They took him out of pass coverage and allowed him to relentlessly attack.

The positive results were immediate. Tippett recorded a ridiculous 12 sacks in the last seven games with at least one in each and finished with a team-record 18.5. That assertive style continued in 1985 and played a critical role in New England dominating in the playoffs and reaching its first Super Bowl. He had blossomed into the premier pass rusher in the AFC and arguably the sport alongside Giants superstar Lawrence Taylor. Tippett developed a philosophy about his aggressive style based on fear. It required a violent style. That approach resulted in four three-sack games in 1985, including two in a nine-sack blitz in a six-game winning streak during which opponents averaged fewer than 12 points.

Then it happened. Coming off the most prolific sack game of his career with 3.5 against Buffalo in Week 8, he hurt his knee and missed the next five games. The injury sapped his speed and quickness upon his return. Tippett came back with a vengeance in 1987, finishing first in the AFC with 12.5 sacks. He again missed time to injury the next year and lost the 1989 season to shoulder surgery. Though he remained an effective pass rusher through 1993, he was no longer among the league's elite. But he was named to the NFL All-Decade Team of the 1980s.

Tippett, who was promoted in 1988 to first-degree black belt, maintained his passion for karate after he retired from football. He was enshrined into the Patriots Hall of Fame in 1999 and into the Pro Football Hall of Fame nine years later. Tippett also worked with the Patriots as Executive Director of Community Affairs and served in Pop Warner coaching football to kids.

HIS GREATEST GAME

The Patriots were trying to stay in the AFC playoff race when they played at Buffalo in Week 8 of the 1986 season. Tippett made sure they did with a career-high 3.5 sacks in a 23–3 victory that again proved his dominance and that of his defense.

SIDE STORY

Tippett married a Jewish woman and converted to Judaism after learning more about the religion. He wanted his family, which included three daughters and one son, to practice the same faith. They took a trip to Israel together.[2]

WHAT TIPPETT SAID

"There isn't a game I'm not scared. These big linemen could really hurt me. That's why I look at some games like a fight. I know I'm gonna have to fight, so I might as well get myself to that way of thinking. I gotta be violent."[3]

WHAT WAS SAID ABOUT TIPPETT

"Anything LT (Lawrence Taylor) could do, Andre could do it just as well. He could rush the passer just as well, stop the run just as well, cover backs out of the backfield just as well. He just never got the notoriety of LT because we played up in New England." —Patriots teammate Irving Fryar[4]

CHAPTER 16

Patrice Bergeron

"St. Patrice"

Patrice Bergeron in 2016. Wikimedia Commons, Lisa Gansky photo

ESSENTIALS
Sport: Hockey

Born: July 24, 1985

Years Active: 2003–2023

Years with Boston: 2003–2023

Position: Center

KNOW THE CAREER NUMBERS
427 Goals

613 Assists

1,040 Points

87.4 Offensive point shares

38.2 Defensive point shares

6 Selke Trophies

3 All-Star appearances

1 Stanley Cup championship

WHY BERGERON IS NO. 16
That a player selected six times as the best defensive forward in the NHL earned a mere three trips to the All-Star Game is a negative reflection on the writers and fans who prioritize prolific scoring over complete talent in their voting. Bergeron seemed destined for the Hall of Fame upon his retirement in 2023 despite the annual snubs.

Bergeron went out on top to cement his standing as one of the best two-way centers in league history, earning the Selke Trophy his last two seasons and helping the Bruins to the best regular season record ever in the NHL his final year before the disappointing playoff loss to Florida. He was also celebrated throughout his career for his leadership and sportsmanship.

Despite his focus on defense, Bergeron racked up more than 1,000 points. His consistent performance was a major factor in the Bruins earning playoff berths in all but four of his seasons and snagging the Stanley Cup in 2011.

ALL ABOUT BERGERON BEFORE BOSTON

For someone afraid to skate as a young child Bergeron certainly reached the big time fast. He was too scared to lace them on until age five—rather late in life for a future NHL player—but was pumping pucks past goaltenders for the Bruins just 13 years later.

It all started in 1990, five years after Bergeron was born in Ancienne-Lorette, a suburb of hockey-crazed Quebec City. Parents Gerard and Sylvie would drive Patrice to a rink in their old stomping grounds of nearby Sillery. But the child would not skate with the rest of the children. He would instead crawl into the net and sit. He was the only kid not skating.

That fear lasted about three months. One December day his parents were stunned to see Patrice wave at them, smiling and skating. After emerging from his shell he became obsessed. He not only loved skating but became an ardent Quebec Nordiques fan. He was also a fine piano player, but when his instructor suggested he quit hockey to focus on the 88 keys, it was over. Such daring and silly advice resulted in the end of his music career.

Bergeron was far from flashy on the ice. He played the ultimate team game with intelligence and competence. But he was small. He struggled at first in the professional ranks. He was cut from his first team at age 16. Then he blossomed. He required only two years in the Quebec Major Junior Hockey League to establish himself as an NHL prospect. Bergeron totaled 73 points in 70 games during the 2002–03 season. The 2003 draft was loaded, and he slipped to the second round. The Bruins recognized his potential. They found a spot for him as an immediate contributor.

IN A BRUINS UNIFORM AND BEYOND

In the five seasons preceding the 2004–05 lockout, only Atlanta star Ilya Kovalchuk outscored Bergeron among rookies who stepped into the NHL right after being drafted. The 18-year-old Bergeron scored 39 points that year and nearly doubled that total in both of the seasons that followed the lockout. He remained unrecognized on a poor team, then lost nearly the entire 2007–08 season to a shoulder injury.

Bergeron hit his stride two years later. He performed particularly well in the 2011 Stanley Cup run with 20 points in 23 postseason games, including two goals in the Game 7 blanking of Vancouver that clinched their first crown in 39 years. He won his first Selke Trophy in 2012, and it could have been renamed the Bergeron Trophy thereafter. He earned five more through 2023. No other forward had won it more upon his retirement.

He indeed finished his career with a flourish, teaming up for several seasons as center flanked by Brad Marchand and David Pastrnak to form a well-oiled machine known as the Perfection Line. It was generally considered the best in the NHL and that was proven on the ice. They were the three leading scorers on every Bruins team from 2017–18 until Bergeron retired after the disappointing 2023 playoffs.

His linemates were quite appreciative. Bergeron had a knack for keeping opponents guessing. "Every team knows he's there," said Pastrnak, "and he's still able to move and find the open ice and get that pass in the slot."[1]

Bergeron reached the 1,000-point plateau in his final season. His 58 points that year were typical of his annual output. He was 37 years old on a one-year contract, but it seemed he could thrive forever—and still be underappreciated. He finished with the most career overtime goals in Bruins history. He scored the game-winner in Game 7 of the 2011 Stanley Cup. He won half the Selke Trophies over 12 years. His greatness was based on durability—he often played through injuries—and steady productivity. His lack of All-Star Game appearances was a testament to a style that was easily overlooked.

His Greatest Game

Bergeron had eight career hat tricks, including two four-goal games. The second—against Detroit near the end of his career in 2021—was achieved in five shots on goal. Given the importance of his two goals in Game 7 of the 2011 Stanley Cup finals against Vancouver, that one deserves the thumbs-up. He gave the Bruins the lead for good late in the first period, then added a short-handed goal with two minutes remaining in the second to all but clinch the title.

SIDE STORY

Bergeron displayed his charitable side with an annual Pucks and Paddles event during which Bruins players and fans competed in table tennis for various causes. The final match in 2023 pitted Bergeron and Brad Marchand against David Pastrnak and David Krejci in a doubles battle. It featured playful trash talk and long rallies. Money raised went to the Special Olympics and Boston Bruins Foundation.[2]

WHAT BERGERON SAID

"I had a dream at 12 years old, and through hard work and perseverance my dreams came true more than I ever could have imagined."

WHAT WAS SAID ABOUT BERGERON

"The other team can't wait for his mistakes to be able to counter attack because it's not going to happen. Yet he can wait for his offense to come because the other team will make the mistakes eventually. That's when he'll pounce." —Toronto Maple Leafs assistant coach Scott Gordon[3]

CHAPTER 17

Pedro Martinez

"Pedro el Grande"

Pedro Martinez at his 2025 Baseball Hall of Fame induction. Wikimedia Commons, Arturo Pardavilla III photo

ESSENTIALS
Sport: Baseball

Born: October 25, 1971

Years Active: 1992–2009

Years with Boston: 1998–2004

Position: Starting pitcher

KNOW THE CAREER NUMBERS
219–100 Win–loss record

2.93 ERA

3,154 Strikeouts

7.1 Hits per nine innings pitched

1.054 WHIP

5 ERA titles

3 Cy Young Awards

8 All-Star appearances

1 World Series championship

WHY MARTINEZ IS NO. 17
The brilliant right-hander would have ranked higher had he pitched longer with Boston. His seven-year stay in an 18-year career warrants less consideration. But those seven years? Wow!

Martinez mastered major league hitters during a Koufaxian blitz. His best seasons were with the Red Sox after leaving Montreal and before joining the Mets. His dominance proved particularly incredible given the steroid era in which he performed. While the best of his peers struggled to keep their earned runs averages under 4.00, he was routinely recording ERAs half that.

It wasn't just velocity. Martinez fired baseballs at between 95–98 miles per hour. That was fast but it was matched by other fireballers. His key to success aside from a burning competitiveness was late movement. His fastball, wicked changeup, and deceptive breaking balls danced before they reached home plate. They were virtually impossible to square up.

The result was ridiculous numbers. Martinez compiled a 117–37 record in a Boston uniform. He won four of his five ERA titles and two of his three Cy Young Awards with the Red Sox, as were all three of his strikeout titles. Ironically, his worst season was 2004, but he still helped the Sox break the Curse of the Bambino by winning all three of his postseason decisions.

ALL ABOUT MARTINEZ BEFORE BOSTON

It all started for Martinez where it all started for so many major leagu-ers—in the baseball hotbed of the Dominican Republic. He was raised in a dirt-floor home in the poverty-stricken town of Manoguayabo. His father, Paolino, once a fine pitcher who was invited to try out with the New York Giants, barely made ends meet working as a janitor while his mother helped by taking in laundry.

Baseball was both an escape and passion for Pedro. Role model older brother Ramon blossomed into an All-Star pitcher with the Dodgers. The two children could not afford bats, so they improvised with tree branches and other sticks and popped off doll heads (much to the dismay of their sisters) to use as makeshift baseballs.

Pedro tagged along with Ramon after the latter signed a contract with Los Angeles and joined its baseball academy. Dodgers scout Raphael Avila noticed the 13-year-old kid brother firing a baseball and clocked him at 80 miles per hour. Avila urged him to keep pitching. Three years later he signed Pedro as well.

The dominance began immediately. He overwhelmed Dominican Summer League hitters for two seasons before dominating rookie league competition. He struggled a bit with his control, a problem he fixed early in his major league career. He rose rapidly through the organizations, going 8–0 with a 2.05 ERA at Class A Bakersfield and 7–5 with a 1.77 ERA at Double-A San Antonio.

By that time Ramon was a mainstay in the Dodgers rotation and had peaked in 1990 winning 20 games and finishing second in the Cy Young Award voting. Pedro was also receiving great attention. He debuted with

Los Angeles in September 1992, pitching twice against Cincinnati and providing a glimpse of his future greatness. Soon, general manager Fred Claire was proclaiming that he had no intention of trading the young stud.

Promises are meant to be broken—and Claire broke his. Needing a second baseman after a contract squabble with Jody Reed, he sent Martinez to Montreal for Delino DeShields. It was a transaction Claire would bitterly regret. The Dodgers feared that Martinez had neither the size nor strength to succeed long term as a starter. It was not the only regretful swap of his career. After he won his first Cy Young Award in his fourth season with the Expos, that cash-strapped team, knowing they couldn't afford him, dealt him to Boston for pitching mediocrities Carl Pavano and Tony Armas.

Martinez had blossomed into one of the premier pitchers in baseball. He had also earned a nickname—"Senor Plunk"—for his penchant for throwing at hitters and getting into fights on the field. He had merely scratched the surface of his potential. He was about to establish himself as the king of all hurlers.

IN A RED SOX UNIFORM AND BEYOND

The Red Sox wasted no time signing Martinez to a six-year contract for $75 million, the heftiest deal for any pitcher in baseball. Then he proved he might have actually been *underpaid*. As the steroid era began, a consequence of the 1994 lockout that nearly killed the sport and the desire of Major League Baseball to turn on turned-off fans again with offensive explosions, Martinez frustrated beefed-up hitters swinging for the fences with his dazzling stuff.

He was merely great in his first year with Boston. Then he became otherworldly. His second and third seasons were among the greatest in baseball history. His combined record of 41–10 and ERA of 1.91 in 1999 and 2000 reminded many of the early 1960s dominance of Dodgers legend Sandy Koufax. Most remarkable was his season-saving surprise relief appearance in Game 5 of the 1999 American League Division Series against a Cleveland lineup considered one of the most powerful ever assembled. He no-hit the Indians over six innings in a scintillating performance that sent the Red Sox into the ALCS against New York. He then blanked the Yankees over seven innings with 12 strikeouts in Game 4. His 1.74 ERA in 2000 was outrageous given that the average ERA in the American League that season was 4.91.

Martinez continued to punch his ticket into the Hall of Fame. A shoulder injury limited him to 18 starts in 2001 but he returned to win his third and fourth ERA titles the next two years. He finished second in the 2002 Cy Young voting despite thoroughly outpitching winner Barry Zito, who simply received more run support.

"He was small," said Yankees slugger Paul O'Neill. "But it didn't stop him from being as intimidating as anybody I ever faced. He had an overpowering fastball. He had the best changeup. And both of those pitches made people forget sometimes how off the charts his breaking ball was. Sometimes he'd just come up for the first two or three innings just showing you his fastball. And, let me tell you, if he got through the order just featuring the fastball, you were in deep, deep trouble. . . . Against Pedro, you never felt as if you were ahead in the count. Never. Didn't matter whether it was 2–0 or 3–1. You always felt as if he had the advantage. In those days, I truly felt that all three pitches, because of the way he could locate them, were the best in the game."[1]

Not all were roses. In Game 7 of the 2003 ALCS against the Yankees, manager Grady Little left him in too long in desperation to win. The result was a blown 5–2 lead in the eighth inning and a defeat clinched when light-hitting Aaron Boone smashed a series-clinching homer.

Martinez stuck around long enough to help Boston break The Curse in 2004, though he did not perform in the regular season nor postseason to his standards. He did come through in his only World Series start, shutting out St. Louis over seven innings in Game 3 of the sweep. That was his last start in a Boston uniform. Martinez opted for free agency and bolted to the Mets. He never again performed close to the level he reached with the Red Sox.

After hanging up his spikes in 2009, Martinez became one of the premier baseball analysts on TV and maintained a foundation that helped Dominican children learn English and music while battling domestic violence and teen pregnancy. He also served as a special assistant to Sox GM Ben Cherington in 2013.

HIS GREATEST GAME

Where do we start? The one-hit complete game with 17 strikeouts against the Yankees in 1999? The three-hit shutout of Toronto with 12 strikeouts two weeks later? The two-hit blanking of Baltimore in 2000 with 15 strikeouts? The eight-inning, 13-strikeout shutout of New York in 2001? Considering the urgency of the moment, let's go with his rare relief appearance in Game 5 of the 1999 ALDS in Cleveland against the powerful Indians. His six no-hit innings snatched victory from the jaws of defeat.

SIDE STORY

Martinez's reputation was marred by his part in an infamous moment during the 2003 ALCS against New York, though some believe he was not to blame. Martinez pushed 72-year-old Yankees coach Don "Popeye" Zimmer to the ground as all hell broke loose in a Game 3 brawl. He claimed it happened too fast and that he did not see Zimmer rushing toward him until it was too late.

WHAT MARTINEZ SAID

"I just try to do what I have to do and let the people out there do what they have to do, which is have fun, scream, yell and jump around. I try to do what I have to do, which is play baseball."

WHAT WAS SAID ABOUT MARTINEZ

"He was a thinker out there. It was just one more element to his genius. Usually when you have the kind of stuff he did, you didn't have to think your way through the order or through a game. But he could, he did."
—Yankees outfielder Paul O'Neill

CHAPTER 18

Kevin McHale

"The Black Hole"

ESSENTIALS

Sport: Basketball

Born: December 19, 1957

Years Active: 1980–1993

Years with Boston: 1980–1993

Position: Power forward

KNOW THE CAREER NUMBERS

17.9 Points per game

7.3 Rebounds per game

.554 Shooting percentage

76 Offensive win shares

37.1 Defensive win shares

1 All-NBA

6 All-Defensive team

7 All-Star appearances

3 NBA championships

WHY MCHALE IS NO. 18

Dependable. Accurate. Quick. Efficient. Tough. Durable. Clutch. Virtually undefendable in the low post because of his long arms and skilled moves but also an excellent defender. He played with intelligence on both ends of the floor. You name it, McHale had it. He was one of the finest all-around big men in NBA history. Not bad considering he spent nearly half his career as a super-sub sixth man.

His annual statistics were not overwhelming, partly because he was a team player. One wonders, however, how impressive those numbers would have been had he not shared the ball with scoring machine Larry Bird and fellow offensive stalwarts such as Robert Parish and Dennis Johnson or not been on a team that valued everyone crashing the boards. McHale could have averaged 25 points and 12 rebounds a game for a lesser squad had that level of production been required.

ALL ABOUT MCHALE BEFORE BOSTON

Larry Bird wasn't the only small-town Midwest boy starring on the 1980s Celtics. McHale arrived via the mining town of Hibbing, Minnesota. His growth spurt from 5-foot-9 to 6-10 in high school proved stunning considering his average-height parents. It also made him a fit for basketball, which was ideal given his love for the sport. His passion was hockey, but his height and hoop talent precluded serious thoughts about a career on the ice.

McHale established his penchant for all-around production at Hibbing High School, scoring and rebounding well enough to earn Minnesota Mr. Basketball honors as a senior. Hibbing coach Gary Addington played a huge role in his development, allowing him to hone his one-on-one skills. He played the high post rather than with his back close to the basket, which helped his passing game. McHale landed scholarship offers at Utah and the University of Minnesota. He chose the latter to stay close to home.

He joined perhaps the most talented roster in Golden Gopher history, but sanctions due to ineligible players destroyed any chance at a national title his freshman year. That disappointed McHale but did not negatively affect his play. He steadily improved through his four-year college career. He led the team in scoring, rebounding, blocked shots, and shooting percentage as a senior.

One year after drafting Bird, Celtics general manager Red Auerbach wanted to add to his front line. He eyed both McHale and young Golden State center Robert Parish but acquiring both seemed an impossibility without a bit of maneuvering. So he traded the first overall pick to Golden State in exchange for the third selection and Parish. He then took McHale with the third selection.

Warriors coach and general manager Al Attles had expressed an interest in McHale. It has been claimed he was turned off when McHale showed his free-spirit side during a pre-draft visit by arriving in a 1966 Plymouth with bad brakes while dressed in jeans and a sweatshirt. Whatever the motivation for what became known as The Trade, the all-time Hall of Fame frontcourt had been established in Boston. It would remain together until McHale hung up his sneakers.

IN A CELTICS UNIFORM AND BEYOND

The first task of Celtics coach Bill Fitch was to sell McHale on a sixth-man role. Fitch wanted scoring off the bench. McHale did not just accept it. He thrived, often dominating bench players in the paint and averaging 10 points in 20 minutes per game. But Fitch cut his court time significantly in the playoffs. McHale scored just one point in the memorable Eastern Conference Game 7 defeat of Philadelphia and played a mere eight minutes in the title-clinching win over Houston.

By his second season McHale had established a remarkable consistency in production. His accuracy improved with added minutes in six consecutive seasons until he led the NBA in shooting percentage at .604 in back-to-back years after landing the starting power forward position. It mattered not if McHale was coming off the bench or starting in the postseason—he had earned starter minutes. He never changed his individual expectations or priorities from the regular season. McHale maintained his focus on efficient scoring and stifling defense.

That defense was even on display as a rookie with a championship hanging in the balance. The Celtics were trailing 3–2 in the Eastern Conference Finals against Julius Erving and the 76ers. Parish had fouled out of Game 6 in Philadelphia. Boston led 99–97 with 14 seconds remaining when McHale blocked an Andrew Toney jumper and caught it off the backboard to keep his team alive.

McHale's playoff performances featured his usual consistency punctuated by brilliance. He averaged 21 points and shot 55 percent of the field in a 1985 playoff series against emerging Detroit, then scored 26 points per game and nailed 60 percent of his shots in the NBA Finals that year against the archrival Lakers. He dominated throughout the 1986 postseason, averaging 25 points and 9 rebounds in 18 games while shooting his incredible but typical 59 percent from the field to play a key role in bringing Boston another NBA championship.

By that time McHale had become unstoppable inside. He used his long arms and nifty moves to hit high-percentage shots but also developed a deft touch on fadeaways. He often drew contact against frustrated defenders, which proved deadly since he was among the premier foul-shooting big men in league history. In 1987 he became the first NBA player ever to hit 60 percent from the field and 80 percent from the line.

McHale was so difficult to handle that he instilled fear in the greatest players in the world. Among them was Hall of Fame forward Charles Barkley, who compared him favorably to his more famous teammate.

"I hated Kevin McHale because he's the best player I ever played against," Barkley said in 2019. "He's the one guy who was so much bigger than me with his long arms and great moves. I had a difficult time guarding him. On the other end, he was so long, it was tough for me to get my shot off if I had to face him up.

"Larry Bird didn't want any of this. He's Larry Legend but not on the defensive end. He was great, great, great. It was a challenge to stop him. Nobody's going to stop a great player, but I'd rather play against him than Kevin McHale. Kevin . . . had the best low-post moves of any power forward to ever play the game. It was a lot easier for me to guard Larry Bird."[1]

Leg and back injuries limited McHale late in his career. He returned to a bench role but maintained his efficiency and productivity until finally fading in his final season and calling it quits in 1993. He was far from done with basketball. He continued his basketball career when he was hired by the Minnesota Timberwolves as a television analyst before landing a job as their general manager. Among his draft selections was future Celtics superstar Kevin Garnett. McHale also coached Minnesota and Houston in the 2000s. He guided the Rockets into the Western Conference finals in 2015.

HIS GREATEST GAME

Most amazing considering his 13-year career was that McHale's two highest-scoring games were played two days apart. His most prolific was a 56-point effort on an incredible 22-of-28 shooting against Detroit at the Garden on March 3, 1985. He also yanked down 16 rebounds with four assists and three blocked shots in the victory. The Celtics then traveled to New York, where McHale tallied 42 points and hit all but six of his 21 shots in another triumph.

SIDE STORY

McHale appeared in two episodes of the legendary Boston-based sitcom *Cheers*. The more memorable episode aired in November 1991 and was titled "Where Have All the Floorboards Gone." McHale plays himself. He becomes obsessed about finding out how many bolts hold down Boston Garden's iconic parquet court after main characters Norm and Cliff raise the question.[2]

WHAT MCHALE SAID

"We played the game, I thought, the way it should have been played. Those were absolutely the best days of my life."[3]

WHAT WAS SAID ABOUT MCHALE

"We were fearful of Bird and McHale, but we were really scared of McHale. You knew Bird was going to be Bird, and we felt that Dominique (Wilkins) might outscore him or you can match that. McHale was a guy we just couldn't get a handle on, and he knew it." —Atlanta Hawks guard and future Celtics coach Doc Rivers[4]

CHAPTER 19

Wade Boggs

"Chicken Man"

ESSENTIALS
Sport: Baseball
Born: June 15, 1958
Years Active: 1982–1999
Years with Boston: 1982–1992
Position: Third base

KNOW THE CAREER NUMBERS
.328 Batting average
1,513 Runs
578 Doubles
.415 On-base percentage
81.4 Offensive WAR
12 All-Star selections
2 Gold Gloves
5 Batting titles

WHY BOGGS IS NO. 19
Boggs was the best pure hitter in the American League over the first eight seasons of his career. In an era in which nonpower hitters receive

short shrift from Hall of Fame voters, his numbers were so overwhelming he landed in Cooperstown on the first ballot.

The third baseman who ate chicken before every game achieved more than four consecutive American League batting titles and five in six years. He paced the circuit in on-base percentage every season from 1985 and 1999 and coaxed more than 100 walks four years in a row. It was no wonder he annually exceeded 100 runs scored and led the league in that category in 1988 and 1989.

Despite that production Boggs finished among the top five in Most Valuable Player voting just once, which is an indictment on those who excluded candidates based on a lack of power. His 24 home runs in 1987 were purely an anomaly—he never again reached double figures in a Red Sox uniform. Boggs was also an above-average defender, and even though he joined the hated Yankees in free agency in 1993, he is deserving of a top 20 spot among the greatest athletes in Boston history.

ALL ABOUT BOGGS BEFORE BOSTON

The home of the College World Series was the home of Wade Boggs as a child. He was the youngest of three siblings born in Omaha, Nebraska, where he began playing little league before his father retired from the military and moved the family to Tampa in 1967. He practiced hitting constantly. The young Boggs would even hit tiny fruits like dates with a broomstick to train his eyes to see smaller objects so baseballs looked larger to him at the plate.

Wade's talent as a hitter was pronounced from the start. Scouts later began paying attention after he batted .522 as a high school junior. He developed patience at the plate after reading *The Science of Hitting* by the master—Ted Williams. Boggs had grown frustrated by pitchers refusing to throw him a strike but the book taught him to lay off balls off the plate. He was a good enough athlete to earn all-state honors as a football kicker but had switched from quarterback to avoid injury as baseball became his first love.

Boggs batted .485 his senior year but some major league scouts were doubtful about his prospects as a hitter and questioned his overall game, including his speed and range. Red Sox scout George Digby believed in him enough to persuade his team to select him in the seventh round of the 1976 draft. The $7,500 offer was far from overwhelming but that passion for baseball motivated Boggs to grab it and try to prove the skeptics wrong.

The doubters appeared justified when Boggs hit just .263 in rookie league ball in his first season but the Sox saw through the struggles and promoted him to Class A Winston-Salem in 1977, where he batted .332 and walked more than he struck out, a statistic he achieved annually until age 40. Though his slowness and lack of power prevented a quick ascension through the farm system, he earned steady promotions and continued to hit at least .300. When he broke his reputation as strictly a singles hitter by slamming 41 doubles at Triple-A Pawtucket in 1981, the Boston brain trust finally decided to bring him to The Show.

Boggs did not just perform as well as he did in the minors upon his arrival. He played even better.

IN A RED SOX UNIFORM AND BEYOND

Boggs had a problem in spring training 1982. His name was Carney Lansford, a solid hitter and starting third baseman. But Boggs hit well enough heading into the regular season to earn a spot as a utility infielder. He became quite familiar with the dugout bench until Lansford sprained his ankle on June 23, prompting manager Ralph Houk to replace him with Boggs, who batted .358 and hit safely in a remarkable 89 or 96 games in his absence. The Sox were convinced. They traded Lansford to Oakland after the season. Boggs was a fixture at third base for the next 10 years.

His development as a hitter stretched beyond batting average, which reached another stratosphere as Boggs grew more familiar with American League pitching. His admirable patience at the plate led to more walks and a rising on-base percentage. His ability to use the entire field, including banging the ball off the Green Monster, and driving it into the gaps and down the line, resulted in Boggs growing into a doubles machine. He was also durable—he played at least 143 games every season from 1983 to 1992.

Boggs became a fan favorite not only for his play on the field. Fans also embraced his superstitious nature and regimentation that became legendary. He most famously ate chicken before every game.

It all worked for Boggs. The superstitions certainly had no negative effects when Boston reached the postseason. Though he didn't hit up to expectations during the 1986 playoffs and World Series, he rose to the occasion in Game 6 of the Fall Classic as the Red Sox moved to within one out of winning it all and breaking the Curse of the Bambino. He slammed three hits, including a double in the 10th inning, and scored twice. He watched in dismay from third base as Bill Buckner allowed a Mookie Wilson dribbler to slip past him as the Mets scored the game-winner. Boggs sat in the dugout and cried when the series ended. He was overcome by emotion, not fueled by defeat but rather by the memory of his beloved mother, who had been killed by a cement truck four months earlier. He was very aware of her absence when he returned home.

Boggs was among the few bright spots in 1988 and 1990 playoff losses to Oakland. The Red Sox dropped all eight games and scored a mere 15 runs in the process. He batted .417 with seven walks in those defeats.

He was not long for Boston. He stunned fans by signing a free-agent contract with the Yankees. They booed him unmercifully when New York visited but time healed those emotional wounds. Age and the loss of favorable dimensions in Fenway resulted in weakening batting statistics, but he did win two Gold Gloves after leaving. He finished his career in Tampa, where he homered for his 3,000th career hit. He had long before punched his ticket into the Hall of Fame.

HIS GREATEST GAME

The Sox were stumbling along in late June 1987 but Boggs was raking. He was batting over .380 when they hosted Baltimore on the evening of the 29th. Boggs, who had moved from the leadoff spot to third in the order to take advantage of his RBI potential, singled in a run in the first inning, tripled in two in the fourth, then capped his momentous performance game with a grand slam in the sixth. Boston beat the Birds, 14–3.

SIDE STORY

Eating chicken before every game was not Boggs's only superstition. He also wore the same socks every game, fielded exactly 150 ground balls in practice every day, and drew the word "chai" ("good luck" in Hebrew) in the dirt before each at-bat.

WHAT BOGGS SAID

"A lot of people have compared hitting to rage. And it's a violent act. I think it's a symphony when it's done well. . . . It's poetry in motion."[1]

WHAT WAS SAID ABOUT BOGGS

"Wade to me was one of the most focused and competitive hitters I've ever been around. Discipline is what comes to mind. He could do a lot of things, but he was steadfast in his approach. He had an idea of what he did best and he had the focus to do it over and over when there was temptation to depart." —Yankees second baseman Willie Randolph[2]

Chapter 20

Eddie Shore

"Old Blood & Guts"

EDDIE SHORE
Star Defense Player of the Boston Bruins

Eddie Shore in 1928. Public domain, attributed to
The Boston Globe

ESSENTIALS
Sport: Hockey

Born: November 25, 1902

Died: March 16, 1985

Years Active: 1926–1940

Years with Boston: 1926–1940

Position: Defenseman

KNOW THE CAREER NUMBERS
103 Goals

176 Assists

279 Points

46.4 Offensive point shares

51.0 Defensive point shares

4 Hart Trophies

8 All-Star appearances

2 Stanley Cup championships

WHY SHORE IS NO. 20
There were other possibilities here—Patriots tight end Rob Gronkowski, Bruins wing Cam Neely, Celtics center Robert Parish, and Sox outfielder Dwight Evans among them. Longevity in a Boston uniform and consistent excellence put Shore over the top. Four Hart Trophies as NHL Most Valuable Player clinched it.

Shore was a defenseman in a low-scoring era decades before Bobby Orr revolutionized the position as an offensive terror. He also competed at a time when teams played fewer than 50 games every year. That added up to about 25 points per season at his peak. His brilliance on defense keyed a run during which the Bruins ranked first in goals against five times in the 1930s.

He also antagonized opponents with his wild style. Shore, who led the NHL in penalty minutes his first two years, was the most controversial player in the sport. Fans streamed to arenas to watch him play. Opposing players sought to rough him up while their owners worked to outlaw him from the game. He was driven to maximize his own effectiveness and that of his teammates. By the time he retired he had 900 stitches in his face and body, as well as several fractures in his back, hip, collarbone, nose, and jaw. The old image of hockey players with all their teeth knocked out? That was Eddie Shore.

All about Shore before Boston

The Shore story began in Fort Qu'Appelle in what was then the Northwest Territories before it became known as Saskatchewan. He was raised on a ranch, planting seeds for his toughness doing such rough-and-tumble chores as breaking horses, herding stock, and hauling grain. The physical labor would prepare him for playing defenseman in the NHL.

Shore first skated on a 44-by-100-foot outdoor rink in nearby Cupar. He cared far less about school than he did hockey—he once correctly spelled just two of 20 words on a test and often skipped class while spending winter days on the ice. He played for a Cupar youth team from 1914 to 1918, though the freezing temperatures and blizzards often wiped out much of the schedule.

His early prospects were dubious. His older brother added insult to injury when he told Eddie he would never make it in hockey after having been cut from the Manitoba Agriculture College team. That merely motivated Eddie to work harder. He soon landed a spot on the Cupar team in the Saskatchewan Intermediate C League and remained there for five years.

Shore quickly gained a reputation as a flake and penalty machine. He retaliated for the slightest physicality on the ice but performed well. His skills began to improve. He earned a place on the WCHL Edmonton Eskimos and was moved from forward to defenseman. His talent helped that team to a first-place finish and a defeat of Vancouver in the championship. Shore continued to compete despite a cut that required 14 stitches. Blood ran down his leg and stained the ice as he skated.

The WCHL folded in 1926. His contract was sold to Boston. A legendary NHL career was about to start.

IN A BRUINS UNIFORM AND BEYOND

Shore immediately displayed his penchant for brawling upon his arrival in Boston. His first fight was with a teammate in training camp. He led the NHL with 130 penalty minutes. He also showed his talent. His 18 points were exceeded only by three other Bruins, all of them forwards.

His influence quickly transformed the team from also-ran into a title contender. The Bruins reached the Stanley Cup final in his first season, won it in 1929, and captured the American Division crown four years in a row. Their 38–5 mark in 1930 remains the best in NHL history.

But it was his brutal style of play that received top billing. He caused injury to opponents and himself. Shore became a target. One Montreal player hit him hard enough to loosen teeth, break his nose, blacken both eyes, gash his cheekbone, open a cut on his forehead, and render him unconscious on the ice for 14 minutes. Shore meted out punishment with equal ferocity. In 1933 he hit Ace Bailey on the back of the head with such force that he knocked out the Toronto wing and sent his body into convulsions. A fractured skull required a four-hour life-saving operation. Bailey was in a coma for 10 days. Had he died, Shore might have been charged with murder. His punishment instead was a 16-game suspension.

Shore gained respect despite his viciousness on the ice. He was the key figure in turning the Bruins into an annual contender and received due recognition. Shore was certainly never considered for the Lady Byng Memorial Trophy that rewarded sportsmanship, but he won the far more important Hart Trophy as the NHL's Most Valuable Player four times in six years during his peak. He was named an All-Star in eight of nine seasons from 1931 to 1939. The lone exception was 1937, when he was sidelined with a broken vertebra.

Shore left on top. He led Boston to a second Stanley Cup in 1939, then retired to buy the AHL Springfield Indians. So desperate were the Bruins for his services that they offered him a then-lucrative $200 per game to return, but after four games he decided his passion for playing had dissipated. Shore was then traded to the New York Americans, for whom he played for six weeks and even assisted on two goals in a playoff defeat. He was not quite done. Shore played two years with the Indians as their owner.

HIS GREATEST GAME
Scoring and assists never came close to defining the impact Shore had on his team and the NHL. He did register one hat trick. That was in a road game against the woeful Philadelphia Quakers on February 24, 1931. He scored one goal in each period in a 5–1 victory.

SIDE STORY
Shore has been credited for helping launch the iconic Ice Capades, once known as the Ice Follies. He and seven other arena managers teamed up to organize the first one in February 1940.[1]

WHAT SHORE SAID
"Most of us are a little crazy one way or another. Some of us admit it. As for me, I'm not sorry about anything I've done in my life. As long as I can be close to hockey I'm happy to be alive."[2]

WHAT WAS SAID ABOUT SHORE
"He antagonized fans, fought opponents and stirred more controversy than any other man in the game. Opponents often teamed to cream him, owners sought to outlaw him and fans came to curse him. But when Shore played, the crowds came. And they saw him play superb, if wild, hockey." —*Sports Illustrated* writer and hockey historian Stan Fischler[3]

CHAPTER 21

Cy Young

"Cyclone"

Cy Young circa early 1900s. George Grantham Bain Collection
(Library of Congress)

ESSENTIALS
Sport: Baseball
Born: March 29, 1867
Died: November 4, 1955
Years Active: 1890–1911
Years with Boston (AL): 1901–1908
Years with Boston (NL): 1911
Position: Starting pitcher

KNOW THE CAREER NUMBERS
511–315 Win–loss record
2.63 ERA
2,803 Strikeouts
1.5 Walks per nine innings pitched
1.130 WHIP
749 Complete games
76 Shutouts

WHY YOUNG IS NO. 21

Denton True Young pitched elsewhere for 11 years before arriving in Boston but still earns this ranking. He performed his best with the Americans, who changed their name to the Red Sox in his final season with the franchise in 1908. Though he won between 21 and 36 games annually with Cleveland and St. Louis, he proved more dominant in Boston by compiling earned run averages such as 1.26 (1908), 1.62 (1901), 1.82 (1905), and 1.97 (1904).

His numbers rivaled those of Pedro Martinez, but Young cannot be rated as high because he pitched in the dead-ball era and before integration greatly strengthened the hitting pool. His all-time major league records are mind-boggling and will never be broken. Included are his 511 wins, 749 complete games, and 7,356 innings pitched.

Young was among the finest control pitchers in baseball history. He began his career as a flamethrower but grew more dependent on hitting his spots as his velocity dissipated. That allowed him to remain dominant. He twice won 21 games for the Red Sox in his 40s. And, hey, MLB named its annual pitching award after him. Enough said.

ALL ABOUT YOUNG BEFORE BOSTON

The Civil War had ended just two years before Young was born in a small farming community 100 miles south of Cleveland. He was the oldest son of a Union soldier who was taught the game of baseball during the war and encouraged him to foster a love for the sport. He often played the game with his kids during lunch breaks and after they had completed their farm chores.

The boy became engrossed in pitching. He organized and played on semipro teams throughout the area into his 20s before capturing the attention of professional clubs. He finally signed with Canton of the Tri-States League at age 23 for $60 a month. It was there he earned the nickname "Cyclone" for his blazing fastball. He also exhibited pinpoint control, walking just 33 batters that season while fanning 201. He tossed a no-hitter in his final game with Canton, walking none and striking out 18. He was ready for the big leagues.

Young was fortunate. Competition from the fledgling Players League forced the National League to search far and wide for minor league talent. Young signed with the local Cleveland Spiders. Chicago Colts legend Cap Anson derisively mocked the newcomer before Young made his debut, calling him "just another big farmer." Young responded with a three-hit victory. By 1891 he was the ace of the Cleveland staff.

Consistent greatness marked his performance throughout the 1890s. He was forced to adapt to the added five feet between the mound and the plate in 1892, which diminished the effectiveness of his fastball, by relying more on throwing quality strikes and keeping hitters off-balance. The change resulted in a higher ERA, but he continued to lead the league in walks per nine innings every season. Young won between 21 and 36 games every year through 1898. He was traded to the new St. Louis Perfectos in 1899 when Cleveland owner Frank Robison, who owned both teams, purged the Spiders. Young maintained his brilliance with the westernmost franchise in the National League.

The birth of the American League in 1901 resulted in another bidding war for top talent. The Americans offered Young a salary of $3,500 that Robison refused to match. Young was on his way to Boston. He was 34 years old. Some believed he was nearing the end of his career. The opposite was true. Young had yet to reach his peak.

IN AN AMERICANS AND RED SOX UNIFORM AND BEYOND

One might argue that the watering down of hitting talent through the creation of the American League aided Young, but then all pitchers were in the same boat. He outperformed everyone in its first season. Young won the pitching "triple crown" by leading the league with 33 wins, 1.62 ERA (at the time his career best), and 158 strikeouts.

Despite waning velocity and greater dependence on off-speed pitches, his strikeout totals increased into his late 30s and reached 210 in 1905. Most importantly, however, was his impact on the earliest Red Sox teams that won the pennant in 1903 and 1904. Young twice defeated the Pirates in the first World Series in 1903 and pitched three consecutive shutouts to help clinch the AL title the next year.

Young maintained his mastery over American League hitters to become the first pitcher in baseball history to gain success into his 40s. He compiled an absurd 93–30 record in pacing the circuit in wins in each of his first three seasons in Boston, then rebounded from an off-year in 1906 to win 21 games in his last two seasons with the club that concluded with a sparkling 1.26 ERA in 1908 before he returned to Cleveland for three years and finished his career with the National League Braves.

That longevity forever inspired comparisons to the all-time greats. Praise during his era centered on focus and offseason work habits on the farm. Among those with whom he was compared was New York Giants pitcher Amos "Thunderbolt" Rusie, who annually led the league in walks and strikeouts and earned a spot in the Hall of Fame despite a comparatively short career. Offered the *Detroit Tribune*, "Rusies have come and gone, in their turn, by Cy Young still pitches on. Perhaps no ballplayer ever lived who paid stricter attention to business and who came out of a long series of honors showered on him with lesser opinion of himself and with such strict attention to temperate habits."[1]

Young finally retired at age 45. He managed briefly in the independent Federal League before returning to his life as a farmer.

His Greatest Game

Young was the first American Leaguer to pitch a perfect game when at age 37 he defeated fellow Hall of Famer Rube Waddell and the Philadelphia Athletics on May 5, 1904. He remained the oldest pitcher ever to retire all 27 batters he faced until 40-year-old Randy Johnson accomplished the feat in the same month exactly 100 years later.

Side Story

The trade that sent Young from Cleveland to St. Louis was among several infamous deals pulled off by Spiders owner Frank Robison, who was angered by a perceived lack of support from fans. The result of the purge was that Cleveland finished the 1899 season with a 20–134 record. It remains the worst mark in the history of major league baseball.

What Young Said

"I thought I had to show all my stuff and I almost tore the boards off the grandstand with my fastball."[2]

What Was Said about Young

"If I were asked who was the greatest pitcher the game ever knew, I would say Cy Young. Cy is now pitching as good ball today as he did twenty years ago." —Sportswriter Francis Richter in 1910[3]

CHAPTER 22

Robert Parish
"Chief"

ESSENTIALS
Sport: Basketball
Born: August 30, 1953
Years Active: 1976–1997
Years with Boston: 1980–1994
Position: Center

KNOW THE CAREER NUMBERS
14.5 Points per game

9.1 Rebounds per game

.537 Shooting percentage

74 Offensive win shares

73 Defensive win shares

2 All-NBA

9 All-Star appearances

4 NBA championships

WHY PARISH IS NO. 22
He was overshadowed by the great centers of his era: Kareem Abdul-Jabbar, Moses Malone, Hakeem Olajuwon. And later Shaquille O'Neal.

He was even overshadowed by his teammates: Larry Bird, Kevin McHale. Robert Parish performed well enough over his long career to step out of that shadow and earn a spot in the Hall of Fame.

His consistency was astounding. Parish averaged between 16 and 20 points per game every season during his 10-year prime. He yanked down between 10 and 12.5 rebounds per game in almost all of them. He shot between 54 and 60 percent from the field in 13 consecutive seasons.

Parish always took the right shot at the right time. He played with ferocity against some of the elite centers in basketball history. He took their punishment and dished it out. He boasted a combination of skill and physicality that helped the Celtics win three NBA championships.

ALL ABOUT PARISH BEFORE BOSTON

Parish was not exactly turning cartwheels in his early youth over the prospect of a basketball career despite sprouting to 6-foot-6 by age 13. As many African Americans grew up in Shreveport, Louisiana, and throughout the segregated South in the 1950s and 1960s, any dreams of a thriving future were stifled.

The oldest of four siblings, Parish was quiet and reserved. He felt more of an obligation to play basketball than a love for the game. He often skipped practice until junior high coach Coleman Kidd inspired him. Kidd often visited the Parish home near still-segregated Union High looking for his pupil. Kidd instilled in him a passion for basketball. By the time Parish arrived at integrated Woodlawn High School he had been transformed into a gym rat. He blossomed into a force on the hardwood.

Scouts flocked to watch him play. Parish led his team to a state championship while receiving more than 400 scholarship offers. His desire to remain close to friends and family motivated him to reject the Dukes and UCLAs of the world and choose close-to-home Centenary College. Playing at the smallest Division I school in the country resulted in little media exposure, but he attracted attention from NBA scouts. He dominated from the start, averaging 23 points and 19 rebounds a game as a freshman while shooting nearly 60 percent from the field. One 50-point, 30-rebound performance helped pique interest. After Parish compiled averages of 25 points and 18 rebounds his senior season, he was snagged eighth overall by Golden State in the 1976 draft.

Despite his all-around talent, he was forced by coach Al Attles to come off the bench in favor of veteran center Clifford Ray. His playing time and production increased but the Warriors collapsed early in his career. Parish became disenchanted while the organization soured on what they perceived as his dispirited play and penchant for straying too far from the basket. They eyed Purdue center Joe Barry Carroll in the draft.

Celtics GM Red Auerbach began scheming. The result was a lop-sided deal (despite Carroll's admirable career) that landed Parish and rookie Kevin McHale in Boston, formed one of the greatest frontcourts in basketball history, and launched an era of greatness at the Garden.

IN A CELTICS UNIFORM AND BEYOND

Unlike Attles, Celtics coach Tom Heinsohn welcomed Parish's mobility and athleticism. Parish exhibited a strong mid-range game without sacrificing physicality near the basket. Using his long arms and high-arching jumper, his shots were nearly impossible to block. He was also a strong defender, continuing to average double figures in rebounds and remaining near the top of the league in blocked shots.

Parish never strayed from the system. He understood and appreciated those with whom he shared the court. Larry Bird. Kevin McHale. Dennis Johnson—the team performed its best when all shared the ball and got their shots. Parish never averaged more than 15 shots per game. His remarkable consistency and accuracy resulted in annual All-Star selections and eventually a spot in the Hall of Fame. Upon retirement he held the record for both defensive and offensive rebounds in the playoffs.

"That's one thing I always liked about us . . . we respected one another," he said. "We talked a lot of trash every day about each other, but there was always that respect. I can't think of one teammate that did not respect one another."[1]

That respect led to fierce loyalty, though that aggressiveness on the court contrasted a mild temperament off it. Parish famously stood up for his teammates in Game 5 of the 1987 Eastern Conference finals against the Bad Boys of Detroit. The incident occurred two days after Bird and Pistons brawling center Bill Laimbeer were ejected for fighting, Parish punched Laimbeer as they battled for a rebound and was suspended for Game 6. He later expressed shame for losing his cool, but he had sent a message to a Detroit team considered the dirtiest in the NBA and returned to help Boston win Game 7.

The talents of Bird and McHale precluded Parish from frequent offensive explosions, particularly in the playoffs. But he had his moments. Among them was Game 5 of the 1982 Eastern Conference semifinals against Washington in which the Bullets staged a remarkable comeback to force overtime. The Celtics survived greatly because of Parish, who led the team with 33 points—a career-high in the playoffs—and 13 rebounds. By that time he had already destroyed the negative reputation he had been saddled with at Golden State.

"In his years in Boston, Parish developed a reputation as a consummate team player who never complained about minutes or shots and who willingly sacrificed his game to become a defensive stalwart," offered *Big Three* author Peter May. "He was little of the above with the Warriors."[2]

Parish outlasted Bird and McHale with the Celtics but was destined to leave by the early 1990s, after both left and the tragic death of young star Reggie Lewis signaled the end of Boston dominance. Parish stuck around as a productive starter until age 40 before leaving for Charlotte in free agency in 1994 and finishing his career with the Bulls. He retired five days before his 44th birthday.

He viewed the last years of his playing career as a coaching role that he hoped would translate into a full-time position. While Bird and McHale realized their NBA goals after retirement, Parish never received the opportunity. He coached only in the United States Basketball League and later mentored big men in Boston.

HIS GREATEST GAME

Parish was often overshadowed by Bird and McHale with the Celtics. It seems appropriate that arguably his finest performance was also overshadowed by another superstar. He scored 40 points on 15-of-23 shooting in a defeat of San Antonio on February 17, 1981. He also led the team with 13 rebounds. Brilliant Spurs guard George Gervin stole the spotlight with a 49-point performance.

SIDE STORY

Parish was by far the best player from Centenary College to reach the NBA. But he was neither the first nor the last. Guard Connie Rea emerged from that school in 1953 to play 20 games with Baltimore. In 1990, guard Larry Robinson was drafted out of Centenary. He played seven seasons in the NBA with eight different teams.

WHAT PARISH SAID

"Boston has some of the best fans in any sport. They are very knowledgeable. They understand me. I was loved, embraced, and supported; what more can you ask for as an athlete?"[3]

WHAT WAS SAID ABOUT PARISH

"He's probably the best medium-range shooting big man in the history of the game." —Hall of Fame center and Celtics teammate Bill Walton[4]

CHAPTER 23

Jim Rice

"Jim Ed"

ESSENTIALS
Sport: Baseball
Born: March 8, 1953
Years Active: 1974–1989
Years with Boston: 1974–1989
Positions: Left field, designated hitter

KNOW THE CAREER NUMBERS
.298 Batting average
382 Home runs
1,451 RBI
.352 On-base percentage
45.8 Offensive WAR
1 Most Valuable Player award
8 All-Star selections
2 Gold Gloves
3 Home run titles

WHY RICE IS NO. 23

Longevity, durability, and production are spotlighted in Rice's Hall of Fame career. He spent all 16 years with the Red Sox and remained one of the most feared power threats in the sport until he finally faded in his last two seasons.

Rice thrice led the American League in home runs and twice in RBI, earning MVP honors in 1978, the season that ended with Sox fans crying "Bucky Freaking Dent!" He fanned often but was no Dave Kingman—he overcame his strikeout totals by consistently making hard contact, as his .298 career batting average attests. Rice became more of a contact hitter late in his career, limiting his strikeouts without sacrificing much power. He exceeded 200 hits three consecutive years at his peak. It was no wonder he finished top five in MVP balloting six times.

Critics claim fairly that Rice thrived at Fenway Park and that his road statistics did not warrant Hall of Fame inclusion. They also cite his mediocre defense and lack of impact on the basepaths. Their disapproval is based partly on analytics. His worth to the Red Sox should not be understated. The purpose of an offense is to score runs. Rice drove in more than 100 eight times. The only players ever to match his average and home run totals were legends Jimmie Foxx, Lou Gehrig, Mickey Mantle, Hank Aaron, Willie Mays, Ted Williams, Stan Musial, and Babe Ruth.

Value proved.

ALL ABOUT RICE BEFORE BOSTON

Rice spent much of his childhood in the segregated South. He was born and raised in Anderson, South Carolina, and attended all-Black Westside High School until the district finally submitted to integration mandates demanded by the Supreme Court 16 years earlier and he transferred to previously all-white T.L. Hanna High. He was embraced immediately by his fellow students. His personality helped soften racial tensions at the school and he was even elected class president.

Rice starred there in baseball and football. The Red Sox selected him No. 15 in the first round of the 1971 draft, but he weighed the opportunity to launch his professional career with scholarship offers to play defensive back or wide receiver at several prominent Division I programs. A $45,000 signing bonus from Boston clinched his decision.

Rice questioned that choice after struggling at Class A Williamsport. He grew frustrated. His was the classic case of a fastball hitter thrown for a loop when fed a steady diet of curves and changeups. He found his groove by his third year, winning the Double-A Eastern League batting title at .317 and bashing 27 home runs. He earned a promotion that season to Triple-A Pawtucket and helped that team capture a Junior World Series title by hitting .378 with four home runs in 10 playoff games.

Sox fans clambered for his ticket to Boston in 1974. They also wanted to see wunderkind Fred Lynn at Fenway. Manager Darrell Johnson was forced to start fading speedster Tommy Harper in left field and unproductive Juan Beniquez in center while his team continued its run of barely over .500 seasons. Rice added fuel to the fire by tearing up the International League that year, by hitting .337 with 25 home runs and winning the *Sporting News* Minor League Player of the Year award. Both Rice and Lynn arrived in time for a September collapse. They were certainly ready for 1975.

IN A RED SOX UNIFORM AND BEYOND

Rice and Lynn formed arguably the greatest rookie-hitting tandem in baseball history. Though Lynn captured Rookie of the Year honors and even won American League MVP, many believed rightfully that Rice would emerge as the superior hitter. Lynn enjoyed a fine career mostly with the Red Sox and Angels. Yet Rice landed in the Hall of Fame.

Rice seethed over the organization starting Lynn, whose minor league credentials in comparison seemed undeserving, over him early that season. Lynn was a superior outfielder, and Rice was earmarked for designated hitter. Manager Darrell Johnson instead started Tony Conigliaro, a fan favorite for whom the nation had been rooting since he was struck in the eye by a pitch in 1967 and was attempting another comeback. But Rice offered in 1978 that the motivation to start Lynn over him had racial overtones. After all, he had outhit Lynn by 55 points at Triple-A the year before.

Conigliaro struggled from the start. Rice slammed two home runs in the eighth game of the season and the experiment was over. He flirted with .300 most of the year, then reached it in late August and maintained it. The Sox and their fans anticipated his impact on the postseason as the team rolled into first place permanently in early July. When he broke his hand on a hit-by-pitch on September 21, he was forced to watch from the bench as his teammates lost a heartbreaking seven-game World Series to the Big Red Machine of Cincinnati.

The all-time greats praised him after the season. Hank Aaron even predicted Rice would break his career home run record. That seemed possible after Rice averaged 41 home runs a season from 1977 to 1979 and earned MVP honors in 1978 by nearly winning the Triple Crown. By that time some considered him the finest hitter in the sport. But his power numbers dropped markedly thereafter. Rice hit more than 30 homers only once more the rest of his career.

His overall productivity waned in the early 1980s but he rebounded to exceed 100 RBI in four consecutive seasons, including 1986, when he helped Boston reach the brink of a World Series championship. His three-run, slump-breaking homer in Game 7 of the ALCS all but clinched a berth in the Fall Classic. Rice then performed well against the Mets with three multi-hit games but did not drive in a run.

Elbow and knee injuries limited Rice in his final seasons while fans and the media debated his Hall of Fame worthiness. A September slump to end 1989 lowered his career batting average under .300, which weakened his case. He received less than 30 percent of the votes in his first year of eligibility. But his support continued to increase. Among those who spoke out about his inclusion after Rice finally made it in 2009 were former teammates. "He always played hurt. He never complained," said pitcher Bob Stanley, who played with Rice for 14 seasons. "He earned his right to that spot in Cooperstown. He was amazing." Rice became the fourth Hall of Famer to spend his entire career with Boston behind Ted Williams, Bobby Doerr, and Carl Yastrzemski.[1]

Rice played for the St. Petersburg Pelicans of the short-lived Senior Professional Baseball Association in 1990 before serving as Red Sox hitting coach from 1995 to 2000. He later worked as a sports commentator for the New England Sports Network (NESN).

HIS GREATEST GAME

Rice twice recorded three-homer games. Both were on August 29. The first was achieved in a defeat to Oakland in 1977. So his greatest must be his second. Rice blasted three in Toronto in 1983. He hit his third in the ninth inning to turn a 7–6 deficit into an 8–7 victory.

SIDE STORY

Rice's reputation as a sullen figure as painted by the Boston media changed in one remarkable moment during an August 1982 game at Fenway after a four-year-old boy was struck by a batted ball. Rice leaped into the stands, picked up the bloody child, and carried him to the trainer's room. Red Sox trainer Arthur Pappas stated years later that Rice's act of heroism with time of the essence might have saved a life.

WHAT RICE SAID

"I was a quiet leader, not a follower. I played through the pain and I suffered."[2]

WHAT WAS SAID ABOUT RICE

"Not only was he one of the best ballplayers this team has ever had, but he may have been the hardest-working ballplayer I was ever associated with. He and I would go out to the park before anyone was even in the stands and I would hit ball after ball to him in left field. He probably had the best work habits I have ever seen, and I've seen a lot of hardworking ballplayers." —Red Sox coach and hitting instructor Johnny Pesky[3]

CHAPTER 24

Rob Gronkowski

"Gronk"

Rob Gronkowski in 2012. Wikimedia Commons, Jeffrey Beall photo

ESSENTIALS
Sport: Football

Born: May 14, 1989

Years Active: 2010–2021

Years with New England: 2010–2018

Position: Tight end

KNOW THE CAREER NUMBERS
621 Receptions

9,286 Yards

15 Yards per catch

92 Touchdowns

5 Pro Bowls

4 Super Bowl championships

4 All-Pro

WHY GRONKOWSKI IS NO. 24
Gronkowski might have been considered the most prolific tight end in NFL history had a series of injuries not severely limited his playing time. He only played full seasons with New England in his first two years. He lost most of 2013 and 2016 to injury and the rest of his Patriots career was peppered with games sidelined. After Wes Welker left for Denver, he then was Tom Brady's premier receiver.

The Brady-Gronk connection struck fear in the hearts of linebackers and defensive backs throughout the league. Gronkowski did everything well. He had good speed for a tight end, ran accurate routes, rarely dropped the ball, and was also arguably the best run blocker in the NFL at his position. He exceeded 1,000 yards receiving four times and would have likely increased that total to seven had he not been unavailable for much of the 2012, 2013, and 2016 seasons. Gronkowski was a scoring machine. While many pass-catching tight ends thrive between the 20s, he was leading the league in touchdown receptions with 17 in 2011 and reaching double figures in four other years.

ALL ABOUT GRONKOWSKI BEFORE NEW ENGLAND

The odds were that someone among the Gronkowski siblings would emerge as a football star. Brothers Dan, Chris, and Glenn all reached the NFL and Gordie played professional baseball. None competed long enough to get their uniforms dirty. Only Rob earned that distinction.

They certainly experienced enough family competition to hone their skills. Their father was a former University of Syracuse guard and grandfather to a record-setting Olympic cyclist. The boys were raised in Western New York. Heated competition between the brothers often resulted in fights their dad had to break up.

Rob dominated in football, basketball, and baseball while thriving in the classroom at Williamsville North High School near Buffalo after giving up hockey at age 14 despite his talents in that sport. He played tight end and defensive end on the gridiron, center on the hardcourt (averaging 21 points and 18 rebounds in 2006), and first base on the diamond. In one game he scored all of his team's points on a touchdown reception, long fumble recovery return, and strip-sack safety.

The separation of his parents forced Gronkowski to move in with his father in Pittsburgh for his senior year. Soon he was receiving offers from the most prestigious college football programs in the country. He chose the University of Arizona. That is where illness and injury curtailed his NFL prospects. Gronkowski missed time his sophomore year with strep throat and mononucleosis but most threatening was a lost junior season to a bulging disk in his back that required surgery. An MRI indicated possible spinal cord damage.

That did not deter Gronkowski from bypassing his senior year and declaring himself draft-eligible. He even turned down a $4 million insurance policy had he been forced to retire due to injury. Some NFL teams removed him from their draft boards, but the Patriots took a chance. They selected him in the second round as the second tight end taken overall. It was a bold move they would never regret despite physical problems that continued to cost Gronkowski playing time.

In a Patriots Uniform and Beyond

Gronkowski scored four touchdowns in his first preseason and quickly wrested the starting job away from fading veteran Alge Crumpler. He soon developed a connection with Brady and positively impacted the New England offense. By his second year, he had emerged as the premier tight end in the league. Gronkowski caught 90 passes for 1,327 yards and an NFL-best 17 touchdowns in 2011.

The Brady-led Patriots were never defined by regular-season statistics. Their playoff and Super Bowl dominance was unparalleled, and Gronkowski played a significant role in that success when healthy. His career was peppered with brilliant performances with championships on the line. He kicked off the 2012 postseason by destroying Denver with 10 catches for 145 yards and three touchdowns. He scored in all three playoff games during the 2015 title run. The following year he scored three touchdowns in two playoff games. He rose to the occasion again in the 2018 Super Bowl, snagging nine passes for 116 yards and two scores.

Gronkowski used speed, strength, and desire to overwhelm defenses. He outran linebackers and even safeties. He caught passes in heavy traffic. He outleaped defenders. He caught seemingly uncatchable passes. That from a tight end deemed too slow and lacking elusiveness by some draft experts before he arrived with the Patriots.

"He makes plays that, it's like in high school, when somebody is far above and beyond the competition," said Patriots fullback James Develin. "That's what he is able to do at the NFL level. Something overtakes him and he just goes off. He just goes crazy."[1]

He certainly went crazy nursing injuries that kept him off the field. A fractured forearm wiped out five games in 2012. Back surgery killed most of his 2013 season. A herniated disk sidelined him from the final eight games in 2016, including the Super Bowl run. Physical issues motivated his retirement in 2019, but he followed Brady to Tampa Bay the following year and helped him with a seventh Super Bowl.

The man affectionately known as "Gronk" used his engaging personality to become a familiar sight in commercials after he permanently called it quits in June 2022.

HIS GREATEST GAME

Gronkowski certainly had a penchant for torturing the Broncos. He not only helped bury them in the first round of the 2012 playoffs but he turned them away on the doorstep of the Super Bowl three years later. He caught eight passes for 144 yards in that AFC title clash and clinched it with a toe-tap touchdown to beat double coverage in the final seconds. He had set up that score with a diving 40-yard reception.

SIDE STORY

How excited was the city of Tampa to have Gronkowski join its Buccaneers in 2020? So excited that ZooTampa named its baby rhinoceros "Gronk" in his honor. Human Gronk even made a video welcoming his namesake into the world.[2]

WHAT GRONKOWSKI SAID

"You're here for a job and it's to win football games. Being on this team, being with the head coach here and the quarterback we have keeps you humble. It keeps you hard working. You can laugh and giggle about stuff, but then at the same time you've got to make sure you're prepared and practicing hard."

WHAT WAS SAID ABOUT GRONKOWSKI

"For a guy to be that big, that fast, that strong, it's not right." —Patriots backup quarterback Jimmy Garoppolo.[3]

CHAPTER 25

Johnny Bucyk

"Chief"

Johnny Bucyk and Andy Brickley being honored at a Bruins game in 2010.
Wikimedia Commons, Danforth Nicholas photo

ESSENTIALS
Sport: Hockey
Born: May 12, 1935
Years Active: 1955–1978
Years with Boston: 1957–1978
Position: Left wing

KNOW THE CAREER NUMBERS
545 Goals
794 Assists
1,339 Points
104.4 Offensive point shares
2 All-Star appearances
2 Stanley Cup championships

WHY BUCYK IS NO. 25
Johnny Bucyk was largely ignored in All-Star voting. He never won a Hart Trophy. His annual statistics did not scream out Hall of Famer. But his teammates and opponents knew he was. By the time he finally hung up his skates, they had seen enough of his pinpoint passes and physicality, particularly those turnover-causing hip checks, to understand his greatness. Opposing puck carriers were doomed if they did not play with their heads up. With Bucyk skating toward them, that disk was as good as gone.

The numbers added up. Upon his retirement in 1978, he was Boston's all-team leader in goals, assists, points, and games played and among the top five in league history in all those categories. His leadership and talent keyed what many believe was the second-best line in the NHL alongside center Fred Stanfield and right wing John McKenzie behind only the teammate trio of Phil Esposito, Ken Hodge, and Ron Murphy (later Wayne Cashman).

ALL ABOUT BUCYK BEFORE BOSTON

Bucyk was born in Edmonton during the height of the Great Depression, but the family burden worsened after World War II with the death of his father. That forced his mother to toil at a factory for a mere 36 cents an hour. She certainly could not afford to buy sporting equipment for young Johnny, who instead used broomsticks for hockey sticks, old magazines for pads, and used skates.

Bucyk was an awkward skater during his youth, but his size and intelligence allowed him to grow as a player. His crisp, accurate shots and hard body checks piqued the interest of coaches and motivated them to maximize his skills as a skater to give him a better all-around game.

He thrived at the junior level, scoring 67 points during the 1953–54 season and landing a pro contract with Detroit's Western Hockey League affiliate in Edmonton. Bucyk dominated with 30 goals and 58 assists. He earned his nickname "Chief" through his tomahawking method of stealing pucks using a chop with his stick.

The Red Wings promoted Bucyk for the 1955 Stanley Cup, which they won without his services. Though he never played, he was presented with a championship ring and an invitation to camp the following year. Yet the wing-heavy Wings rarely used him. Bruins GM Lynn Patrick eyed Bucyk. He convinced Detroit to trade him to reacquire goalie Terry Sawchuk. It was a deal the Red Wings would regret for years.

IN A BRUINS UNIFORM AND BEYOND

Bucyk played on the most anemic offensive teams in the lowest-scoring era in NHL history early in his career. Averaging 2 to 3 goals per game and often ranking last in the league in that category kept Boston out of the playoffs eight consecutive years. Bucyk led the team in scoring four times from 1962 to 1967, but a lack of surrounding talent prevented him from reaching his potential productivity.

Then it happened. The arrivals of Phil Esposito and Bobby Orr transformed the Bruins from doormats to contenders and allowed Bucyk to maximize his impact in all facets of the game. His goal and assist totals not only soared but his veteran leadership inspired his young teammates.

"Johnny was a great help to me making the transition from junior hockey to the pros," Orr wrote in his autobiography. "He came to work every day and set the standard with his level of play. He always set the bar high for us, and it made you want to follow suit and set your own example for others. There can be no doubt that his leadership was a key part of the success the Bruins would enjoy in the years that followed."[1]

Coach Harry Sinden paired the veteran left wing with Stanfield and McKenzie in 1967. His scoring skyrocketed. He earned his first All-Star spot that season and averaged 34 goals and 48 assists over the next nine years. Bucyk saved his best for last with point explosions peppering playoff stat sheets. He tallied seven in back-to-back defeats of Toronto in the 1969 quarterfinals. His hat trick keyed a Game 1 victory over St. Louis in the 1970 Stanley Cup finals during which he lit the lamp in every game of the sweep. He tallied six goals in another four-game blitz of the Blues in the 1972 semifinals. His nine-point performance helped put away Chicago in the 1974 semis.

His numbers never fully defined his contributions. His passes, steals, and hard checks did not always lead to goals. They impacted victories and proved his greatness. So did his durability and longevity. Bucyk maintained his excellence nearly as long as any player ever. He scored 83 points at age 40 and continued to play for two more seasons.

Bucyk was inducted into the Hall of Fame in 1981 and 17 years later ranked No. 45 on *The Hockey News* list of all-time players. He remained with the Bruins in their front office and as a radio broadcaster. His 69 years in professional hockey is the longest tenure in the history of the sport.

HIS GREATEST GAME

Bucyk tortured St. Louis in the postseason. His successive four-point performances destroyed the Blues in 1972, but his most important domination had already been accomplished in Game 1 of the 1970 Stanley Cup finals. Bucyk set the tone for the sweep by scoring Boston's first two goals, including one early in the second period that put his team ahead to stay, then added another in the third for the hat trick.

SIDE STORY
Edmonton Oil Kings junior coach and former NHL goalie Ken McAuley took an unusual tact in helping Bucyk overcome his awkwardness on the ice. He arranged figure skating lessons for him in an attempt to improve his balance and coordination. It obviously worked.

WHAT BUCYK SAID
"I threw my weight around and always played a physical game. The other players respected me because they knew if they had their head down, I'd hit them pretty hard."[2]

WHAT WAS SAID ABOUT BUCYK
"He made the Boston power play work from the corner because he could thread the needle with the pass. He could put it through your skates, under your stick, over your stick, and he'd just put that big body between you and puck, protect it, shovel it off. He was a key ingredient on the power play." —New York Rangers defenseman Brad Park[3]

CHAPTER 26

Dave Cowens

"Big Red"

Dave Cowens in a 1976 game. Sporting News, attributed to
Robert Kingsbury but not copyrighted

Essentials
Sport: Basketball

Born: October 25, 1948

Years Active: 1970–1980, 1982–1983

Years with Boston: 1970–1980

Position: Center

Know the Career Numbers
17.6 Points per game

13.6 Rebounds per game

.460 Shooting percentage

35 Offensive win shares

55.8 Defensive win shares

3 All-NBA

8 All-Star appearances

1 Most Valuable Player award

2 NBA championships

Why Cowens Is No. 26
The Celtics pretty much started three Hall of Fame centers consecutively with Cowens bridging the gap between Bill Russell and Robert Parish (though the immortal Henry Finkel played that position for one season before Cowens arrived). The difference was that Cowens was undersized and boasted neither their talent nor physical gifts. He had to work tirelessly to achieve greatness. His constant motion on the court and hyper-aggressive style resulted in a series of broken ankles, feet, and legs. The physical and emotional drain of competing at that level against bigger and stronger centers forced him to retire in 1980.

Cowens played all out all the time. He was driven. He used his strengths to frustrate opponents. Cowens understood that at 6-foot-9 he could not succeed playing a traditional back-to-the-basket style. He developed a short-range and mid-range game to score on jump shots and drives to the hoop. Despite his lack of size he was a tremendous rebounder. He averaged at least 14 rebounds in each of his first eight seasons in Boston.

Big Red was a winner. He was arguably the best player on Celtics teams with less talent than those that preceded and followed them, though the abilities of teammates such as Jo Jo White and a still-viable John Havlicek (as well as Charlie Scott for two seasons) should not be understated.

ALL ABOUT COWENS BEFORE BOSTON

Cowens was born and raised in Newport, Kentucky. He lived just three blocks from the Ohio River. The boy enjoyed a Tom Sawyer childhood, fishing in the Ohio River and hopping trains that chugged over the bridge to Cincinnati. Sometimes he walked or biked to the big city. He would attend Cincinnati Reds games at Crosley Field with his friends.

Cowens developed a work ethic that proved invaluable in his career. He took a paper route that none of the other kids wanted. He collected bottles to cash in and did yard work around the neighborhood. He also played baseball and basketball. He enjoyed the latter but switched to swimming and track and field during his freshman year in high school after a conflict with the coach.

Cowens was a mere 6-1 at the time. His hoops career seemed to be over. A growth spurt motivated a comeback in his junior year. He averaged 13 points and 20 rebounds a game that season to lead Newport to the state tournament. He received attention from Ohio Valley Conference schools but not from legendary coach Adolph Rupp and the University of Kentucky. He felt slighted, but rather than take his father's advice and remain in Kentucky he took a chance and chose Florida State, which was on probation for recruiting violations.

It was the right decision. Cowens not only averaged 19 points and 17.2 rebounds per game but he ran the court better than any college center and helped transform the Seminoles into a national power. Celtics general manager Red Auerbach yearned for a standout center to replace Russell and he was impressed with Cowens's dedication and work ethic.

Auerbach overlooked a lack of height and selected him fourth overall in the 1970 draft.

IN A CELTICS UNIFORM AND BEYOND

Most rookies dip their toes in the water before taking the plunge and becoming a major contributor to team success. Not Cowens. He totaled 16 points and 17 rebounds in his NBA debut, followed it with a 27-point, 21-rebound performance, averaged 21 rebounds in his first five games, and rolled to a Rookie of the Year award he shared with Portland guard Geoff Petrie.

Cowens and an emerging White played the most critical roles in turning the Celtics back into a winner that season and a perennial title contender for several years thereafter. Cowens battled Hall of Fame centers night after night, including Kareem Abdul-Jabbar, Wilt Chamberlain, Bob Lanier, Wes Unseld, and Nate Thurmond. He effectively countered bigger and stronger players by boxing out for rebounds, passing to open teammates, shooting high-percentage jumpers, and working his way inside for tough baskets against the wider and taller trees of the NBA.

His all-around performances, value to the Celtics, and respect earned around the league were reflected in postseason awards voting. Cowens won MVP in 1973 despite averaging a comparatively paltry 20.5 points per game and finished among the top four in voting four consecutive years.

When most consider the best Boston teams, those featuring Bill Russell and Larry Bird often come to mind. However, the Celtics achieved their best record at 68–14 behind Cowens. Though they were upset by the Knicks in the Eastern Conference finals, he certainly could not be blamed. He averaged 24 points and pulled down between 13 and 15 rebounds in that series while shooting 50 percent from the field.

Cowens indeed performed his best with titles on the line. His 28-point, 14-rebound effort in Game 7 of the 1973 finals against Milwaukee in which he outscored and outrebounded Abdul-Jabbar sealed the championship. Two years later, he stuffed the stat sheet to subdue Phoenix to clinch the crown with 21 points, 17 rebounds (including seven offensive), three steals, and 10-for-16 shooting.

The battering, as well as the mental and emotional toll, prevented Cowens from maintaining the intensity with which he played the game. Stung by the trade of close friend Paul Silas to Denver, he lost his enthusiasm. His retirement at age 28 lasted a mere 30 games but he never returned to peak form. Neither did the team, which struggled mightily, failing to make the playoffs in 1978 and 1979. Cowens became player-coach after a 2–12 start to the 1978–79 season as Boston limped to last place.

He felt overwhelmed by the task. Cowens finally retired in 1980, though he made a brief comeback with the Bucks as a favor to coach and former teammate Don Nelson. He contributed for half the regular season and the playoffs mostly as a starter. Included was a sweep of Boston.

Cowens warmed up to the idea of coaching following his permanent retirement. He coached Charlotte to winning records and the playoffs in the late 1990s and a terrible Golden State squad for two seasons.

His Greatest Game

Though his performance in Game 6 of the 1976 finals clinched the championship, his effort in Game 4 of the Eastern Conference semis the following year tied that series and produced mind-boggling numbers. Cowens led both teams with 37 points and 21 rebounds in the Boston victory. He shot an efficient 16 of 24 from the field.

Side Story

Cowens had been a Democrat but ran as a Republican for Massachusetts Secretary of the Commonwealth in 1990. He was forced off the primary ballot because he failed to register in time. Rather than embark on a write-in campaign, he dropped out of the race.[1]

What Cowens Said

"I never thought of myself as a superstar. I represent the working class of the NBA. I'm honored they've selected me [to the Hall of Fame] because I could name a whole lot of guys who were better than Dave Cowens. You have to play with the right people and get picked by the right team. Let's face it—I was pretty lucky."[2]

What Was Said about Cowens

"I thought he was a wild man. I'd never seen anybody with that much talent play that aggressively." —Celtics teammate Paul Silas

CHAPTER 27

Jayson Tatum

"Taco Jay"

Jayson Tatum in 2022. Wikimedia Commons, All-Pro Reels

Essentials
Sport: Basketball

Born: March 3, 1998

Years Active: 2017–

Years with Boston: 2017–

Positions: Small forward, power forward

Know the Career Numbers
23.0 Points per game

7.3 Rebounds per game

.461 Shooting percentage

.375 Three-point percentage

28.1 Offensive win shares

26.0 Defensive win shares

3 All-NBA

5 All-Star appearances

Why Tatum Is No. 27
Seven seasons were enough to determine the worthiness of Tatum. Despite the legendary greatness of Celtics basketball extending back eight decades, he had by that time already earned a ranking among the franchise's best through his all-around play. Tatum was far more than one of the most prolific scorers of his era. He was a sticky defender and tough rebounder whose passing and court awareness led to an increase in assists every year. He played with a high level of intensity.

The only drawback through 2023—particularly after an Eastern Conference finals upset by Miami in which he struggled in Game 7 (though he had hurt his ankle)—was that he had yet to lead Boston to a championship and hadn't played his best in the postseason. Blame, however, should never be heaped on one player in any sport for team failures. Tatum still averaged 25 points and 10 rebounds in that series. The Celtics would not have advanced if not for his 51-point explosion on 17-for-28 shooting in Game 7 of the semifinals against Philadelphia.

ALL ABOUT TATUM BEFORE BOSTON

That Tatum survived a childhood of abject poverty to gain success was a triumph. For him to blossom into an NBA superstar was downright amazing.

There were bills left unpaid for months. There was a foreclosure notice on the door of the family home in the diverse University City neighborhood of St. Louis. There were the years of living with no furniture and being forced to sleep in the same bed as his mother. There was always the threat of homelessness.

There was also the dream. Young Jayson told his first grade teacher he wanted to be an NBA player. The reply? Pick a more realistic profession. His mother reacted angrily, lecturing the teacher about the value of goals in life. She had her own. She went to college. She studied property law. She earned her law degree. She encouraged her son to pursue a basketball career.

It was not an unfounded quest. He arose early every morning and displayed his talent, averaging 25 points per game in fifth grade competing in a league against adults. His father, a former college player who was coaching the St. Louis University men's team, became a big part of his life. As a child, he visited the Netherlands when his dad was playing professionally there.

Tatum's environment became conducive to basketball growth. He played small forward at Chaminade College Preparatory School in St. Louis and dominated, averaging 30 points and 9 rebounds a game his senior season, and was named Gatorade National Player of the Year. Tatum graduated as the school's all-time leading scorer and rebounder.

Tatum played in an era during which only a brief tour of the college hardwoods was required. He played one year under Mike Krzyzewski at Duke, where he averaged 16.8 points and 7.3 rebounds as a freshman. He added muscle to his lean frame. Boston selected him third overall in the 2017 draft. The dream had become a reality.

IN A CELTICS UNIFORM

Tatum learned in his first two NBA seasons what his peers already understood: When Kyrie Irving plays point guard on your team, expect your own shooting opportunities to be limited. The immensely talented ballhandler and finisher never recorded impressive assist totals or raised the performance level of his teammates.

That was certainly true during his short stint with the Celtics. Irving averaged seven more shots than anyone else on the roster during Tatum's first season and five more the following year. As a rookie, Tatum displayed his potential, shooting .434 from three-point range. The departure of Irving allowed Tatum to explode into an All-Star in 2020 and steadily improve thereafter. His scoring average, rebounds, and assists all rose in each of the next four seasons. By his fifth year, he had grown into a perennial MVP candidate.

Tatum asserted his confidence but never in a boastful way. He also understood that through 2023 he had never led Boston to its ultimate goal. Tatum was aware that he could not be uttered with the same reverence as other Celtics legends until he took his team to a title.

"I would love to be on the Mount Rushmore of Celtics. Bird, Russell, Paul Pierce and those guys," he said. "They paved the way. The one thing all those guys have is chips. I have to get to the top of the mountain to even be considered one of those guys. I want to be an all-time great, I want to be known as a winner, and I believe I will be."[1]

That might have happened in 2023 after the Celtics roared back from a 3–0 deficit in the Eastern Conference finals against upstart Miami. But Tatum hurt his ankle on the first play of Game 7 and limped around the court in a lopsided defeat.

Tatum had just turned 26 as the 2024 playoffs approached. He was proving that season his unselfishness and drive toward team success, limiting his shot totals to allow newcomer Kristaps Porzingis and longtime standout teammate Jaylen Brown to maximize their offensive contributions.

HIS GREATEST GAME

Tatum tallied a career-high 60 points in a defeat of San Antonio in 2021, but the importance of performance in playoff battles must take precedence. His 51-point effort to polish off the 76ers in Game 7 of the 2023 Eastern Conference semifinals must be placed on top. He not only buried Philadelphia with his scoring barrage but added 13 rebounds and 5 assists.

SIDE STORY

Jason's father Justin did not reach the NBA but was certainly a stand-out on the court. He played three seasons for St. Louis University from 1998 to 2001 before launching a two-year career professionally in the Netherlands. He then spent 16 years coaching high school basketball, winning three state championships along the way.

WHAT TATUM SAID

"Maybe I've kinda grown into my own in a sense. I'm still young, 25, but it's my seventh year in the league. I'm very confident because I know how hard I work and how much I put into this game. I know how badly I want to be one of the best and how badly I want to win. Why wouldn't I be confident? I know how hard I work."

WHAT WAS SAID ABOUT TATUM

"Right now, the best American in the league is Jayson Tatum. You look at his growth and what he's done over the past couple of years, he's been first-team All-NBA, hit you with the 55 in the All-Star, hit you with another 50 in Game 7 versus Philly, and I'm looking around. I think he's passed [Kevin Durant], I think he's passed LeBron." —Paul Pierce[2]

CHAPTER 28

Dwight Evans

"Dewey"

ESSENTIALS
Sport: Baseball
Born: November 3, 1951
Years Active: 1972–1991
Years with Boston: 1972–1990
Position: Right field

KNOW THE CAREER NUMBERS
.272 Batting average
385 Home runs
1,470 Runs
1,384 RBI
.370 On-base percentage
60.5 Offensive WAR
3 All-Star selections
8 Gold Gloves

WHY EVANS IS NO. 28
Had Dwight Evans retired around 1980 he would have been remembered as a cannon-armed right fielder with little punch at the plate.

While he continued to pile up Gold Gloves (despite modern metrics such as WAR claiming mediocre defensive prowess), his hitting evolved. He grew more selective at the plate, consistently approaching or surpassing a .400 on-base percentage and adding significant doubles and home run power.

Evans peaked offensively in his mid-to-late 30s. That run of success changed his legacy to one of durability, consistency, and productivity. It also had many wondering why Evans had yet to be voted into the Hall of Fame through 2023. His career does not warrant a ranking among the greatest Boston athletes of all time but it certainly merits a spot in the top 30.

All about Evans before Boston

Evans spent much of his childhood on foreign soil—Hawaii before statehood. His family moved there from Santa Monica and remained until he returned to California at age nine and began his career journey after accompanying his father to a Dodgers game and catching the baseball bug.

His passion and talent as a third baseman and pitcher led to All-Star selections in his youth but did not translate to immediate success at the next level. Evans was cut from the high school team but continued to work on his game and blossomed his junior year, not only earning a spot on the varsity but all-conference honors before winning its MVP award as a senior.

Evans, who heard from several major league teams but not Boston in high school, wasted no time launching his professional career after the Sox surprisingly picked him in the fifth round of the 1969 amateur draft. Considering he had yet to celebrate his 18th birthday, his .280 average at Class A Jamestown proved quite remarkable. He ascended rapidly through the Boston system, showing a sure glove, a keen eye at the plate, and decent power. Evans skipped Double-A in 1972 and remained unfazed, batting .300 with 95 RBI at Triple-A Louisville that season to earn a September callup to the big leagues. He would remain a fixture in right field for nearly two decades.

In a Red Sox Uniform and Beyond

The Red Sox were motivated in 1973 to move Carl Yastrzemski to first base, switch Reggie Smith to center field, and open up right for Evans. The full potential of the Boston outfield wasn't realized until 1975 when rookies Fred Lynn and Jim Rice joined him—all were 23 or under. Evans had gained a reputation as a solid, defense-first right fielder but had taken a back seat to the wunderkinder.

Though he compiled a significantly better slugging percentage at home than on the road, his lack of doubles and home run power at Fenway Park considering his classic hitter's build, short porch in right, and inviting Green Monster puzzled many for years. His starting job might have been in jeopardy had the Sox not featured plenty of potent bats around him. They could afford to employ a fine defender with one of the game's most powerful arms in right. His sprinting grab of a Joe Morgan blast in the 11th inning helped keep the Sox alive in Game 6 of the 1975 World Series. The organization and Red Sox Nation continued to hope that Evans would reach his offensive potential.

They waited years, but it finally came to fruition in the strike-shortened 1981 season when Evans batted .295, led the American League with 22 home runs, and finished third in the MVP voting. He eventually emerged as one of the premier all-around hitters in the sport. He gained power without sacrificing average. And his walk totals soared. He led the American League in that category three times from 1981 to 1987 and exceeded 100 runs scored four times during that span. He slugged at least 20 home runs nine consecutive seasons after previously never reaching that total yet remained an infrequent invitee to the All-Star Game. That lack of recognition became more pronounced post-retirement as he continued to be ignored by Hall of Fame voters.

One reason was his frequent offensive struggles with seasons on the line. Evans batted just .100 during the 12-game September Sox collapse of 1978 and barely .200 in the 1986, 1988, and 1990 playoffs combined. He rose to the occasion in the World Series with seven hits in 1975 and a team-high nine RBI in 1986.

Major back problems limited his playing time in 1990 and resulted in his release after the playoffs that year. He played well for one season with Baltimore but was let go the following spring. He later toiled as a minor league coach with the White Sox and Rockies before hooking back up with the Red Sox as a roving hitting instructor and later a major league batting coach.

His Greatest Game
Evans was on a roll when the Sox returned home on June 28, 1984, for a series against Seattle. He had slammed seven hits in his previous four games, but nobody could have anticipated his explosion that Thursday night. He doubled and tripled in his first two at-bats, singled in the 10th, then smashed a walk-off homer over the Green Monster in the 11th to complete the cycle.

Side Story
Dwight and wife, Susan, suffered a tragedy when sons Justin and Timothy both died 10 months apart from neurofibromatosis, which is a condition that causes tumors to form in the brain, spinal cord, and nerves. Both were diagnosed with the disease in the 1980s.

What Evans Said
"Red Sox fans are great. I learned early in my career that if you give an all-out effort they will always support you. If a player lets up, even briefly, fans are all over him. And that's fair."[1]

What Was Said about Evans
"Dwight Evans is also one of the most underrated players in baseball history, because he did many things well, rather than having one central skill that people could use to explain his excellence." —Analytics guru Bill James[2]

CHAPTER 29

Ty Law

"T-Leezy"

ESSENTIALS
Sport: Football
Born: February 10, 1974
Years Active: 1995–2009
Years with New England: 1995–2004
Position: Cornerback

KNOW THE CAREER NUMBERS
53 Interceptions
828 Interception yards
7 Touchdowns
845 Tackles
5 Pro Bowls
3 Super Bowl championships
2 All-Pro

WHY LAW IS NO. 29
Durability, consistency, and longevity with the Patriots were tiebreakers here. Other candidates for this sport did not play as long for their teams or did not boast the credentials as this Hall of Famer, though he was

forced to wait 10 years beyond his retirement to gain his spot in Canton. He missed just five games from 1997 to 2003 and started all the others.

Law was a football thief. He twice led the NFL in interceptions (once with the Jets). He had a knack for reading quarterbacks, jumping routes, and snagging footballs. Those are traits more related to free safeties but Law remained a sticky defender whose aggressive play rarely resulted in losing his man. He was most often assigned the opponent's premier receiver. His playoff and Super Bowl performances helped the Patriots build their dynasty.

ALL ABOUT LAW BEFORE NEW ENGLAND

Many kids figuratively embrace a role model athlete as inspiration. Ty Law was lucky. He could embrace one literally during his summer visits to Texas. He embraced Uncle Tony. That is, Cowboys superstar running back Tony Dorsett.

"I used to just stare at that Heisman, stare at his Hall of Fame bust," Law recalled. "It meant the world to me because I realized dreams do come true. He walked the same streets that I did, so why can't I? Why not me? But, I knew there had to be a lot of sacrifice to get to that point."[1]

Both were born and raised in the football hotbed of Aliquippa, Pennsylvania. The tough neighborhood and strong competition on the gridiron strengthened Law as he pursued his sports dreams and more generally in life. He accepted every challenge at Aliquippa High School, playing a myriad of offensive and defensive positions to pique the interest of college scouts and earning a scholarship to Michigan.

Most must cool their heels to gain playing time at that level of college football but not Law. He played in every game from the beginning and landed a starting spot midway through his freshman season. Law soon established his reputation as a ball hawk, snagging five interceptions as a sophomore. A strong belief in his talent motivated him to declare for the draft after his junior year. His dream? Induction into the Pro Football Hall of Fame. It was a justified goal. He began to prove it after the Patriots picked him No. 25 overall in the 1995 draft.

In a Patriots Uniform and Beyond

Law followed the same path to stardom as he did at Michigan, earning a starting job halfway through his rookie year and keeping it through his 10 seasons as a Patriot and beyond. He emerged as one of the stingiest shutdown cornerbacks in the sport with the size to stifle bigger, rangier receivers and the speed to hang with the faster ones.

He became a mainstay on the greatest New England teams ever, including three that celebrated Super Bowl championships. Teammates marveled at his physicality, conditioning, and confidence that bordered on cockiness. Among the many excellent defenders on those sensational Patriots teams—Willie McGinest, Rodney Harrison, Ted Bruschi, Mike Vrabel, and Richard Seymour—only Law was inducted into the Hall.

"He was a big corner that wasn't just a cover-2 corner," Vrabel said. "He was . . . a man-matchup corner, could play man coverage, could play zone coverage, could jam, reroute, could tackle. But just his energy and excitement for life and playing a game, it was always fun hanging out with Ty."[2]

It was more fun celebrating championships, and Law contributed mightily to those, including the playoff runs that led to the ultimate triumphs. His interception of Steve Young while guarding legendary receiver Jerry Rice played a role in a 1998 victory over San Francisco that clinched a playoff spot. His pick-six against NFL MVP Kurt Warner gave his team the lead for good in a Super Bowl XXXVI defeat of the Rams. He blanketed prolific Colts wide receiver Marvin Harrison and intercepted Hall of Fame quarterback Payton Manning three times in the 2003 AFC title game.

Yet despite those acts of athletic heroism, the Patriots decided his $12.5 million annual salary scheduled for 2005 was too expensive. He was sidelined by a foot injury for much of 2004 and was soon released. He was signed by the Jets, leading the league with a career-best 10 interceptions, including a long pick-six of Brady, and earning a Pro Bowl spot in 2005. After two seasons as a starter with Denver, he finished out his career in 2009.

Law finally gained his place in the Pro Football Hall of Fame in 2019.

HIS GREATEST GAME
New England and Indianapolis battled for a Super Bowl berth on January 18, 2004. It was no contest—greatly because of Law. He intercepted Peyton Manning's passes in the second, third, and fourth quarters to thwart the Colts. His last pick came deep in New England territory and preserved a 21–7 lead.

SIDE STORY
Law opened a chain of entertainment facilities called Launch Trampoline Park around New England following his retirement.

WHAT LAW SAID
"I said from day one that my goal by the time I'm done was to be a Hall of Famer. I set that bar that high. And everything else, to get to that point, I had to work harder, I had to study harder, I had to compete harder."[3]

WHAT WAS SAID ABOUT LAW
"Ty was tough, he would tackle, he could play against big receivers and he was physical against guys. You know, the Marvin Harrisons of the world that were maybe a little quicker, but Ty had great instincts and size and playing presence, and he matched up well with those type of players, too." —Patriots coach Bill Belichick[4]

CHAPTER 30

Cam Neely

"Bam Bam Cam"

ESSENTIALS
Sport: Hockey
Born: May 12, 1935
Years Active: 1983–1996
Years with Boston: 1986–1996
Position: Left wing

KNOW THE CAREER NUMBERS
344 Goals
246 Assists
590 Points
53.3 Offensive point shares
4 All-Star appearances

WHY NEELY IS NO. 30
One of the most popular Bruins ever helped change the power forward position with a combination of size, speed, skill, and physicality. He was an enforcer who worked as his career advanced to limit his penalty minutes and prevent power plays against Boston while becoming a more prolific scorer. His 50 goals in 49 games during the 1993–94 season was a remarkable feat. Though his Bruins never won a Stanley Cup, they

reached two finals and he could not be blamed for the failure to conclude with a crown. Neely performed his best in the postseason.

Neely's quick release, fast and accurate shots, and hard body checks marked his career. His style and effectiveness have been credited as the archetype of the modern power forward. Flyers superstar Eric Lindros, who arrived in the NHL as Neely's career was winding down, was often compared to him.

Knee and hip injuries prevented Neely from playing full seasons and shortened his career. His retirement at age 31 after 13 years, the last 10 with Boston, did not cost him a spot in the Hall of Fame. He ranked third in the league in average goals per game during that time.

ALL ABOUT NEELY BEFORE BOSTON

Neely first played in the NHL for the team he rooted for as a child. He was born in Comox, British Columbia, before moving to Maple Ridge, a Vancouver suburb, where he became an ardent Canucks fan. Among his childhood friends was future major league slugger Larry Walker, who dreamed of a career as a hockey goaltender. The two honed their skills on the local rinks.

While others dipped their toes into the waters of junior hockey before blossoming, Neely exploded onto the scene at age 17 with the Portland Winter Hawks. He scored an amazing 120 points—56 goals and 64 assists—in just 74 games during the 1982–83 season and maintained the furious pace early the following year before the hometown Canucks selected him ninth overall in the 1983 draft. They wasted little time promoting him to make his NHL debut at age 18.

Neely was young and healthy, and he was aggressive. He attacked the goal and dished out punishment to any defender in his path. He did not, however, emerge as a prolific scorer in Vancouver. He averaged nearly four minutes in the penalty box per game during his two full seasons with the Canucks. He had yet to develop the game that would make him a four-time All-Star.

It would not happen in his hometown. Canucks coach Tom Watt had grown disenchanted with Neely, who he believed lacked grit on the defensive end. In what some consider the worst trade in Vancouver history, he was shipped on his 21st birthday along with a first-round pick that Boston used to draft defenseman Glen Wesley for fading center Barry Pederson, who was coming off shoulder surgery.

That was a tough period for Neely, whose lack of playing time in Vancouver resulted in waning confidence. He had also learned that his parents were diagnosed with cancer. They were both gone by 1993. But his hockey career had been saved.

In a Bruins Uniform and Beyond

Neely led the Bruins with 36 goals in 1986–87, more than his previous two seasons combined. He also compiled 143 penalty minutes, many for fighting, raising concern from teammates and new coach Terry O'Reilly. He could only hurt the team from the box and create power plays. Neely kept fighting and the punishment time increased, reaching 190 minutes two years later.

Only when he limited his penalty minutes did Neely peak as a scorer and all-around player. He led Boston in scoring with 55 goals and 92 points in 1989–90 after chopping 77 minutes off his time in the box, then added 91 points the next season, earning spots on the All-Star team both years.

He would not enjoy another fully healthy season, but by that time he had already earned a reputation as a prolific scorer who performed his best in the playoffs. He tallied a hat trick and scored eight points in a four-game sweep defeat to Montreal in his first postseason series with the Bruins. His five goals in five games against the Sabres vaulted Boston into the 1989 conference finals. He exploded for nine points in a five-game victory over Washington to lead the Bruins to the brink of a Stanley Cup championship before falling to Edmonton. He added another hat trick in a playoff victory over Montreal in 1991.

A knee-to-knee collision with Pittsburgh defenseman Ulf Samuelsson in the next series planted the seeds for his career demise and the run of Bruins playoff success. Neely suffered one devastating injury after another, losing significant playing time every year. He played in just 22 games combined the following two seasons and 49 in 1993–94, but not before scoring 50 goals in 44 games. Only the immortal Wayne Gretzky had lit the lamp that often in fewer games. A torn knee ligament ended Neely's best year. That ailment resulted in frequent scratches, and then a degenerative hip condition forced his retirement after the 1995–96 season at age 31.

Neely attempted a brief comeback with the Bruins in 1998 that ended before he played a game. He returned to the organization as its vice president in 2007—two years after his induction into the Hockey Hall of Fame—and was promoted to president three years later. He was still at that post into 2024.

His Greatest Game

Neely will always be remembered for his postseason accomplishments but his finest performance was on October 16, 1988. That is when Neely scored three goals and added four assists in a 10–3 defeat of Chicago. He amazingly didn't tally a point until four minutes remained in the first period. Then he exploded. He recorded two goals and one assist in the second and flip-flopped those totals in the third.

Side Story

After losing both his parents to cancer, Neely launched the Cam Neely Foundation in 1995 in conjunction with the Tufts Medical Center in Boston. That year he asked comic Denis Leary to arrange a comedy benefit show fundraiser that later became known as Comics Come Home. It has been held annually ever since.[1]

What Neely Said

"I have been always a very determined person. I'm pretty black and white. There's no gray area. At least people know what they're dealing with. . . . I see what I want and I go after it."[2]

What Was Said about Neely

"If I was going to build a hockey player, I'd start with [Neely]." —Bruins defenseman Don Sweeney

CHAPTER 31

Sam Jones

"Mr. Clutch"

ESSENTIALS

Sport: Basketball

Born: June 24, 1933

Died: December 30, 2021

Years Active: 1957–1969

Years with Boston: 1957–1969

Position: Shooting guard

KNOW THE CAREER NUMBERS

17.7 Points per game

4.9 Rebounds per game

2.5 Assists per game

.4561 Shooting percentage

48.6 Offensive win shares

43.7 Defensive win shares

3 All-NBA

5 All-Star appearances

10 NBA championships

WHY JONES IS No. 31

That Jones compiled the statistics he did sharing the ball with Bill Russell, Bill Sharman, Bob Cousy, and Tom Heinsohn is phenomenal. He certainly benefited from their passing and the fast-break style instituted by coach Red Auerbach, but he also had to share the ball with brilliant teammates who lessened his scoring, rebounding, and assist numbers. The "bank was open" with Jones on the floor—he popularized the bank shot.

Jones earned his "Mr. Clutch" nickname. He played significant parts in the annual championships his Boston teams won in the 1950s and 1960s by performing his best with victory and defeat hanging in the balance. Included was his most famous shot, a buzzer-beater over Wilt Chamberlain to eliminate Philadelphia in the 1962 Eastern Conference finals. Jones was among the deadliest shooters of his era—46 percent accuracy in that era was rare. Russell even praised him as "the purest shooter I have seen."[1]

ALL ABOUT JONES BEFORE BOSTON

Jones was born and raised in segregated Wilmington, North Carolina, during the Jim Crow era. His father died during his childhood. Jones spoke years later about positive family influences helping him avoid negative temptations in life. He played well enough at Laurinburg Prep to gain the attention of Basketball Hall of Fame coach John McLendon, who at the time headed the program at all-Black North Carolina College. Jones made an impact in four seasons there, averaging 18 points per game.

By the time he had played out his college career he was 24 years old, having spent two years in the military, which fielded a basketball team that allowed Jones to hone his skills. Among those whom he had impressed at NCC was former Wake Forest coach Bones McKinney. When asked by Celtics coach Red Auerbach to name the best college player in North Carolina, he replied that it was Jones. That was heady praise considering North Carolina had just beaten Chamberlain and the University of Kansas to win the NCAA championship. Auerbach gave the relative unknown a shot, selecting him eighth overall in the first round of the 1957 draft.

Jones was stunned and disappointed at being chosen by Boston as the first African American selected in the first round of any major American sport because he did not play in a prominent college program. "I carried a burden on my shoulders that felt very similar to what Jackie Robinson must have felt," he said. "I wanted to succeed. I wanted to make good so that others could follow me, and so that the people in this country could see that we had some good basketball players in our black collegiate institutions."[2]

The disappointment revolved around the depth of the Celtics and a fear that he would be relegated to a bench role for the defending NBA champions. At that time teams carried just 10 players. Jones even considered shunning basketball for a teaching career. But he performed well enough in training camp to beat out two-time ACC Men's Player of the Year Dick Hemric for the last roster spot. Jones was not destined to make an immediate impact. When he did receive an opportunity, he ran with it all the way to the Hall of Fame.

IN A CELTICS UNIFORM AND BEYOND

Jones had one obstacle after earning a spot on the Celtics. His name was Bill Sharman. Sharman was a shooting guard in the midst of a Hall of Fame career. Jones spent most of his rookie season watching the veteran from the bench or playing in garbage time after another Boston victory was in the bag.

Auerbach could not keep Jones down. The coach recognized how valuable he could be to the fast-breaking offense and stifling defense. Jones tempered speed with body control and a calming effect in the most harrowing of game circumstances. He bolted downcourt a split second after a Russell rebound and awaited the outlet pass. Soon he was headed to the rim for a layup or draining one of his trademark bank-shot jumpers with a smooth and quick release.

Jones averaged 20 minutes per game in his second and third seasons and 26 in his fourth while his scoring, shooting accuracy, and assist totals increased. He then landed a starting role upon Sharman's retirement and earned his nickname. Jones played a key role in a monumental comeback in the 1962 finals against the Lakers, scoring 10 points in a six-minute flurry to erase an eight-point deficit in Game 6, then scoring half his team's points in a dramatic overtime to win Game 7 and the championship. Three years later he scored 37 points in the iconic "Havlicek stole the ball" defeat of Philadelphia to clinch the Eastern Conference title. The aging guard rose to the occasion again in his last season with Russell as player-coach. He won a critical Game 4 of the finals against Los Angeles with an off-balance buzzer-beater, then scored 24 points in his career finale that helped Boston win Game 7 and the crown.

Upon retirement he served as athletic director and basketball coach at Federal City College in Washington, D.C., before landing a job as an assistant coach with the expansion New Orleans Jazz. He later worked as an athletic director at various D.C. schools.

HIS GREATEST GAME

That no Boston player had ever scored 50 points in a game until 1965 was a testament to their ball-sharing, balance, and depth. Jones finally broke the mold with a 51-point performance that year against Detroit. The importance of his effort against Oscar Robertson and the Cincinnati Royals in Game 7 of the 1963 Eastern Conference Finals trumps it. The Celtics needed a victory to advance and Jones came through as usual. He scored 47 points on 18-of-27 shooting and added seven rebounds in a 142–131 triumph.

SIDE STORY

Sam Jones was not the first notable American athlete named Sam Jones. Another was a pitcher who was among several stars reviled Red Sox owner Harry Frazee sent from the Red Sox to the Yankees (including Babe Ruth), helping New York launch its dynasty. "Sad" Sam Jones won 21 games for the Yankees in 1923 as that team won its first World Series. He finished his career with 229 victories.

What Jones Said

"If I can get to the spot I like on the floor before the man who is guarding me, I'm going to score."[3]

What Was Said about Jones

"Sam was one of the great shooters of all time. But he was team-oriented. All he wanted to do was win." —Red Auerbach[4]

CHAPTER 32

Richard Seymour

"Hulk"

ESSENTIALS
Sport: Football
Born: October 6, 1979
Years Active: 2001–2012
Years with New England: 2001–2008
Positions: Defensive end, defensive tackle

KNOW THE CAREER NUMBERS
498 Tackles
91 Tackles for losses
57.5 Sacks
7 Pro Bowls
3 Super Bowl championships
3 All-Pro

WHY SEYMOUR IS NO. 32
Those unfamiliar with Seymour must do double-takes when they learn he played mostly defensive end at nearly 320 pounds, though he spent two seasons with New England as a tackle. His speed and quickness belied his size. He rushed with power but developed the moves to shed linemen and sack or at least disrupt quarterbacks. Seymour could play with equal

effectiveness in the interior. His career-high eight sacks were achieved in a 2003 season during which he played more tackle than end.

Patriots coach Bill Belichick emphasized in a push to get Seymour voted into the Pro Football Hall of Fame that his team would not have won three Super Bowls in a four-year stretch without him. Teammate Andre Tippett concurred. "I saw Richard rise in big moments, as well as sacrifice his personal goals so others around him could make contributions," Tippett wrote. "Richard in my opinion was truly a difference maker. He had the power and explosiveness, as well as the quickness, to cause quarterbacks to worry. . . . But Richard's greatness isn't in the numbers or the scheme; it was his ability to do whatever was asked of him."[1]

ALL ABOUT SEYMOUR BEFORE NEW ENGLAND

A turbulent relationship with his father began during his childhood in Gadsden, South Carolina. Though his parents were separated he depended on his dad for advice on life and sports. Richard woke up early to watch his father at his contracting job and learn about his work ethic. Little could he have imagined that Richard Seymour Sr. would kill his girlfriend and commit suicide in 2004.

The younger Seymour displayed his talents at Lower Richland High School in nearby Hopkins, earning all-region honors as a senior. He landed a scholarship to the University of Georgia, where he blossomed into a defensive force. He exploded in 1999 with 74 tackles—no small feat for a defensive lineman. Seymour became only one of two Bulldogs who didn't play linebacker to ever lead the team in that category. The respect he gained as a player and leader inspired his teammates to vote him captain.

It came as no surprise when Seymour was twice chosen All-SEC first team and named an All-American in 2000. He finished his college career with 233 tackles, including 26 for losses, 9.5 sacks, and 35 quarterback pressures.

The Raiders fan growing up hoped to be drafted by a team on the West Coast or the South. He was initially disappointed when the Patriots selected him ninth overall. He arrived in time to help launch a dynasty.

IN A PATRIOTS UNIFORM AND BEYOND

Seymour found his groove as a rookie after missing time to a leg injury and showed flashes of future greatness in the postseason, playing a role in the team's first Super Bowl championship with a sack of Kurt Warner and two tackles for losses in the taut victory over the Rams. He soon blossomed into a Pro Bowl regular, earning five consecutive trips.

A switch to a 3-4 defense motivated his move to the outside despite his size, though he also played nose tackle. He used his rare combination of power and quickness to overwhelm offensive linemen and record a career-high eight sacks, a second-place finish in the 2003 AFC Defensive Player of the Year balloting behind Ravens linebacker Ray Lewis, and a first-team All-Pro selection. Seymour had taken his first major step into the Hall of Fame. "Richard had a tremendous skill set," said Patriots coach Bill Belichick. "Great length, explosive, very quick for his size. Very smart and very aware."[2]

Seymour battled through injuries during his last four seasons with the Patriots but continued to earn postseason awards. The New England defense was designed for defensive linemen to hold the fort and focus on the ground game while the linebackers tracked down quarterbacks, so Seymour never managed more than eight sacks in a season.

That lack of showy statistics resulted in a longer wait than deserved for NFL Hall of Fame induction—he was not voted in until his fifth year of eligibility. During their dynasty, the defense enjoyed its best seasons with him on the field. He was rated New England's most valuable player statistically by Pro Football Reference in 2006 despite playing with an ailing left elbow. He even played fullback occasionally on short-yardage situations.

The Patriots shocked Seymour by trading him to Oakland for a first-round pick in 2008. He continued to play at a high level, earning two more Pro Bowl spots before retiring while on the free agent market waiting for an acceptable contract offer in 2013.

HIS GREATEST GAME

Seymour wreaked havoc on the Steelers with the New England defense devastated by injuries on September 25, 2005. He twice sacked hard-to-bring-down Pittsburgh quarterback Ben Roethlisberger and added three tackles for losses. His contributions keyed a 23–20 victory.

SIDE STORY

Seymour turned his passion for poker into a second career. He participated in the 2019 and 2023 World Series of Poker events, though he did not finish in the top 100 in either one.[3]

WHAT SEYMOUR SAID

"Together, we were in constant pursuit of that edge. We called ourselves the edgers. That edge was our culture. We felt a sense of responsibility to each other, a sense of obligation. None of us wanted to be the person to let the team down, to let our brothers down. That defined us. We never cared who got the accolades as long as we got the W."[4]

WHAT WAS SAID ABOUT SEYMOUR

"He laid the foundation for a defense that helped propel the Patriots to three Super Bowl championships in his first four seasons in the NFL. Richard was the consummate professional and leader, always accepting the roles he was assigned, putting team goals ahead of personal ones, and in turn, raising the game of everyone around him." —Patriots owner Robert Kraft[5]

CHAPTER 33

Bill Sharman

"Bull's-Eye Bill"

Bill Sharman around 1960. Public domain, photographer unknown

ESSENTIALS
Sport: Basketball

Born: May 25, 1926

Died: October 25, 2013

Years Active: 1950–1961

Years with Boston: 1950–1961

Position: Shooting guard

KNOW THE CAREER NUMBERS
17.8 Points per game

3.9 Rebounds per game

3.0 Assists per game

.426 Shooting percentage

.883 Free throw percentage

61.4 Offensive win shares

21.3 Defensive win shares

7 All-NBA

8 All-Star appearances

4 NBA championships

WHY SHARMAN IS NO. 33
Sharman was one of the greatest shooters in an era during which most guards struggled to hit 40 percent of their shots. He became the first NBA guard to exceed that milestone when he hit 43.6 percent from the field during the 1952–53 season. He was also among the deadliest ever at the foul line. He helped drive the Celtics dynasty in the mid-1950s with his mid-range accuracy.

The advent of the 24-second clock in 1954 increased his value. The faster tempo of the game playing for a team that had already established the fast-break as its primary offensive weapon allowed Sharman to increase his scoring average and hit shots before defenses could properly set up to defend him. He was also a fine, fiercely competitive defensive player who was particularly adept at preventing drives to the basket.

ALL ABOUT SHARMAN BEFORE BOSTON

That Sharman would become a pro athlete was a given. The only question was which sport he would choose. He excelled in several. Born and raised in Abilene, Texas, he was the son of a *Los Angeles Examiner* newspaper distributor. He won 15 varsity letters at Porterville High. He starred in football, baseball, tennis, track, boxing, and basketball. One day he won both the discus throw and shot put at a morning track meet, then pitched the baseball team to victory that evening.

Sharman landed at the University of Southern California after serving in the Navy and earned All-American honors in basketball. The Brooklyn Dodgers hoped he would forge a baseball career. They signed him as an outfielder in 1950. Sharman played several seasons in the minor leagues before and during his time with the Celtics and excelled, twice driving in 77 or more runs and finishing his stint with a fine .281 batting average after reaching the Triple-A level. He yearned to succeed in baseball but never got his shot in the majors. So he turned to basketball.

Sharman had played one NBA season with the Washington Capitols. That team folded and he was selected in the dispersal draft by Fort Wayne. That's when Boston GM Red Auerbach, always one to make shrewd deals, traded the draft rights to eventual journeyman Charlie Share for Sharman. It materialized as one of the greatest steals in NBA history.

IN A CELTICS UNIFORM AND BEYOND

Auerbach had coached Washington for three seasons before Sharman arrived and had taken over the Celtics when the rookie played with the Capitols. He was quite aware of Sharman's strengths and how he would fit into the fast-break system he had created. The 25-year-old had yet to maximize his talent and sometimes struggled in his first year with Boston.

By 1952 he had hit his stride. Sharman and Cousy emerged as the most potent backcourt in the sport. They teamed with string bean center Ed Macauley to average 56 points a game, nearly two-thirds of the team total. Sharman was far more efficient a scorer than Cousy, and he certainly took advantage of his teammate's passing and ballhandling wizardry. He struggled in the playoffs, hitting just four of 20 shots in back-to-back losses to New York that destroyed their championship hopes.

Thereafter Sharman blossomed into a deadeye from the field and line with titles hanging in the balance, though the Celtics continued to falter before Bill Russell transformed them into a powerhouse. There were exceptions such as the 3-for-20 effort in the legendary Game 7 defeat of St. Louis in the 1957 Finals. Sharman peaked in the four-game sweep of Minneapolis for the 1959 crown, averaging 22.5 points per game and tallying 29 in the clincher.

Sharman grew into a more prolific scorer late in his career, exceeding 20 points a game for the first time in 1957 and hitting that mark in both of the next two seasons. He also led the NBA in free throw percentage seven times, including his last year at .921. He hung up his sneakers to pursue a coaching career—an equally impressive endeavor as he led Boston archrivals such as the Warriors and Lakers. He managed seven winning records in his first eight seasons, including a then-record 69–13 mark with title-winning Los Angeles in 1972.

He was not done with basketball after retiring from coaching in 1976. He served as general manager and president of the Lakers from the late 1970s into the early 1990s and constructed the championship teams featuring Magic Johnson and Kareem Abdul-Jabbar.

HIS GREATEST GAME

The original Baltimore Bullets were not long for the world—they posted a losing record every year of their existence—but what Sharman achieved against them on December 11, 1952, strangely in Philadelphia, was still quite impressive. It was needed given that Cousy missed 15 of 17 shots in that game. Sharman nailed 17 of 25 for 42 points, nearly half his team's total in a 94–88 victory. His career-best 44 came five years later, but Sharman needed 37 shots to do it.

Side Story

Sharman was on the Brooklyn Dodgers bench in the Polo Grounds in 1951 after signing with the team when Bobby Thomson hit the most famous home run in baseball history, a blast against Dodgers pitcher Ralph Branca that sent the New York Giants to the World Series.[1]

What Sharman Said

"It's a game of habit, or repetition. You can't play one way in practice and another way in a game. It's a reflex. The game is so quick you don't have time to think."[2]

What Was Said about Sharman

"He was the best athlete I've ever played with or against." —Bob Cousy[3]

CHAPTER 34

Milt Schmidt

"Uncle Milty"

Bobby Bauer, Woody Dumart, and Milt Schmidt from a 1942 Bruins team photo. Attributed to *The Los Angeles Daily News*, photographer unknown, public domain

ESSENTIALS
Sport: Hockey
Born: March 5, 1918
Died: January 4, 2017
Years Active: 1936–1955
Years with Boston: 1936–1955
Positions: Center, defenseman

KNOW THE CAREER NUMBERS
229 Goals
346 Assists
575 Points
50 Offensive point shares
13.4 Defensive point shares
1 Hart Trophy
4 All-Star appearances
2 Stanley Cup championships

WHY SCHMIDT IS NO. 34
Schmidt centered one of the most prolific trios in NHL history, playing beside fellow Hall of Famers Woody Dumart and Bobby Bauer to form the legendary "Kraut Line," which played nearly 1,900 games together for the Bruins. He led the team in scoring five times despite missing three years to fight with the Royal Canadian Air Force during World War II.

One of those seasons in which Schmidt paced Boston in scoring was 1939-40. The Kraut Line placed 1-2-3 in NHL scoring that year—a distinction achieved only twice since in league history. Schmidt could have scored more goals but he embraced a pass-first, score-second mentality that allowed his linemates to also rack up goals.

All about Schmidt before Boston

The Kraut Line wasn't thrown together when the three arrived in Boston. They were childhood friends who sharpened their skills on the ice growing up in Kitchener, Ontario. Schmidt experienced a tough upbringing. He was forced to leave school during the Great Depression in 1932 to help support his family after his father fell ill. The boy landed a job at a shoe factory earning just 18 cents an hour.

Schmidt loved to skate as a child. Once chastised for a stronger focus on the ice than his studies by his elementary school principal, who questioned his future, he replied that he planned to become a professional hockey player. He also excelled as a youth in baseball. He played with The Kitchener Empires and Kitchener Greenshirts junior teams alongside Dumart and Bauer. His talents earned him a spot on the Bruins' AHL affiliate Providence Reds. Schmidt also received a tryout with the MLB St. Louis Cardinals but concluded that he lacked the power to thrive at that level.

He developed a reputation for his toughness and goal-scoring more than his passing. Schmidt scored an amazing 26 goals in 29 games for the two Kitchener teams then added eight more for Providence after signing a contract with Boston in October 1935. Soon the Bruins had seen enough. He played only 23 games for the Reds before his promotion in 1937. Schmidt was the second of the three Kraut Line stars to hit the NHL. By the 1937–38 season the three had been established. They would terrorize opponents for seven years. Only World War II would stop them.

In a Bruins Uniform and Beyond

Schmidt began his NHL career before the Original 6 even existed. His relentless style on the rink contrasted with his congenial personality off it. He quickly earned the distinction as the premier two-way player of his generation.

One of the top scorers of his era, Schmidt blossomed along with the Kraut Line before the war. He averaged nearly a point a game in those three seasons before he and his two compatriots joined the Canadian military. Schmidt led the NHL in assists and points to land his first All-Star berth in 1940.

His time away from hockey certainly sapped none of his skills. He became more productive upon his return. Schmidt tallied a career-high 62 points in just 59 games during the 1946–47 season and continued to fight through knee injuries as his career progressed. He won his only Hart Trophy as league MVP in 1951 after scoring 39 goals. Schmidt played in his fourth All-Star game the following year.

Most impressive was his playoff heroism. Schmidt performed his best with Stanley Cups up for grabs. He scored seven points during the four-game sweep of Detroit for the crown in 1941, including two assists in the 3-1 clincher. He added 21 points in 24 playoff games over four seasons after the war.

Schmidt retired as a player after a 1954 game against Chicago during which he fell and struggled to rise back to his feet. That retirement did not end his affiliation with the Bruins—far from it. He immediately took over as head coach and guided them to the Stanley Cup finals in 1957 and 1958. Monumental struggles followed. Boston suffered through terrible seasons under Schmidt through 1966. However, he returned to Boston as general manager for 11 years and made a hugely positive impact. He drafted and acquired key pieces to the 1970 and 1972 Stanley Cup champions. His blockbuster deal that landed Phil Esposito and Ken Hodge from Chicago remains one of the biggest heists in hockey history.

Schmidt left the Bruins to serve as the first general manager for the expansion Washington Capitals. That team set a record for futility with a mark of 8–67–5, motivating Schmidt to take over as coach. He was fired in 1976 after his team opened the season at 3–28–5.

HIS GREATEST GAME

Given his penchant for scoring it seems amazing that Schmidt never managed a hat trick during his illustrious career. He did, however, score two goals and an assist in Game 3 of the 1946 Stanley Cup semifinals against Detroit. His first-period goal gave Boston the lead to stay. He then assisted on another to make it 2–0 and put the victory away with another goal early in the third. The Red Wings did not die easily in that series. The Bruins needed overtime in Game 5 to clinch it.

SIDE STORY
Schmidt forged one of the most bitter individual rivalries in hockey during his career. That was with Canadiens legend Maurice "The Rocket" Richard. The animosity was heightened one night when a high-sticking Richard broke Schmidt's nose. Schmidt returned to the game and targeted Richard for a vicious body check. "(Richard) starts skating toward me and he says, 'Why you do dat?'" Schmidt recalled years later. "I just pointed at my nose and said, 'Because you do dat!'"[1]

WHAT SCHMIDT SAID
"You have friends—although you are bitter enemies, you had friends in the National Hockey League."[2]

WHAT WAS SAID ABOUT SCHMIDT
"A case could be made for (Schmidt) being the greatest all-around hockey person in the history of the sport." —Dick Johnson, historian and curator for the Sports Museum of New England[3]

CHAPTER 35

Jimmie Foxx

"The Maryland Strong Boy"

Jimmie Foxx early in his career with Boston. Wikimedia Commons, Charles M. Conlon photo

ESSENTIALS
Sport: Baseball

Born: October 22, 1907

Died: July 21, 1967

Years Active: 1925–1945

Years with Boston: 1936–1942

Positions: First base, outfield

KNOW THE CAREER NUMBERS
.325 Batting average

534 Home runs

1,751 Runs

1,922 RBI

.428 On-base percentage

90.7 Offensive WAR

9 All-Star selections

3 Most Valuable Player awards

2 World Series championships

1 Triple Crown

2 Batting titles

WHY FOXX IS NO. 35
Granted, this all-time legend is more closely associated with the Philadelphia Athletics, for whom he played his first 11 years. But he was so dominant during his six-plus seasons in Boston that he earned a spot on this list. Had he achieved his career numbers with the Red Sox he would have fallen comfortably in the top 10.

Foxx was a premier masher in the golden age of offensive baseball. He had already led the American League in home runs three times and RBI twice when he was purchased from the A's by the woeful Sox, who were still reeling more than a decade after owner Harry Frazee's fire sales that sent Babe Ruth and Hall of Fame pitchers Herb Pennock and

Waite Hoyt to the Yankees. Foxx and Hall of Fame pitcher Lefty Grove, an earlier acquisition from Philadelphia, helped bring Boston back to respectability.

The slugger averaged nearly 40 home runs and 135 RBI in his first five years with the club. His 175 RBI in 1938 remains a Sox record. So feared were pitchers at the prospect of facing Foxx that they often pitched around him. The result was 100 walks per season and an on-base percentage that soared above .400. He was simply among the greatest hitters in baseball history.

ALL ABOUT FOXX BEFORE BOSTON

The eldest son of tenant farmers in Sudlersville, a farming village in northeast Maryland with a population barely over 200, James Foxx benefited from his father's passion for baseball. He embraced athletics far more than academics, adding soccer and track to his list of talents. Rugged work on the family farm built the muscular physique he eventually used to slug baseballs a long way. He displayed an impressive combination of power and speed in his early years playing organized ball.

His talent caught the eye of local legend Frank "Home Run" Baker, who led baseball by hitting a "whopping" 11, 10, and 12 dingers in consecutive seasons during the dead-ball era from 1911 to 1913. Baker, from nearby Trappe, Maryland, arrived as manager of a new Easton team in the Eastern Shore League. Baker invited Foxx, who was rewriting the record books at Sudlersville High School, for a tryout as a catcher. Foxx batted .296 for Easton that summer, motivating legendary manager Connie Mack and the Athletics to purchase his contract. He was even allowed to watch late-season Philadelphia games from the bench to whet his appetite. It was quite a treat for a 16-year-old.

Foxx was just 17 when he singled in his Philadelphia debut on May 1, 1925. He was dispatched to Providence of the Eastern League to gain more experience. He didn't need it. Foxx had already batted an absurd .667 in 10 major league games. He was stuck behind Hall of Fame catcher Mickey Cochrane, which in 1926 relegated him to pinch-hitting duties and spot starts in the outfield.

A move to first base in 1927 increased his playing time. He batted .323 that year, then took off. By 1929 he was among the top sluggers in the sport. That season was the first of 13 consecutive in which he exceeded 100 RBI. He exploded for a team-record 58 home runs in 1932 to threaten Babe Ruth's single-season record of 60. He won the rare Triple Crown the following year by hitting .356 with 48 home runs and 163 RBI.

By that time the Great Depression had depressed attendance and Mack's bank account. He began to sell off top talent, including Al Simmons, Lefty Grove (to Boston in 1934), and Cochrane. Only Foxx remained. He continued to mash, gaining a spot in the first MLB All-Star game in 1933. But he grew disenchanted with the direction of the now-woeful team and even battled Mack for the slightest pay increase. The loss of Cochrane forced Mack to move him back to catcher. The cellar-dwellers finally sold Foxx to the Red Sox after the 1935 season. Soon he was handed a $7,000 raise. Fenway Park and the Green Monster were tailor-made for the right-handed power bat.

IN A RED SOX UNIFORM AND BEYOND

Foxx was merely 28 years old upon his arrival in Boston despite having played 11 seasons with Philadelphia. He was in his prime and hit like it, establishing single-season franchise records in his first year with 41 home runs and 143 RBI.

Sinus problems limited Foxx in a disappointing 1937 in which his average plummeted to .285, but he returned with a vengeance the next year by winning the American League batting title by hitting .349, and setting a Sox record that stood through 2023 with 175 RBI, and a third MVP. So fearful were AL pitchers of his fearsome bat that they walked him 119 times that year as Foxx paced everyone in baseball with a .462 on-base percentage. The arrival of rookie Ted Williams in 1939 gave Foxx better pitches to hit. The result was a career-best .360 batting average and .464 OBP.

His production tailed off as the new decade began but he remained an All-Star and triple-digit RBI machine. Foxx, however, grew increasingly critical of Red Sox manager Joe Cronin, whom he respected far less than Mack. Meanwhile, his popularity waned as Sox fans became increasingly enamored with Williams. Foxx was traded to the Chicago Cubs on June 1, 1942. After being rejected by the military to fight in World War II due to his sinus condition, he played out his career with the Phillies three years later.

Plagued by alcoholism, Foxx toiled in various odd jobs after his retirement. He was elected into the Hall of Fame in 1951.

HIS GREATEST GAME

The Red Sox came to the plate just five times against the Yankees on September 7, 1938. They had clinched an 11–4 rain-shortened victory. Foxx had by then out-bombed the Bronx Bombers. He had hit three-run homers in the third and fourth innings and a two-run double in the fifth for eight RBI. Foxx was not done torturing the Yankees that year. He concluded the season with a two-homer, seven-RBI finale on October 1.

SIDE STORY

The tiny town of Sudlersville, Maryland, had a life-sized bronze statue erected of Foxx in 1997. It is located in the heart of the town at the intersection of Main and Church Streets.[1]

WHAT FOXX SAID

"If I had broken Ruth's record it wouldn't have made any difference. Oh, it might have put a few more dollars in my pocket, but there was only one Ruth."

WHAT WAS SAID ABOUT FOXX

"When Neil Armstrong first set foot on the moon, he and all the space scientists were puzzled by an unidentifiable white object. I knew immediately what it was. That was a home run ball hit off me in 1973 by Jimmie Foxx." —Hall of Fame pitcher Lefty Gomez[2]

CHAPTER 36

Wes Welker

"The Slot Machine"

ESSENTIALS
Sport: Football
Born: May 1, 1981
Years Active: 2004–2015
Years with New England: 2007–2012
Position: Wide receiver

KNOW THE CAREER NUMBERS
903 Receptions
9,924 Yards
11.0 Yards per catch
50 Touchdowns
5 Pro Bowls
4 Super Bowl championships
2 All-Pro

WHY WELKER IS NO. 36
Welker earned his nickname. He caught passes with machine-like frequency and consistency, peaking in his six seasons with New England. He was considered the original slot receiver and a reliable outlet for

quarterback Tom Brady early in his career. Welker led the NFL in receptions three times in five seasons to keep the chains moving. Well over half his catches resulted in first downs. Had he played with the Patriots longer he certainly would have ranked higher.

Considering the wide array of targets from which Brady had to choose during Welker's time with New England, including Rob Gronkowski, Aaron Hernandez, several pass-catching running backs, and the virtually unstoppable Randy Moss, his numbers were remarkable. Though he never won a championship with the Patriots, his playoff and Super Bowl contributions were substantial.

ALL ABOUT WELKER BEFORE NEW ENGLAND

It seems Welker was born with a drive to succeed and a competitive spirit. One needs only ask his older brother Lee, who witnessed it on trampoline battles and wrestling matches in the yard. The two sometimes jumped off the second-story balcony onto a couch below. Young Wes even snuck up from behind and smashed him over the head with a crystal ashtray.

Welker's sport of choice as a youth growing up in Oklahoma City was soccer. His parents insisted he wait until junior high to play organized football. He watched others compete on the football field and thirsted for action. So his folks permitted him to start a year early. He was a natural. He led his youth team to a championship by scoring five touchdowns in the finals.

He was about to attend private Heritage Hall High School, but he demonstrated such gifts on the gridiron that his parents considered sending him to a bigger school with a stronger football program. Welker, however, wanted to stick with Heritage. Good idea. He won a state title there and two Oklahoma Player of the Year awards.

Where were the college scholarship offers? They never came. Scouts felt he lacked the speed and athleticism to thrive at that level. The snub was painful. He finally landed one at Texas Tech after another recruit backed out of his. Red Raiders coach Mike Leach would not be sorry. Welker dominated as a receiver and punt returner. He averaged 92 receptions and 1,077 yards in his last two seasons. He scored 29 receiving touchdowns during his four years there, including an amazing eight taking punts into the end zone. He set an NCAA record with 1,761 punt return yards.

Even that did not impress scouts. A stunned Welker went untaken in the 2003 draft. He signed a contract with San Diego but failed to make the team. He finally received a chance to play in Miami, first on special teams then as a receiver. But the Dolphins employed no quarterback who could maximize his potential. Welker was traded to the Patriots in 2007 for two draft picks. It was a steal for New England. An incredible run was about to begin.

IN A PATRIOTS UNIFORM AND BEYOND

The Patriots obviously needed receivers heading into the 2007 season. After all, the rather forgettable Reche Caldwell had been their top player at the position the year before. They traded for prolific pass-catcher Randy Moss. Welker was considered by most an afterthought.

He was no afterthought to Brady. One can argue that no quarterback in NFL history better utilized his surrounding talent, and Welker became his go-to receiver. Welker nearly matched Moss in targets and catches. He took advantage of defensive attention on Moss to snag 112 passes for 1,175 yards and eight touchdowns to help New England complete an undefeated regular season. He caught two more scoring strikes from Brady in the AFC playoffs then grabbed 11 more passes in the Super Bowl defeat to the Giants.

Welker continued to provide remarkable consistency and production over the next several years. He finished four of the next five seasons with at least 1,165 yards receiving, peaking in 2011 with a league-best 122 catches for 1,569 yards. He set the tone for that season with a 99-yard touchdown reception to help beat Miami in Week 1.

Most importantly he thrived in the playoffs despite somehow experiencing no Super Bowl victories during the team's incredible run. Welker scored five postseason touchdowns and averaged nine catches for 82 yards in three Super Bowls. He left the Patriots in free agency in 2016, but by that time had established an NFL record for 100-catch seasons with five.

The Brady-Welker combination destroyed opponents. He could not replicate that success elsewhere, though he did set a career-high with 10 scoring receptions with Denver in 2013. Welker faded thereafter, retiring at age 34 after playing out his career with St. Louis. Welker began a coaching career in 2017, serving as a special teams and wide receiver mentor for Houston, San Francisco, and Miami.

HIS GREATEST GAME
The Patriots and Welker were on the roll to start the 2011 season. The team won four of its first five games. Welker averaged nine catches for 148 yards during that stretch. Oddly, however, his greatest game came in the lone defeat. Welker caught 16 of 20 targets for a career-high 217 yards and two touchdowns in Buffalo. His score with three minutes left tied the game at 31–31 before the Bills won it on a last-second field goal.

SIDE STORY
Welker is part of the Cherokee Nation. He was officially recognized as a Cherokee citizen during a Tribal Council meeting on January 14, 2013. His grandmother lived in Sequoyah County within the Cherokee Nation's tribal jurisdiction.[1]

WHAT WELKER SAID
"I thought I would be returning kicks and punts my whole career. I thought that was going to be my deal, and I was fine with that."

WHAT WAS SAID ABOUT WELKER
"There was nobody who could define what being a great teammate was, what doing the right thing was, like Wes." —Tom Brady

CHAPTER 37

Roger Clemens

"Rocket"

Roger Clemens delivers a pitch at Fenway in 1996. Wikimedia Commons, Jerry Reuss photo

ESSENTIALS
Sport: Baseball

Born: August 4, 1962

Years Active: 1984–2007

Years with Boston: 1984–1996

Position: Starting pitcher

KNOW THE CAREER NUMBERS
354–184 Win–loss record

3.12 ERA

4,672 Strikeouts

7.6 Hits per nine innings pitched

1.158 WHIP

7 ERA titles

7 Cy Young Awards

11 All-Star appearances

WHY CLEMENS IS NO. 37
It would not take a thorough examination of statistics to indicate a much higher ranking, but the allegations of steroid use knocked Clemens down on the list, though it must be cited that if his numbers and health were indeed bolstered by performance-enhancing drugs much of that happened after he left Boston. Inconsistency late in his time with the Red Sox also weakened his case.

Clemens dominated like no other in his generation when he was on top of his game. His breakout 1986 season was among the greatest in baseball history and marked the first of four ERA titles and three Cy Young Awards he achieved in Boston. His upper-90s fastball and hard splitter overpowered hitters. He concluded his career third in MLB history in strikeouts behind only Nolan Ryan and Randy Johnson. Yet he continued to be snubbed by Hall of Fame voters through 2023 for his connection to the steroid era as one of the most polarizing figures in the history of the sport.

ALL ABOUT CLEMENS BEFORE BOSTON

Among the most fanatically competitive pitchers ever was merely five months old when his father left the family, then eight when the man his mother married died. That bolstered the influence of older brother Randy on his life. He idolized the budding baseball and basketball standout. Roger embraced Randy's outlook that one is either a winner or a failure. That philosophy remained with him throughout his career.

The younger Clemens failed early to gain the same athletic success. At age 15 he joined Randy, who had moved to suburban Houston. That is where he honed his craft and earned a record of 12–1 as a high school sophomore. Clemens transferred to a school with a stronger baseball program that played in elite competition. The move had mixed results. He learned more about pitching mechanics but seldom got a chance to play as a junior. Even as a senior he was considered a soft-tosser and nonprospect.

Clemens drew little attention from college scouts. He pitched instead for San Jacinto Junior College. Coach Wayne Graham transformed him into a fireballer through sage advice about finishing his delivery with greater force. Clemens improved so much that he was selected by the Mets in the 12th round of the 1981 draft. He rejected that team to transfer to the University of Texas. That angered Graham, who anticipated another season with Clemens.

Though not overwhelmingly dominant with the Longhorns, his stock rose. He finished 12–2 with a 1.99 ERA in his first year there, then grew so frustrated by his lack of success the following season that he threatened to quit the team. He still didn't throw quite hard enough to overpower hitters. Yet the Red Sox saw enough potential to snag him 19th overall in the 1983 draft.

Clemens rocketed through the organization. He sported an ERA under 2.00 and struck out more than a batter per inning at every stop. He landed at Triple-A Pawtucket a year after launching his professional career. He also gained a reputation as a hypercompetitive and intimidating pitcher who threw at hitters or at least brushed hitters off the plate with a fastball that was gaining velocity and whose "winner or failure" mentality became more pronounced. It would be severely tested in his first three months as a big leaguer.

In a Red Sox Uniform and Beyond

The view that Clemens required more minor league seasoning gained credibility after his promotion to the Red Sox in May 1984. He was pounded for 11 hits in five innings by Cleveland in his debut and managed just three quality starts in his first 12, after which his ERA had ballooned to 5.94, and was briefly removed from the rotation. Clemens responded with a vengeance, shutting out the White Sox and continuing to lower his ERA through August.

Shoulder problems ended his season early and plagued him severely in 1985. He grew frustrated and even tearful as he experienced pain and was forced to undergo surgery to remove cartilage, cutting his 1985 season short as well. Some wondered if shoulder issues would wreck his career.

They wondered no longer in 1986. He vaulted from prospect to superstar in one memorable performance on April 29 after setting a major league mark by striking out 20 batters to beat the Mariners at Fenway Park and raise his record to 4–0. During one early stretch that year, he fanned 51 in 32 innings. By the end of June, he owned a 14–0 record and 2.18 ERA as the Sox were steamrolling to the pennant. Clemens finished the year 24–4, not only winning the Cy Young Award unanimously but beating National League wunderkind Dwight Gooden in the All-Star Game by pitching three perfect innings, then winning AL MVP honors as well.

Such a dominant season was impossible to repeat but Clemens was a perfectionist. Being great was not good enough. He had to settle for mere greatness and occasional mediocrity thereafter. He won 20 games and another Cy Young in 1987, led the league in ERA every year from 1990 to 1992 despite a contentious relationship with the organization that began when he bolted spring training over a contract dispute, then experienced a period of mediocrity in the mid-1990s. He became antagonistic with the media and fans, both of whom criticized him for being what they perceived as an entitled, pampered athlete and for his postseason inconsistency. His 4.02 playoff and World Series ERA with Boston was deemed unworthy of his talent. Clemens was even ejected in the second inning of one 1990 playoff game in Oakland for charging one umpire and pushing another. The incident was seen as another example of his me-first, team-second outlook.

Despite his struggles in the mid-1990s, Boston GM Dan Duquette still offered him a three-year, $24.75 million contract. Clemens turned it down to join Toronto in free agency. He silenced those who claimed he was fading by winning four more Cy Young Awards pitching for the Blue Jays, Yankees, and Astros, though charges of steroid use if true certainly helped his arm stay healthy and perform at a high level. He remained effective until finally retiring at age 44. Like others spotlighted in the steroid era such as Barry Bonds and Mark McGwire, he was shunned by Hall of Fame voters for at least the next 16 years.

His Greatest Game

Granted, Detroit was terrible in 1996. Granted, Clemens was on his way out of Boston. But on September 18 he not only matched his own baseball record with 20 strikeouts but shut out the Tigers in the process. It was his third-last start and final victory in a Red Sox uniform. He fanned tough hitter Travis Fryman to clinch the victory.

Side Story

The most infamous moment of Clemens's career came in Game 2 of the 2000 World Series—otherwise known as the Subway Series—between the Yankees and Mets. That was when Clemens, who had once bounced a fastball off Piazza's skull and concussed him, threw a jagged shard of a sawed-off bat at the superstar catcher. Both benches emptied and a near-brawl ensued. The perplexingly furious reaction to a harmless broken-bat grounder for which Piazza could not be blamed strengthened claims that Clemens was on steroids and that a "roid rage" event had been witnessed. Piazza refused to forgive Clemens years thereafter.[1]

WHAT CLEMENS SAID

"I went out to play the game of baseball because I love to play it. I did it right. I did it the right way. I worked hard doing it."[2]

WHAT WAS SAID ABOUT CLEMENS

"He's the Rolls Royce of pitching. He competes, has good stuff. He knows how to pitch. You don't win 300 games by accident." —MLB manager Lou Piniella[3]

CHAPTER 38

Joseph White
"Jo Jo"

ESSENTIALS
Sport: Basketball
Born: November 16, 1946
Died: January 16, 2018
Years Active: 1969–1981
Years with Boston: 1969–1979
Position: Point guard

KNOW THE CAREER NUMBERS
17.2 Points per game
4.0 Rebounds per game
4.9 Assists per game
.444 Shooting percentage
20.3 Offensive win shares
33.7 Defensive win shares
2 All-NBA
7 All-Star appearances
2 NBA championships

WHY WHITE IS NO. 38

Jo-Jo White did nothing brilliantly but everything well. He handled a huge adjustment running a slow-down offense at the University of Kansas and directing the famed Celtics fast-break upon his arrival. He made the transition quickly and displayed his all-around talents and steady influence on his teammates early in his career.

White ran the break as well as anyone in the NBA as a scorer or distributor. He also displayed an underrated jump shot and played defense with intensity, fighting through picks, and rarely allowing his man to beat him to the basket. He focused less on scoring and more on passing after coming to the realization he could help Boston without averaging 20 points per game.

The result was a steadiness that marked his time with the Celtics, who could count on him for 17–20 points and 5–6 assists per game every season. He generally performed his best with championships on the line.

ALL ABOUT WHITE BEFORE BOSTON

Injuries are rarely fortunate, yet one to his hand paved the way for a Hall of Fame basketball career. White hurt it playing football, prompting his mother to suggest he try a different sport. He tried shooting hoops and became obsessed, often jacking up jumpers at a St. Louis recreation center until midnight.

White was the youngest of seven children to a Baptist minister. He did not give up football completely as a teenager—he starred as a wide receiver in high school. He even got drafted out of college by the Dallas Cowboys. White even excelled in baseball, motivating the Cincinnati Reds to take him in the early years of the Major League Baseball draft. However, he chose to pursue a basketball career. He was recruited to the University of Kansas—former home of Wilt Chamberlain—by legendary NFL running back and alumnus Gale Sayers.

The rest is history. White displayed his greatness for the Jayhawks, averaging 15.3 points per game during his four-year career, improving every season and intriguing NBA scouts with his ball-handling and defense. He started for the US team in the 1967 World University

Games and Pan American Games in 1967, then with the 1968 Olympic team that won the gold medal.

Celtics coach Bill Russell urged general manager Red Auerbach to grab White when he remained available at No. 9 in the first round of the 1969 draft. Neither would regret it.

IN A CELTICS UNIFORM AND BEYOND

White arrived in the NBA with a score-first mentality, but the Celtic style under coach Tom Heinsohn and pairing with legend John Havlicek precluded that mindset from lasting. He had gone from a Kansas offense predicated on pick-and-rolls to one in Boston fueled by the fast-break while the team transitioned from the Bill Russell and Sam Jones era. As his point totals shrunk, his passing skills and defense strengthened. His scoring average dropped from 23.1 points per game in his third season to 18.1 two years later yet he had become a more accurate shooter from the field and the foul line.

White earned a reputation as a streaky, inconsistent shooter but Heinsohn understood that it was related to a focus on his all-around game. His role changed from season to season and he took pride in living up to expectations. "It's been difficult," he said in 1976, "because each year I'm asked to do something different. I just looked to score my first year in the league. That made things simple. But now, I have to play both ends of the floor."[1]

He certainly did that in the playoffs. White showed his focus, along with his mental and emotional toughness by performing his best with titles on the line. His career postseason scoring average of 21.5 was four points higher than what he achieved in the regular season. He nailed his trademark mid-range jumper and drove to the basket relentlessly to frustrate opponents despite the natural fatigue resulting from playing 43 minutes per game.

That overall playoff brilliance was overshadowed by one legendary performance in arguably the greatest NBA game ever. He played a ridiculous 60 of the 63 minutes in the triple-overtime Game 5 of the 1976 finals against Phoenix and scored 33 points with nine assists to lead the

Celtics to the key victory in their championship run and win the Most Valuable Player award in the series.

"It was a very fast-paced game, so early on I realized that conditioning was going to be key," White said. "This played into my strengths because I considered myself the best-conditioned athlete on the floor. My mental approach was, 'If I'm tired then everyone else on the court must be dead tired.'"[2]

Yet that effort was hardly shocking given White's established penchant for playoff success. He shot 58 percent from the field and averaged 24.2 points and six assists per game in his first postseason series, a defeat of Atlanta. He remained a dependable cog throughout his career in the playoffs, including two steamrolls to NBA championships.

White did not get a chance to play with Larry Bird. He was traded to Golden State during the pre-Bird collapse of the Celtics during the 1978–79 season for a first-round pick the team eventually used to land aging Hall of Fame scoring machine Bob McAdoo. White played out his career with the Warriors and Kansas City Kings. He later worked as director of special projects for the Celtics.

HIS GREATEST GAME

A no-doubter. It was Game 5 of the 1976 NBA Finals against Phoenix in which White scored 33 points and led both teams with nine assists. His clutch shooting in the first two overtimes kept Boston alive.

SIDE STORY

White played on the 1968 US Olympic basketball team in Mexico City. It was not expected to win the gold medal after superstar college players Lou Alcindor (later Kareem Abdul-Jabbar) and Elvin Hayes stayed away as part of a Black boycott and fellow standouts Pete Maravich, Calvin Murphy, and Dan Issel were not invited. White helped the Americans sweep nine games and take the gold. He averaged 11.7 points per game, second on the team to future NBA star Spencer Haywood. That was the last of seven consecutive Olympic championships for the US team.

WHAT WHITE SAID

"It's all really quite simple. I just concentrate on getting the ball over the front rim and shooting the same way every time."[3]

WHAT WAS SAID ABOUT WHITE

"He was under the gun to perform and be an all-around player from the moment he stepped into the league. He had more pressure put on him than Havlicek as a rookie. Remember, John was the Celtics' sixth man for several years." —Tom Heinsohn[4]

CHAPTER 39

Dustin Pedroia

"Muddy Chicken"

Dustin Petroia in a 2012 game at Baltimore. Wikimedia Commons, Keith Allison photo

ESSENTIALS
Sport: Baseball

Born: August 17, 1963

Years Active: 2006–2019

Years with Boston: 2006–2019

Position: Second base

KNOW THE CAREER NUMBERS
.299 Batting average

140 Home runs

922 Runs

725 RBI

.365 On-base percentage

41.4 Offensive WAR

1 Most Valuable Player award

4 Gold Gloves

4 All-Star selections

2 World Series championships

WHY PEDROIA IS NO. 39
This feisty second baseman was the heart and soul of the 2007 and 2013 World Series champions and strong Boston clubs before and after. He played with passion while producing consistently strong numbers annually. He began his career with a bang as a potential Hall of Famer, winning Rookie of the Year and MVP honors in successive seasons.

Though it seemed unlikely in 2024 that Pedroia would make it to Cooperstown because knee injuries weakened his play and shortened his career, he remained one of the best all-around players in the game with a combination of speed, power, and defensive dependability. He played only with the Red Sox and finished his career with nearly as many walks as strikeouts.

ALL ABOUT PEDROIA BEFORE BOSTON

Pedroia was born and raised in California but nowhere near the southern region where so many modern-era major leaguers honed their skills. He was from the tiny agricultural village of Woodland, which rests 20 miles northwest of Sacramento. He spent much of his childhood playing baseball with his older brother Brett and modeling his game after hero Barry Bonds. Their skill sets, paths to stardom, and legacies would prove quite dissimilar.

That his budding career as a football quarterback was ruined by injury his freshman year at Woodland High School might have been a blessing in disguise. It allowed him to focus solely on baseball. He batted at least .445 in all three seasons while adding power every year to win league MVP as a senior. His lack of size—he was a mere 5-foot-2 and 140 pounds—turned off college and pro scouts. It only takes one believer and for Pedroia, it was Arizona State University coach Pat Murphy, who appreciated his scrappy on-field approach and attitude.

Pedroia sprouted to 5-foot-8 before his first year. He proved his worthiness with a brilliant first season, slamming an ASU freshman record 82 hits and driving in 45 runs.

He was merely scratching the surface of his talent. He led the PAC-10 in hits, runs, and doubles in both of his next two seasons. He checked the last box as a five-tool player as a junior when he hit nine home runs. He was ready to play pro ball after the Sox snagged him 65th overall in the 2004 draft.

Though it took two years for Pedroia to exhibit the decent power he eventually showed with the Red Sox and had yet to blossom into a consistent base stealer, his bat spoke volumes in the minors and led to quick promotions. He reached Triple-A Pawtucket in 2005 after batting .324 at Double-A Portland. After hitting .305 with the PawSox in 2006 the organization could wait no longer. After a five-game sweep to the Yankees and during a 3–14 stretch in August that pushed Boston out of the race, he was deemed ready for "The Show."

IN A RED SOX UNIFORM AND BEYOND

Red Sox manager Terry Francona did not dip Pedroia's toes in the major league waters upon his arrival. He pushed him into the water. Pedroia was forced to sink or swim in the waning days of the 2006 season—and for a while, he was drowning. His average sunk to .122 in mid-September before an 11-for-30 stretch raised it to .205. Few could have predicted the heights he or his team would reach in 2007.

The commendable patience of Francona paid off that year. Pedroia struggled mightily in April, but the manager maintained his commitment as a starting second baseman. A 14-game hitting streak sent his batting average soaring to .331 by early June and it remained over .310. Pedroia dominated the Rookie of the Year balloting. His batting skills were ideal for the leadoff and second spots in the order. He did not shrink from the pressure of the postseason, slamming 11 hits, including two home runs and four doubles during one torrid stretch in the ALCS and World Series to help Boston to its second crown in four years.

That was merely a prelude to his finest season. He embarked on a 17-game hitting streak in mid-June and amazingly had no successive hitless games the rest of the year. The 25-year-old affectionately nicknamed "Pedey" by his teammates led the league with 213 hits and 54 doubles, earning the AL Most Valuable Player award. Some pegged him as a future Hall of Famer. He became the first player in baseball history to win Rookie of the Year, MVP, Gold Glove, and World Series within his first two seasons.

Perhaps he would have fulfilled that Hall of Fame goal that appeared destined to elude him had a series of injuries and ailments not resulted in absence from the lineup and limited productivity. After pacing the league again in runs scored in 2009, foot surgery prematurely ended his next season. Pedroia rebounded to drive in a career-high 91 runs in 2011 and continued to thrive, finishing seventh in MVP voting in 2013 to help Boston to another title.

"He was the ultimate team player," praised Francona, who was the Red Sox's manager during the first six seasons of Pedroia's career. "He always seemed to save his very best plays for the most important time of the game. He seemed to will himself at times to lead us to victory."[1]

He could not will the Sox to victory from the operating room. He eventually needed six surgeries on his knee resulting from an injury sustained when Baltimore star Manny Machado slid into him trying to break up a double play in 2017. Pedroia worked diligently to continue his career but after managing just 31 at-bats the next two seasons combined finally announced his retirement in 2021. Four months later he was inducted into the Red Sox Hall of Fame. Perhaps only injuries would keep him out of Cooperstown.

His Greatest Game

Pedroia had five five-hit games in his career, but given the importance of a three-hit game in 2007 that must be considered his best. It was Game 7 of the ALCS against Cleveland. The Red Sox had rebounded from a 3–1 deficit in the series to force an all-or-nothing battle at Fenway. Pedroia certainly rose to the occasion. He singled and scored in the first inning, blasted a two-run homer in the seventh to break open a tight game, and then drove in three more with a bases-loaded double in the eighth to put it away and clinch a trip to the World Series that Boston parlayed into a championship.

Side Story

Pedroia beat out future MLB standout Ian Kinsler for the starting shortstop job at Arizona State, causing the latter to transfer to the University of Missouri. Kinsler briefly played with Pedroia on the Red Sox in 2018 as both neared the end of their careers.

What Pedroia Said

"People always ask me if I wish I were bigger. I tell them no. I always wanted to be a miniature badass."[2]

What Was Said about Pedroia

"Dustin came to represent the kind of grit, passion and competitive drive that resonates with baseball fans everywhere, and especially with Red Sox fans. He played the game he loves in service to our club, its principles and in pursuit of championships." —Red Sox owner John Henry[3]

CHAPTER 40

Gino Cappelletti

"The Duke"

ESSENTIALS
Sport: Football
Born: March 26, 1934
Died: May 12, 2022
Years Active: 1960–1970
Years with Boston: 1960–1970
Positions: Wide receiver, defensive back, kicker

KNOW THE CAREER NUMBERS
292 Receptions
4,589 Yards
15.7 Yards per catch
42 Touchdowns
176 Field goals
5 Pro Bowls (AFL)
1 Player of the Year

WHY CAPPELLETTI IS NO. 40
Those who either do not know or recognize the greatness of this Boston
Patriot either lack knowledge of franchise history or appreciation of his

talent, versatility, and impact. Cappelletti even played defensive back his rookie season and intercepted three passes in one game. He was the all-time leading scorer in AFL history and one of the last two-way football standouts.

Cappelletti did everything well as one of three men to play in all of his team's AFL games (along with Raiders Jim Otto and George Blanda). He became a shining light in an era of darkness for a Boston team that stumbled to a 13–42 record in his last four seasons.

ALL ABOUT CAPPELLETTI BEFORE BOSTON

Cappelletti didn't need time to become acclimated to the cold climes of Boston upon his arrival. He was born and raised in the northern Minnesota town of Keewatin, where he worked on the railroad and iron ore mines as a teenager while playing on the high school football team.

He performed well enough to land a spot on the University of Minnesota squad and eventually served as backup quarterback to All-American Paul Giel. Though he played some wide receiver, his specialty was placekicking. His 31 consecutive successful extra points set a school record. He finally took over as the starting quarterback in 1954 and led the Golden Gophers to a 7–2 mark.

Cappelletti waited in vain for a call during the 1955 NFL draft. He then played quarterback for Sarnia and Toronto of the Ontario Rugby Football League before joining the Army. He spent time with Winnipeg and Saskatchewan of the Canadian Football League. His career was going nowhere.

Then fate and the AFL stepped in. Original Patriots coach Lou Saban, who later guided Buffalo to back-to-back league championships, found Cappelletti tending bar during a scouting mission to Minnesota. The 27-year-old was only playing touch football with his friends at that time but he begged Saban for a tryout. Saban eventually relented. Cappelletti showed the confidence to announce his intention to earn a roster spot as a defensive back. Indeed he secured it. It would be his kicking and receiving that transformed him into an all-time great.

IN A PATRIOTS UNIFORM AND BEYOND

Cappelletti did not last long as a defensive back—he lost that spot in the AFL kickoff game (September 9, 1960)—but he did make history by booting the first field goal in league history, a 34-yarder in a loss to Denver at Nickerson Field, home of Boston College. But he impressed assistant coach Mike Holovak after replacing an injured wide receiver in practice and started the last game at that position.

Cappelletti took that job and ran with it. He overcame a case of hepatitis the following training camp and caught a touchdown pass from quarterback Babe Parilli in the final exhibition game, during which he also booted three field goals to lock up the placekicker job. Cappelletti blossomed in 1961 with eight touchdown catches and achieved the first of six consecutive 100-point seasons.

He also helped turn the Patriots into a winner for several years under Holovak, who had replaced Saban in 1961. His talents played a significant role in four straight seasons over .500, including a title-game berth against the eventual champion San Diego Chargers in 1963. Cappelletti nailed the first franchise playoff field goal in that defeat.

Cappelletti led the AFL in field goals three times and played in four Pro Bowls from 1961 to 1966. His 51-yard field goal in 1961 was the longest in the league that year, as was his 53-yard kick the following season. He also caught at least 34 passes every year from 1961 to 1967, peaking with 49 catches for 865 yards in 1964 to win AFL Most Valuable Player honors.

His retirement in 1970 did not mark the end of his affiliation with football. Cappelletti became a Boston icon. He toiled as an assistant coach with the team before becoming the voice of the Patriots on radio for three decades and also serving as color commentator for Boston College football.

HIS GREATEST GAME

Cappelletti caught more passes in games than he did on November 15, 1964. He gained more yards and kicked more field goals in other games. But he destroyed Buffalo that afternoon with three touchdown receptions. He caught a 35-yard scoring strike from Parilli in the second quarter to give his team the lead and led a comeback from a 14-point deficit with two more scores in the fourth quarter, including a 34-yarder from Parilli that put it away. He also kicked four extra points in the victory.

SIDE STORY

Cappelletti was working as a color commentator on one of the most famous college football games ever. He was in the booth when Boston College quarterback Doug Flutie heaved his game-winning Hail Mary touchdown to beat the University of Miami in 1984. Cappelletti could be heard yelling "He got it! He got it! I don't believe it!" as he broadcast the game alongside play-by-play partner Don Davis.[1]

WHAT CAPPELLETTI SAID

"We were true pioneers and part of an era that helped establish the Patriot franchise."[2]

WHAT WAS SAID ABOUT CAPPELLETTI

"He is small and slow, but he has good moves and sure hands and catches a lot of passes." —*Sports Illustrated* writer Edwin Shrake[3]

CHAPTER 41

Tris Speaker

"The Gray Eagle"

Tris Speaker in 1912. Library of Congress

ESSENTIALS
Sport: Baseball
Born: April 4, 1888
Died: December 8, 1958
Years Active: 1907–1928
Years with Boston: 1907–1915
Position: Center field

KNOW THE CAREER NUMBERS
.345 Batting average
3,514 Hits
1,882 Runs
1,531 RBI
.428 On-base percentage
792 Doubles
222 Triples
125.1 Offensive WAR
436 Stolen bases
1 Most Valuable Player award
3 World Series championships

WHY SPEAKER IS NO. 41
Yes, Speaker played longer with Cleveland than Boston. Yes, it can be argued he performed better with the Indians than the Red Sox. Yes, he played in the dead-ball era. Each of those arguments calls for counterarguments. Speaker did play nine years with Boston—long enough to earn a spot among the top 50. His numbers with the Red Sox scream out inclusion despite improving in Cleveland. He was among the best power hitters—weak as they were—in the pre-Ruthian period.

Speaker was a hitting and on-base machine. He even led the league in doubles and homers in 1912 when the Sox christened Fenway. His .464 on-base percentage that year helped him win the AL Most Valuable

Player award. His best years as a base stealer were in a Boston uniform. Had he played his entire career with the Red Sox he would easily be a top 10 selection.

ALL ABOUT SPEAKER BEFORE BOSTON

The son of a former Confederate soldier, Speaker was born and raised in the tiny railroad town of Hubbard, Texas. His father died when he was 10 years old.

His athletic talents were pronounced. He played football and captained the baseball team in high school before pitching for what is now Texas Wesleyan University. He kept himself quite busy playing semipro ball while adding funds toiling as a telegraph lineman and cowpuncher.

His future as a pitcher was doomed shortly after landing a spot on Cleburne of the Texas League for the whopping sum of $50 per month. He reportedly once yielded 22 consecutive extra-base hits in losing six straight decisions. Thankfully, he showed promise as an outfielder. In 1907 he raised his batting average to .314 and stole 36 bases. That piqued the interest of the Americans—soon to be Red Sox. They provided a cup of coffee for Speaker late that year. But he choked on it.

IN AN AMERICANS AND RED SOX UNIFORM AND BEYOND

Speaker did not exactly have Boston brass turning cartwheels over his prospects in 1907. His .158 batting average had him waiting in vain for a contract before the next season. His pleas to Giants manager John McGraw and other major league teams fell on deaf ears. So he paid his own way to Americans training camp in Little Rock and hoped for the best.

He did not have to go far from there. Speaker was sent to the Southern Association team in that town to play in 1908. And he tore it up. He batted .350 with 28 stolen bases there and played flawlessly in the outfield. That drew interest from many big-league organizations but Little Rock sold him to Boston. At age 21 in 1909 he was ready to fly.

The perennially strong Sox—at least until the day after Christmas in 1919 when they sold Babe Ruth to the Yankees—welcomed Speaker into their lineup. He batted .309 and led the team in home runs and RBI.

But that was merely the tip of the iceberg. His production grew in time and peaked when Fenway opened in 1912. Speaker not only established career-bests in batting average, runs, hits, doubles, homers, RBI, and on-base percentage, but he helped his team beat McGraw and the Giants in the World Series by hitting safely in eight of nine games. It was sweet revenge on the manager who had rejected him.

It also endeared him to Boston fans. Speaker became immensely popular. Boston Garters named a straw hat after him. Speaker trading cards showed him running the bases. But team president Joe Lannin did not feel the same level of appreciation. When Speaker struggled to match his 1912 numbers, Lannin tried to cut his annual salary in half to $9,000. The angry star staged a holdout that resulted in a trade to the Indians.

His loss was Cleveland's gain. Speaker led the league with a .386 batting average in his first season there and helped the Indians win the World Series in 1920 as a player-manager after batting a career-high .388. He served in that capacity until 1926 and later worked as a radio broadcaster on Cubs and White Sox games.

HIS GREATEST GAME
Speaker managed one five-hit game for Boston in 1915, but one must reach back to his finest season for his best performance. Granted, it was in St. Louis against the lowly Browns but Speaker did something special on June 9, 1912. He hit for the cycle in a 9–2 victory. He tripled in the first inning, homered in the fourth to make it 1-0, doubled in a run in the fifth, and singled in another in the ninth.

SIDE STORY
Speaker taught himself how to throw left-handed as a child when he twice broke his right arm after being thrown from a bronco.

WHAT SPEAKER SAID
"Success is not the result of spontaneous combustion. You must set yourself on fire."[1]

What Was Said about Speaker

"You can write him down as one of the two models of ball-playing grace. The other was Napoleon Lajoie. Neither ever wasted a motion or gave you any sign of extra effort. . . . They had the same elements that made a Bobby Jones or the Four Horsemen of Notre Dame—the smoothness of a summer wind." —Sportswriter Grantland Rice[2]

CHAPTER 42

Brad Marchand

"Little Ball of Hate"

Brad Marchand before a game in 2016. Wikimedia Commons,
Lisa Gansky photo

ESSENTIALS
Sport: Hockey
Born: May 11, 1988
Years Active: 2009–
Years with Boston: 2009–
Position: Left wing

KNOW THE CAREER NUMBERS (THROUGH 2023–24)
401 Goals

528 Assists

929 Points

88.2 Offensive point shares

32.2 Defensive point shares

4 All-Star appearances

1 Stanley Cup championship

WHY MARCHAND IS NO. 42
Marchand blossomed late after spending his early career in the shadow of Patrice Bergeron. He did not break out as a scorer until age 28 but that did not stop him from emerging as a superstar. He did not score more than 61 points nor earn an All-Star spot until the 2016–17 season. But over the next eight seasons his assist totals skyrocketed and he made four All-Star teams while placing among the top seven in Hart Trophy voting four times.

His greatest talent was creating offense for himself and his teammates through elusive skating and tricky stickhandling. The Bruins simply gained more quality shots and goals with Marchand on the ice. His goal-scoring did not vastly improve over the years but his assist numbers did. He blossomed into one of the premier left wings in the game and in Bruins history.

ALL ABOUT MARCHAND BEFORE BOSTON
Marchand was born and raised in Halifax, Nova Scotia. By seventh grade he was dreaming of hockey greatness. Rather than focus on his

homework he practiced signing autographs. The feisty, rambunctious youth and oldest of four siblings gave little effort in his schoolwork. Unlike others who dreaded hockey workouts he could not wait to get to the rink. He began skating when he was two years old and soon gained confidence to the point of cockiness that he was a future star.

One problem was his temper. He had trouble controlling it. He even underwent anger management as a child. He sought to harness that temper and transfer it to aggression on the ice. He began speaking with a sports psychologist. It worked.

His talent was pronounced but he never rose to the top level of the prospect pool. After scoring 29 goals for the Moncton junior team he was selected in the third round of the 2006 draft by the Bruins. Marchand continued to improve, tallying 80 points the following season for Val d'Or Foreurs at age 18. By 2008 he had reached the doorstep of the NHL. He scored 59 points for the AHL Providence Bruins and added 32 points in just 26 games the next year before earning a 20-game stint with Boston during which he rarely played. Though other prospects showed more promise he was soon ready for the big time.

IN A BRUINS UNIFORM

Marchand finally found an opening-game spot in Boston in 2010 and ran with it. He was placed on the energy line, also known as the Merlot Line for their dark-red practice sweaters. He fits well with the rough styles of linemates Gregory Campbell and Shawn Thornton.

Coach Claude Julien was impressed enough by Marchand to promote him into a top-six role alongside stars Patrice Bergeron and Mark Recchi. The result was an offensive explosion and all-around improvement, particularly on the penalty-killing unit specializing in shorthanded goals. His 21 goals overall ranked fifth among NHL rookies.

He indeed showed star potential, but nobody could have predicted how much impact Marchand would make in the playoffs that season. He scored 19 points, including 11 goals, in 25 games as the Bruins skated their way to the championship. Marchand tallied three points to open the second-round sweep of Philadelphia but saved his best for last. In the winner-take-all Game 7 of the Stanley Cup finals in Vancouver against the heavily favored Canucks, he scored or assisted on three of the four goals in a shutout victory.

But Marchand did not progress as hoped. He appeared destined to blossom into superstardom after producing 36 points in 45 games during the lockout-shortened 2012–13 season but his scoring stagnated. He went scoreless in the Cup final against Chicago that year and managed just 103 points combined over the next two regular seasons. He was putting pucks into the net but failing to consistently set up his linemates.

Then it happened. Marchand arrived as a superstar during the 2016–17 season when given more opportunities on the power play. He had been pegged based on his numbers as only a scorer who could not distribute the puck, but he proved his doubters wrong that year. The result of his increased minutes with Boston on the advantage was 46 assists, nearly double his previous career high, and 85 points.

Marchand was unleashed. He matched that point total the following year and then reached 100 in 2019. He totaled at least 67 points every season through 2024 while becoming an annual All-Star contributor until 2022. Age had begun to take a toll as he approached his mid-30s but he was still going strong. He took over as captain of the team when Bergeron retired in 2022 and even scored eight points in the first four games of the 2024 playoffs against Toronto.

His Greatest Game

Given the enormity of the winner-take-all Game 7 of the Stanley Cup finals against Vancouver in 2011, that must be listed on top. Marchand assisted on a Bergeron goal to open the scoring then put the crown away with goals in the second and third periods.

Side Story

Marchand was most famously called "Little Ball of Hate" by President Obama when the team visited the White House after winning the 2011 Stanley Cup. Obama had taken it from former NHL star Pat Verbeek. Marchand had several other nicknames, including Rat, Tomahawk, Squirrel, and Weapon of Mass Destruction.[1]

WHAT MARCHAND SAID

"My compete level probably is what separates me. I think that I just find ways to compete to win. And so I think I've learned how to get better in a lot of other areas, and I can win battles and make plays over the corners or whatever it is."[2]

WHAT WAS SAID ABOUT MARCHAND

"His leadership is untouched. He's just a tremendous, tremendous athlete. And . . . he's a pain in the butt to play against." —Wayne Gretzky[3]

Chapter 43

Charles Nichols

"Kid"

Kid Nichols of the Boston Beaneaters. Library of Congress

Essentials
Sport: Baseball
Born: September 14, 1869
Died: April 11, 1953
Years Active: 1890–1906
Years with Boston: 1890–1901
Position: Starting pitcher

Know the Career Numbers
362–208 Win–loss record
2.96 ERA
1,881 Strikeouts
8.8 Hits per nine innings pitched
2.3 Walks per nine innings pitched
1.224 WHIP

Why Nichols Is No. 43
Pitchers from the dead-ball era, particularly those who thrived before the turn of the twentieth century, are difficult to judge. But Nichols, who played for the Beaneaters of the National League, was one of the premier hurlers of his generation. He used a fluid, straight-overhand delivery and pinpoint control to stay healthy and retire batters. Nichols led the National League in wins three consecutive seasons and won between 27 and 35 games every year from 1890 to 1898. His seven 30-win seasons remains a major league record—and given the modern five-man rotations and focus on pitch counts will likely stand forever. He even won 27 as a rookie. There were no awards as measuring sticks such as the Cy Young back then—after all, Young was still pitching!

Nichols completed all but 30 of the 562 games he started. Such durability was not a rarity in the early days of major league baseball, but it certainly proves he did not get rocked often enough to be removed from the mound. Aside from two anomaly seasons in 1894 and 1895 he consistently allowed fewer hits than innings pitched, no small feat given the era in which hitters eschewed power and focused on slapping line drives around the park.

ALL ABOUT NICHOLS BEFORE BOSTON

The guns of the Civil War had only been silenced for four years when Charles Nichols was born the son of a butcher in Madison, Wisconsin, in 1869. Half-brothers James and John played for the Capital Cities baseball club of the National Association of Base Ball Players. The family moved to Kansas City around 1881.

Soon Charles competed with the Blue Avenue club along with his siblings. He pitched his team to one amateur championship. His talents helped other local clubs and gained attention from the Kansas City Cowboys of the Western League in 1887. He pitched his first professional game on June 14 that year at the age of 17 and won it, 7–6. His youthful look inspired teammates to give him his iconic nickname—Kid. At just 135 pounds some speculate that he had been mistaken for the batboy upon his arrival.

He didn't pitch like a kid. He won 18 games that season, then posted a 16–2 record and league-leading 1.14 ERA the following year with another Kansas City club. Nichols soon gained his baseball freedom and signed with an Omaha club managed by Frank Selee. He posted a ridiculous record of 39–8 in 1889. Selee was then hired to lead the NL Boston Beaneaters and yearned to take Nichols with him in 1890. He rejected offers from other teams to pitch for Selee. A wonderful marriage had been launched.

IN A BEANEATERS UNIFORM AND BEYOND

Nichols began with a bang. In one notable performance he pitched 12 shutout innings against the Players League Giants, which boasted many of the top players who had abandoned the NL champion Giants for the new circuit and consistently outdrew their established counterparts. Nichols lost the shutout and game in the 13th innings on a solo home run.

That did not deter him from a brilliant rookie year. He emerged as ace of the staff with a 27–19 record and a team-best 2.23 ERA. Nichols completed all but one of his 48 starts. He followed that with the first of his seven 30-win seasons and led his team to pennants every year from 1891 to 1893.

Boston's chief rival in that era was the Baltimore Orioles, who captured three straight titles after the Beaneater run. The two teams forged a wire-to-wire battle for the crown in 1897. A critical three-game series began in late September in Baltimore. Nichols won twice, including the clincher on the last day of the season despite terrible Boston defense. His efforts inspired praise from sportswriters.

Baseball historian Bill James recognized his contributions a century later. Using a formula to determine the impact a player makes on his team, James concluded that Nichols contributed the third-most to pennant winners in baseball history behind Babe Ruth and Mickey Mantle. Among those championship contributions was in 1898, when Nichols went 31–12 (his last 30-win season) with a 2.12 ERA.

Nichols faded in the early 1900s and in 1904 managed the St. Louis Cardinals to a fifth-place finish. He later worked as a minor league manager and major league scout.

HIS GREATEST GAME

Box scores from the 1890s are nonexistent but Nichols received much praise for his performance on October 13, 1899, against tough Philadelphia southpaw Wiley Piatt in a battle of 20-game winners. Brooklyn had already clinched the pennant but Boston and Philadelphia were fighting for second place. Nichols tossed a three-hit shutout in a taut 1–0 victory.

SIDE STORY

Nichols was a tremendous bowler. He opened up a bowling academy and some alleys in the Kansas City area. He even won that city's Class A bowling championship at age 64.

WHAT NICHOLS SAID

"Never used a swing in my delivery. Always pitched straight away. Using same delivery when men were on base. Never did I use trick pitching."[1]

WHAT WAS SAID ABOUT NICHOLS

"The features of his pitching are speed, headwork, and control of the ball. He has never been troubled with a glass arm, which he attributes to the fact that he delivers the ball with a long easy swing and not a jerk."
—*Kansas City World*[2]

CHAPTER 44

Tom Heinsohn

"Tommy Gun"

Tom Heinsohn driving to the basket in a game against Philadelphia in 1962. Public domain, photographer unknown

ESSENTIALS
Sport: Basketball

Born: August 26, 1934

Died: November 9, 2020

Years Active: 1956–1965

Years with Boston: 1956–1965

Position: Power forward

KNOW THE CAREER NUMBERS
18.6 Points per game

8.8 Rebounds per game

.405 Shooting percentage

18.3 Offensive win shares

41.7 Defensive win shares

4 All-NBA

6 All-Star appearances

8 NBA championships

WHY HEINSOHN IS NO. 44
Heinsohn deserves praise for simply remaining memorable in competing with Bill Russell, Bob Cousy, Bill Sharman, Sam Jones, and John Havlicek. He also played an integral role in the Boston dynasty as a dependable scorer, strong rebounder, and one of the league's toughest defenders. His deadly running hook shot became legendary. Heinsohn would have earned a higher ranking had nagging foot and knee injuries not ended his career at age 30.

The Celtic success was based greatly on chemistry, and Heinsohn fit perfectly. He was the leading scorer on teams with tremendous balance offensively and he helped Russell clear the boards. His numbers would have been gaudier had he not shared playing time with others on that deep roster.

ALL ABOUT HEINSOHN BEFORE BOSTON

Heinsohn spent his early youth in Jersey City, New Jersey, during the waning days of the Depression before his family moved to nearby Union City at the height of World War II in 1944. He credited his interest in sports to local basketball standout Perry Del Purgatorio, who was in the midst of his career at Villanova. Del Purgatorio took the young Heinsohn under his wing and piqued his fascination with basketball.

He was a natural. Heinsohn received a scholarship from St. Michael's, a small Catholic high school. He helped his team win the Metropolitan Catholic Championship. His talent was so pronounced that he was selected to play in an All-Star game held in Kentucky, which attracted a bevy of college scouts. Heinsohn earned a spot on an All-America team and 350 college offers. He gained more experience playing highly competitive semipro basketball. Soon he committed to Holy Cross, which boasted arguably the best basketball program in the country at that time.

Heinsohn dominated. He averaged 16 points and 11 rebounds as a mere sophomore, playing a key role on a team that won the NIT and remained ranked No. 1 or 2 all season. By the following year, he was considered a prized pro prospect. The All-American peaked as a senior, averaging 27.4 points and a whopping 21.1 rebounds per game.

It was the mid-1950s, an era in which the NBA held a territorial draft. The Celtics held his exclusive rights if they wanted him—and Red Auerbach wanted him. Heinsohn arrived in time to help Boston launch its dynasty.

IN A CELTICS UNIFORM AND BEYOND

Heinsohn was one of three Hall of Famers the Celtics drafted that year. The others were Bill Russell and K. C. Jones, all of whom eventually coached Boston. Though Cousy ran the famed fast-break, the team required strong rebounding to kick the ball out to him. Heinsohn averaged 9.8 rebounds that season to complement his 16.2 points per game in winning NBA Rookie of the Year.

He was certainly ready for the pressure of the postseason. Heinsohn saved the Celtics in Game 7 of the finals against St. Louis in perhaps the most dramatic finish in NBA history. While Cousy and Sharman struggled mightily with their shots, Heinsohn scored 37 points and added 23 rebounds. Every one of them was needed for the 125–123 double-overtime victory during which Russell fouled out while Cousy and Sharman hit a shocking 5 of 40 shots combined.

Heinsohn improved every year until his foot injury began weakening his performance and lowered his minutes in the early 1960s. He consistently averaged about 21 points and 10 rebounds as a steady contributor to annual championship teams. One of his crowning moments was achieved in the 1960 Eastern Conference finals against Wilt Chamberlain and the Philadelphia Warriors. Heinsohn quieted a raucous crowd at Convention Hall with a buzzer-beating, game-winning tip-in to clinch the series. He then led Boston in scoring during another finals defeat of the Hawks.

Though his court minutes dissipated late in his career and his knee problems worsened, Heinsohn continued to play nearly every game and remained a regular on the All-Star team. By the mid-1960s, his scoring and rebounding diminished (and being a heavy smoker didn't help).

Heinsohn retired at age 30 in 1965 but his name continued to be synonymous with Boston basketball. He spent three years doing radio broadcasts of Celtics games before coaching the Dave Cowens–era team from 1969 to 1978, winning championships in 1974 and 1976. He had by then been instrumental in forming the NBA Players Association. Heinsohn later worked on national TV games for CBS, then returned to the local broadcast booth to work Boston games from 1990 to 1999.

HIS GREATEST GAME

Heinsohn recorded some gaudy numbers in the regular season during his career, but no performance proved stronger and more important than Game 7 of the 1957 NBA final when he scored a team-best 37 points and yanked down 23 rebounds in a thrilling two-point triumph over St. Louis.

SIDE STORY

Heinsohn once pulled a prank on legendary Celtics Coach Red Auerbach. He was motivated by a fine he received from Auerbach for being late to practice after a particularly bad day that included a parking ticket, speeding ticket, and stolen wallet. Auerbach told him that he would feel better if he smoked a cigar. So he handed Heinsohn one that later exploded in his face. Heinsohn vowed revenge. He bought Auerbach legitimate cigars for weeks so he would not be suspicious. During the playoffs, Auerbach asked Heinsohn to light one for him in front of the media. He took two puffs and it exploded. "He literally chased me out of that place . . . up the stairs, on the court, everywhere," recalled Heinsohn with a laugh.[1]

WHAT HEINSOHN SAID

"You don't do things because people will like you. Because I've found out playing basketball that forty percent of the people will hate you no matter what. Forty percent of the people will love you no matter what. And twenty percent of the people will actually be influenced by what you truly do. So you've got to find something that you like to do, that you have fun doing, and then do it."[2]

WHAT WAS SAID ABOUT HEINSOHN

"Tommy symbolizes, more than any other Celtics that has come through this thing since 1950, the Celtics dynasty." —Bob Cousy[3]

CHAPTER 45

Carlton Fisk

"Pudge"

ESSENTIALS
Sport: Baseball
Born: December 26, 1947
Years Active: 1969, 1971–1993
Years with Boston: 1969, 1971–1980
Position: Catcher

KNOW THE CAREER NUMBERS
.269 Batting average
2,356 Hits
1,276 Runs
1,330 RBI
.341 On-base percentage
421 Doubles
376 Home runs
66.3 Offensive WAR
17.1 Defensive WAR
11 All-Star appearances

Why Fisk Is No. 45

Some might believe Fisk belongs higher on this list. But it must be cited that he spent more years with the White Sox than the Red Sox, lost significant playing time to injury, and managed just one 100-RBI season with Boston. He was, however, an emotional sparkplug and Hall of Famer. He also slugged the most iconic home run in Sox history.

Fisk was both a tough and intelligent backstop. He often yelled at his pitchers to motivate them. He demanded that they intimidate batters with inside fastballs. His desire to win was unmatched. Often compared to and contrasted with Yankees star catcher Thurman Munson, his production and style played a role in strengthening the burgeoning rivalry between the two teams in the 1970s.

All about Fisk before Boston

Fisk was a New Englander all the way. He was born in Vermont but considered himself a native of Charlestown, New Hampshire. His toughness and athleticism were handed down from his parents. His father toiled as a tool-and-die engineer when not working the family farm. He stayed fanatically busy, even finding the time to win local tennis matches and play competitive basketball. His mother was also a standout athlete, dominating in candlepin bowling, tennis, and softball. Fisk's siblings proved themselves in various sports as well. His parents were not demanding while grooming their children as athletes but they certainly promoted high expectations.

Carlton did not stand out among them athletically as a child. He was a bit chubby, which led to the "Pudge" nickname. And he could slug a baseball. He famously mashed a home run in his first at-bat for the Bellows Falls American Legion team in a game at legendary Doubleday Field in Cooperstown, home of the National Baseball Hall of Fame, where he would return 35 years later to be inducted.

Fisk starred in soccer and basketball at Charlestown High School. Despite his comparative lack of height at 6-foot-2, he impressed many on the court, once scoring 42 points in a tournament game. Although the cold weather annually limited the high school baseball schedule, it lasted long enough for Fisk to prove it was his best sport. He was a fine pitcher before gaining skills behind the plate.

Major league scouts took notice, though they wondered if Fisk showed the bat speed to succeed at that level. His home runs were hit to the opposite field. He needed to work on pulling the ball to maximize his power. Fisk decided to hone his talents at the University of New Hampshire.

It seemed surprising when the Sox selected him in the first round of the draft in January 1967. The gamble paid off. Fisk batted .338 with Class A Waterloo in 1968. Yet he was unhappy because the team sported a losing record. That was Fisk. While the sole motivation of other prospects was to be promoted to the next level and eventually the big leagues, the ultracompetitive Fisk valued winning above all else. Fisk played at Double-A Pittsfield the following year and batted just .243. A surprise awaited him in September.

IN A RED SOX UNIFORM AND BEYOND

That proverbial cup of coffee? Fisk tasted it in 1969 with five hitless at-bats in two games 10 days apart. It was the old "can't hit the curve" syndrome that returned him to the minors in 1970 and most of 1971. He had matured for his stint with Boston that year, batting .313. Only journeyman catcher Duane Josephson stood in his way of the starting position in 1972. An injury to Josephson in the third game paved the way for Fisk.

He took the job and ran with it. In an era with few slugging catchers, his offensive onslaught gained attention. One writer offered a comparison to an emerging Johnny Bench. He was named to the American League All-Star team. When he finished the year batting .293 with 22 home runs and .370 on-base percentage, the mystery was over. He was unanimously named Rookie of the Year.

Fisk, however, was not immune to the so-called sophomore jinx. His average plummeted during the second half of 1973. Then came the injuries that would often limit his playing time and production for much of his career. A collision at the plate with Leron Lee of the Indians in

June 1974 not only ended his season but threatened to destroy his career. Doctors warned him that he might never play again.

Others might have called it quits. Heck, baseball players didn't make big money back then anyway. Free agency had barely begun. Fisk was just too strong-willed. He focused on his recovery because he loved the competition on the field. He returned in late June 1975 on fire at the plate to help the Red Sox cruise to the division title. Fisk concluded the regular season on a 16-game hitting streak, then hit safely in three more as the Sox swept Oakland to secure a World Series matchup against the powerful Big Red Machine of Cincinnati.

That's when it happened—one of the most iconic moments in baseball history. Game 6. Fenway Park. Reds up in the series, 3–2. Bottom of the 12th inning. Score tied at 6. Pat Darcy on the mound. Fisk launches a pitch down the left-field line. It's gone if it's fair. He hops up and down on both feet toward first base, waving his arms like an air traffic controller trying to *will* the ball fair. Clank! It hits the foul pole. Home run. Boston wins. Though Fisk went hitless in Game 7 in a Cincinnati comeback victory, he would always be cherished by Red Sox Nation for that moment in time.

Fisk never played another postseason game for Boston. That would have seemed unfathomable in August 1978, a year after he had enjoyed his healthiest and most productive campaign, the only year during which he exceeded both 100 runs scored and RBI and also batted .315. Fisk could not be blamed for the epic September swoon when the Sox lost 14 of 17 to blow a seven-game first-place lead to the Yankees. He maintained his near-.300 batting average and even managed five hits in the four-game sweep by New York at Fenway immediately dubbed "The Boston Massacre."

By that time he was consistently playing through pain. It was no small feat for a catcher to spend so much time crouching behind the plate and playing the game with physical abandon. In July 1978 he broke a rib hurtling into the stands for a foul ball. He played on. He injured his elbow trying to make throws while compensating for the pain in the ribs. Fisk spent much of his final seasons in Boston as a designated hitter. Meanwhile, he roundly criticized the organization over contract disputes and a perception that it was not trying hard enough to put a championship team on the field after Butch Hobson, Rick Burleson, and Fred Lynn had been traded. He grudgingly accepted an offer in free agency from the White Sox in 1981 that paid him nearly double what the Sox proposed.

Fisk played 13 seasons in Chicago but only once played in more than 135 games as injuries continued to threaten his career. He remained productive and steadfast in his desire to keep going. Remarkably, he did not hang up his spikes until age 45.

His Greatest Game
It was Opening Day at Fenway Park in 1973 with the hated Yankees in town. In the first game of a three-game sweep, Fisk tied the game with a two-run homer in the second inning off New York ace Mel Stottlemyre, doubled in the third, and hit a grand slam in the fourth. He also managed a two-home run, seven-RBI game against Milwaukee in 1975 but, hey, this was Opening Day against the Yankees at Fenway.

Side Story
Fisk was honored for his game-winning home run in Game 6 of the 1975 World Series at a Fenway Park ceremony on June 13, 2005. The left-field foul was renamed the Fisk Foul Pole during a pregame ceremony before a game against Cincinnati, which was returning to Boston to play the Sox for the first time since that classic Fall Classic.[1]

What Fisk Said
"There's nothing better than playing in front of a crowd who loves and supports you. It's what gives you that extra motivation to go out there and give it everything you've got."

What Was Said about Fisk
"No catcher of our time looks more imperious than Carlton Fisk, and none, I think, has so impressed his style and mannerisms on our sporting consciousness: his cutoff, bib-sized chest protector above those elegant Doric legs; his ritual pause in the batter's box to inspect the label on his

upright bat before he steps in for good; the tipped back mask balanced on top of his head as he stalks to the mound to consult his pitcher; the glove held akimbo on his left hip during a pause in the game. He is six-three, with a long back, and when he comes straight up out of the chute to make a throw to second base, you sometimes have the notion that you're watching an aluminum extension ladder stretching for the house eaves." —Author and baseball historian Roger Angell[2]

CHAPTER 46

Mike Haynes

"Luxury"

ESSENTIALS
Sport: Football
Born: July 1, 1953
Years Active: 1976–1989
Years with New England: 1976–1982
Position: Cornerback

KNOW THE CAREER NUMBERS
46 Interceptions
688 Interception yards
8 Touchdowns
9 Pro Bowls
1 Super Bowl championship
2 All-Pro

WHY HAYNES IS NO. 46
Haynes intercepted 19 passes in his first three seasons but only once more than five thereafter, greatly because quarterbacks learned their lesson and refused to throw to his side of the field. He boasted all the requisite qualities for greatness at his position—speed, quickness, physicality, toughness, durability.

He blanketed receivers throughout his career, often jumping routes for picks and returning them deep into enemy territory. His athletic picks were fodder for highlight reels. He could leap high to snag passes away from receivers or dive to catch what seemed to be the uncatchable. It was no wonder he made annual trips to the Pro Bowl and landed a spot in the Pro Football Hall of Fame.

All about Haynes before New England

Haynes was born in Denison, Texas, but spent most of his youth in Los Angeles, where he displayed his impressive athleticism and starred in both football and track and field at Thomas King Middle School and John Marshall High School. He set a school long-jump record that still stood 50 years later. He was also the premier player on a winless football team. Haynes earned Athlete of the Year honors at the latter his senior year.

Despite playing both quarterback and cornerback for the Barristers neither was his favorite position. Haynes yearned to be a wide receiver when he arrived at Arizona State University. He explained that desire years later. "Like a lot of kids playing football, you want to see your name in lights and people reading about you in the papers," he said. "At wide receiver, quarterback, running back, you can get that, that can happen for you. Not a lineman . . . not at defensive back, usually. It's usually defensive backs getting beat in those news highlights, and some wide receiver is looking pretty good."[1]

Haynes continued to thrive in both sports with the Sun Devils. He won a Western Athletic Conference (WAC) championship in the long jump and earned all-league recognition in football three out of four years. He also returned two punts for touchdowns as a senior, a role he would continue to play with New England.

Coach Frank Kush always lined him up across from the opponent's top receiver without a thought of double-teaming. That allowed the free safety to help the other cornerback or blitz. Haynes emerged as a shutdown corner on one of the best defenses in college football in 1973. He gained his reputation as a ball-hawk the following season with 11 interceptions.

The Patriots needed one. They had managed just 13 picks in 1975 during a 3–11 season. They chose Haynes fifth overall in the 1976 draft. That marked the highest selection of a defensive back since Jerry Stovall was taken second by the St. Louis Cardinals in 1963. Haynes was about to play a key role in one of the most significant turnarounds in NFL history.

In a Patriots Uniform and Beyond

The additions of Haynes and fellow defensive back Tim Fox transformed the New England secondary. Haynes intercepted eight passes in 1976, ranking second in the league. He picked seven during a ridiculous four-game stretch, including three against the Jets. He twice intercepted Hall of Fame quarterback Joe Namath, who praised him for his coverage range. Haynes, who contributed to an 11–3 record and playoff berth, earned first-time All-Pro status and won Defensive Rookie of the Year.

Haynes had already blossomed into one of the most feared cornerbacks in the sport. He also established himself as one of its best punt returners. He led the AFC with 608 yards as a rookie, which included touchdown runs of 89 and 62 yards. Haynes continued to shut down wideouts and pile up picks until quarterbacks found it wiser to simply stay away from his side of the field. He intercepted 11 more passes in 1977 and 1978 combined, returning one the latter year in a blowout of the Jets 50 yards for a touchdown. During one stretch in 1977, however, not one pass was thrown in his direction.

His career with New England took a hit when he held out from the first three games in 1980 due to a contract dispute. He returned in time to earn all-league honors and play in his fifth consecutive Pro Bowl. He continued to feud with the front office over a contract. Haynes sat out the first 11 games in 1983 before playing out his option and forcing a trade to the Los Angeles Raiders, who had to pay a heavy price. The Patriots received a first and second-round pick for him. Haynes, who never won a playoff game with New England, helped the Raiders win the 1984 Super Bowl. He even intercepted a pass in the title-game blowout of Washington.

HIS GREATEST GAME

Haynes became the third Patriot to intercept three passes in a game and first since 1962 when he achieved it his rookie year on November 21, 1976. It was the first time a New England player picked three since the franchise joined the NFL. Two of those interceptions were off passes by legendary New York quarterback Joe Namath.

SIDE STORY

NFL Network ranked the Top 100 NFL players of all time in 2010. Haynes placed 49th. The only Patriots players ranked higher were Tom Brady and John Hannah.

WHAT HAYNES SAID

"(Playing defense) You're always either bad or great. There are no in-betweens. I wish the public was more educated about defenses but they're not. . . . I've had some of my best games when I've completely shut out a guy and it goes unnoticed."[2]

WHAT WAS SAID ABOUT HAYNES

"When I was coaching at North Carolina State, we played against Haynes at Arizona State, I went up to him in the pre-game warmups that day and told him he was the best collegiate defensive back I'd ever seen. It was the first time I ever did something like that. I also told him he wasn't going to see much of the ball because we were throwing away from him. As it turned out, the only time he touched the ball all game was when he returned a kickoff 97 yards for a touchdown." —New York Jets head coach Lou Holtz[3]

CHAPTER 47

Drew Bledsoe

"The Statue"

ESSENTIALS
Sport: Football
Born: February 14, 1972
Years Active: 1993–2006
Years with New England: 1993–2001
Position: Quarterback

KNOW THE CAREER NUMBERS
44,611 Yards passing
251 Passing touchdowns
206 Interceptions
1 Super Bowl championship
4 Pro Bowl selections

WHY BLEDSOE IS NO. 47
Some claim that Steve Grogan was the second-best quarterback in Patriots history behind Tom Brady and he was certainly more athletic and mobile. After all, Bledsoe's "Statue" nickname was a jab at his lack of mobility in the pocket.

Bledsoe was more effective during his stint with New England before famously losing his job to Brady due to injury. He was among the most prolific quarterbacks in the NFL early in his career, even leading the league in completions and yards in 1994. He also threw the most interceptions that year but cut down dramatically on his picks as his career progressed. He would have been ranked higher on this list had he not thrown so many interceptions in the playoffs and Super Bowl.

Bledsoe played a key role in dragging the Patriots out of the abyss. The team sported a record of 14–50 in its five seasons before his arrival. After compiling a 5–11 in his rookie year, the Patriots reached the play-offs in three of the next four and even reached the 1997 Super Bowl.

ALL ABOUT BLEDSOE BEFORE NEW ENGLAND

Bledsoe was born in Ellensburg, Washington. His family moved five times before finally settling in Walla Walla. Both his parents were schoolteachers. His father was also an assistant football coach. He encouraged his son to play football but focused early on refining his talents as a receiver rather than a quarterback.

That did not last long. By eighth grade Drew was thriving at the position in which he would blossom into stardom. Though he also excelled in basketball and track as a discus and javelin thrower, he garnered the most attention in football. He was heavily recruited but chose Washington State, which was only two hours from his home. Cougars coach Jim Price called him the greatest recruit ever signed by that school.

His arm strength, quick release, and ability to read defenses led to a starting job toward the end of his freshman year. He finished that season with 1,386 yards passing and nine touchdowns. Bledsoe continued to improve. He won PAC-10 Offensive Player of the Year honors as a junior after throwing for 3,246 yards and 20 scores. He did toss 15 interceptions. That would remain a problem in his professional career. That did not scare NFL teams away.

It did, however, lead Bledsoe to believe he might require a senior season of seasoning. He was enjoying his time at WSU, yet he finally decided to forgo his last year and make himself eligible for the draft. The lowly Patriots snagged him first overall in 1993. Just as he did at the college level, he wasted no time establishing himself as a starter in New England.

IN A PATRIOTS UNIFORM AND BEYOND

When your four quarterbacks starting games one year are Hugh Millen, Scott Zolak, Tom Hodson, and Jeff Carlson, you're going to need a new starter. New England had finished 2–14 in 1992. Though many rookie quarterbacks—even those drafted No. 1—must wait and learn before being handed the reins, Bledsoe gained that distinction immediately.

He struggled early but improved with time and experience. He overcame a distinct lack of receiving talent in 1993 aside from tight end Ben Coates. He completed fewer than half his passes but still managed to guide the Patriots to a 5–7 record before losing the last four games to a knee injury.

Many expected a step forward in 1994. Few expected him to lead his team to the playoffs. But Bledsoe blossomed. He overcame a spate of interceptions, developing a reputation as a gunslinger on a team with a weak running attack, finding Coates time and again for first downs and winning his last seven games. He paced the NFL with 4,555 passing yards to earn the first of three Pro Bowl berths with New England. His three picks against Cleveland in the playoffs doomed the team, but it remained an encouraging year.

Bledsoe and the Patriots digressed in 1995 but he rebounded the next two seasons to reach his peak, earning Pro Bowl spots in both. A brilliant New England defense and running back Curtis Martin played the most significant roles in the 1996 Super Bowl run—Bledsoe threw just one touchdown pass and three picks in the two playoff games combined. Then he tossed four more interceptions in the Super Bowl loss to Green Bay. Zero scoring strikes and two picks against Pittsburgh dashed his 1997 playoff hopes.

Despite his postseason struggles, he performed well enough to keep his starting job. He remained one of the more effective quarterbacks in the NFL. In 2001 the Patriots took a flyer in the sixth round of the draft on a University of Michigan prospect named Tom Brady. When Bledsoe was blasted in the chest on a clean hit by Jets linebacker Mo Lewis in Game 2 that season and sustained an injury that according to some could have killed him, he was replaced by Brady (though Bledsoe was allowed to remain in the game for one more series, a decision that Patriots coach Bill Belichick reportedly regretted).

The unwritten rule that nobody should lose his job to injury? Forget it, exclaimed Belichick. It was all about the team, and when Brady began displaying the talent that made him arguably the greatest of all time and lead New England to a Super Bowl championship, it was over for Bledsoe as a Patriot.

Yet, it was not over for Bledsoe. Traded to Buffalo he recovered in 2002 to earn his fourth Pro Bowl berth. He played out his career mostly as a starter for the Bills and Cowboys.

HIS GREATEST GAME

It was November 13, 1994, and the Patriots appeared doomed. They owned a 3–6 record. They were down 20–0 to the tough Vikings at Foxboro Stadium. Then Bledsoe went to work. A 31-yard touchdown pass to Ray Crittenden closed the gap to 20–10. He tossed a five-yard scoring strike to Leroy Thompson to make it 20–17. He engineered a drive that resulted in a game-tying field goal. He won it in overtime with a 14-yard touchdown to Kevin Turner. It was perhaps the most important performance of his career. The victory was the first in seven straight that launched New England into the playoffs. In the process he set NFL records with 45 completions and 70 attempts.

SIDE STORY

Bledsoe went into the wine-making business after retiring from football. He cofounded the Doubleback Winery. The vineyards used to grow the grapes for his wines were located around Walla Walla, Washington. His wines placed among the Top 100 in 2010 by lifestyle magazine *Wine Spectator*.

WHAT BLEDSOE SAID

"That was a bitter pill to swallow. I thought I was entitled to get my job back, and it turns out I wasn't, and it doesn't work that way. I did some soul-searching and decided that the only proper way to handle it was to go back to work and be the best teammate I could."[1]

WHAT WAS SAID ABOUT BLEDSOE

"Drew Bledsoe played such an integral role in our efforts to rebuild the Patriots. He gave fans hope for the future." —Patriots owner Robert Kraft[2]

CHAPTER 48

Nomar Garciaparra

"No-Nonsense Nomar"

Shortstop Nomar Garciaparra in a game against the Detroit Tigers in 2017.
Wikimedia Commons, John Gudorf Photography

ESSENTIALS
Sport: Baseball

Born: December 26, 1947

Years Active: 1969, 1971–1993

Years with Boston: 1969, 1971–1980

Position: Shortstop

KNOW THE CAREER NUMBERS
.269 Batting average

2,356 Hits

1,276 Runs

1,330 RBI

.341 On-base percentage

421 Doubles

376 Home runs

66.3 Offensive WAR

17.1 Defensive WAR

11 All-Star appearances

2 Batting titles

WHY GARCIAPARRA IS NO. 48
That debate raged for eight years comparing Garciaparra to Derek Jeter explains all one needs to know about the justification of his inclusion among the top 50 athletes in Boston history. The hitter who reminded Ted Williams of Joe DiMaggio would have ranked far higher had a devastating split wrist tendon not destroyed what appeared inevitably to be a Hall of Fame career.

Few contemporaries matched his combination of average and power. He twice led the American League in hitting yet averaged more than 80 extra-base hits and twice managed more walks than strikeouts. Garciaparra scored and drove in more than 100 runs in four of his seven full seasons. It was no wonder he finished among the top 11 in MVP voting six times during that stretch.

All about Garciaparra before Boston

Born Anthony Nomar Garciaparra, he preferred his middle name, which is "Ramon" (his father's first name) spelled backward. His dad encouraged his versatility on the diamond, teaching him to play every position. He also rewarded every hit with a quarter and levied a fine of 50 cents for every strikeout.

Born in Mexico, Garciaparra eventually attended St. John Bosco High School in Bellflower, California, where he starred in soccer and football. But his near-.500 batting average as a senior punched his ticket to a baseball career.

Though he was chosen in the fifth round of the 1991 draft by Milwaukee and was recruited by nearby UCLA, he chose instead to attend Georgia Tech, which also featured future Red Sox teammate Jason Varitek and had emerged as a national power. Garciaparra blossomed into one of the premier players in college baseball, compiling an outlandish .427 average and .585 on-base percentage with 16 home runs and 73 RBI in just 274 at-bats as a junior. He earned the distinction as just one of two at that level to reach double figures in doubles, triples, and home runs.

Garciaparra had by that time earned a spot on the 1992 US Olympic team as a walk-on. Yellow Jackets coach Danny Hall ranked him as the best defensive shortstop he'd seen with that program before comparing him to future Hall of Famer Barry Larkin, who was then starring with the Cincinnati Reds.

The Red Sox jumped on him when he remained available with the 12th overall pick in the 1994 draft. Varitek went two selections later to Seattle but would soon join Garciaparra in Boston. None of the first 11 choices would approach Garciaparra's achievements on the field. He wasted little time tearing through the system. By 1996 he was destroying Triple-A pitching and forcing the Sox to promote him.

In a Red Sox Uniform and Beyond

The Sox thought enough of Garciaparra to move strong-hitting shortstop John Valentin to second or third base to make room for the rookie. After getting a taste of major league pitching, Garciaparra proved himself as one of the team's best hitters in 1997. He hit safely in 17 of 18 games into early May, slumped briefly, then slowly raised his average back over .300 and kept it there the rest of the season. His 30-game hitting streak in July and August fell four short of the franchise record set in 1949 by Dom DiMaggio.

His cozy new home had both positive and negative effects on his line-drive stroke. He slammed 26 of his 44 doubles at Fenway. But he hit 19 of his 30 home runs on the road. The Green Monster giveth because of its short distance from home plate and the Green Monster taketh away due to its height. Garciaparra led the AL that year in hits and triples. It all added up to a unanimous Rookie of the Year vote.

Sophomore slump? Not for Garciaparra. He cemented a growing reputation as one of the best pure hitters with power in baseball in 1998. He hit with remarkable consistency, maintaining an average between .316 to .328 from late June through the rest of the season, then hitting a grand slam in Game 1 of the ALDS against Cleveland and finishing that otherwise dismal series as the most effective Boston hitter, amazingly driving in 11 of his team's 19 runs. Only a 157-RBI year from Texas slugger Juan Gonzalez prevented Garciaparra from winning AL MVP.

He just kept mashing, winning successive batting titles the next two seasons. Garciaparra even flirted with .400 in 2000, hitting that magical plateau on July 14 last achieved over a full year by Ted Williams in 1941. His .372 average was the best since George Brett hit .390 in 1980 and had not been exceeded since through 2023. So fearful were major league pitchers of Garciaparra that he also paced the AL with 20 intentional walks.

He appeared destined for the Hall of Fame, even after losing nearly the entire 2001 season to the wrist injury that would eventually ruin his chance at Cooperstown. Despite rebounding to hit well in 2002 and 2003, the clouds of discontent had gathered. The vastly underpaid Garciaparra began openly complaining about contract negotiations with the Red Sox and how he was being portrayed by the media. His September and playoff slump in 2003, along with his rejection of a four-year, $60 million offer and impending free agency, placed the writing on the wall. He had grown bitter. Garciaparra was not long for Boston.

Ironically and sadly, he was shipped to the Cubs on July 31 during the curse-breaking season of 2004. The wrist injury sent his career spiraling. He managed just two more relatively healthy seasons, batting .303 with the Dodgers in 2006. But he had lost some of his power and was forced to retire after concluding his career with Oakland in 2009. He later worked as an analyst on Dodgers television broadcasts.

HIS GREATEST GAME
Garciaparra was on one of his many tears at the plate when he arrived at Fenway for a game against Seattle on May 10, 1999. He was in the midst of a 16-game hitting streak. This was ridiculous as he bashed a grand slam to the visitor's bullpen in the first inning, cranked a two-run homer that wrapped about the Pesky Pole in the third, and then capped it off with a second grand slam over the Green Monster in the eighth, after which he emerged from the dugout to wave his cap at the cheering crowd that had demanded a curtain call.

SIDE STORY
Garciaparra married superstar soccer player Mia Hamm in 2003. Twin daughters followed four years later and a son in 2012. The couple met at a promotional event in Boston in 1998 during which Hamm defeated Garciaparra in a soccer shootout. They were divorced in 2021.

WHAT GARCIAPARRA SAID
"People are going to make comparisons and they can do that but I'm definitely not going to compare myself to Derek Jeter."[1]

WHAT WAS SAID ABOUT GARCIAPARRA
"He's very unorthodox, the way he throws the ball, kind of side-armed. But he has all the tools—the power, the hands, deceptive speed.

I'm impressed with his overall game, the way he improved, the hard work. . . . When I met him at the All-Star game the thing that really jumped out is that he is a very nice guy, with respect for the game. You can tell he appreciates being here. And that's refreshing." —Yankees third-base coach Willie Randolph[2]

CHAPTER 49

Cecil Thompson
"Tiny"

ESSENTIALS
Sport: Hockey
Born: May 31, 1903
Died: February 9, 1981
Years Active: 1928–1940
Years with Boston: 1928–1939
Position: Goaltender

KNOW THE CAREER NUMBERS
1.99 Goals against average
252–153 Win–loss record
74 Shutouts
4 Vezina Trophies
4 All-Star appearances

WHY THOMPSON IS NO. 49
By modern goalie standards, Tiny was definitely tiny. He was 5-foot-9, 160 pounds, and was among the larger goalies of his era. He earned his nickname for being the tallest player in a midget league team photo. He certainly played big. He allowed the fewest goals per game in four

seasons and led the NHL in wins five times. It was no wonder he earned four Vezina Trophies as the league's top goaltender in four of nine years from 1930 to 1938.

Thompson was an innovator. He helped establish the practice of catching the puck to make saves and was also adept at using his stick to prevent goals. He is considered the first puck-handling goaltender. Thompson showed the ability to pass pucks to teammates in advantageous positions. He was even the first goaltender ever to record an assist (during the 1935–36 season). Some consider Bruins successor and perennial All-Star Frank Brimsek a superior goaltender, but Thompson allowed a half-goal fewer per game and doubled his number of Vezina Trophies.

ALL ABOUT THOMPSON BEFORE BOSTON

Thompson was born in Sandon, British Columbia, but spent his formative years in Calgary. He played catcher on the baseball diamond with neighborhood kids and became a goaltender so that he could join in on the rink. His experience blocking pitches at the plate served him well as he honed his skills in the crease.

The boy became passionate about goaltending. He studied the positioning and movements of local standout Charlie Reid, who played for the Calgary Tigers team that battled Montreal in the 1924 Stanley Cup. Thompson gained enough skill to earn a spot with the junior hockey Calgary Monarchs and compete in the prestigious Memorial Cup with that team at age 16.

He continued to evolve at the position. Thompson competed for teams in Alberta before joining the Duluth Hornets of the American Hockey Association, pitching 11 shutouts in 45 games before landing with the Minneapolis Millers of the same league for three years. He allowed a mere 1.37 goals in 118 games with 33 shutouts. He was ready for the big time. Thompson had gained such a remarkable reputation that Bruins coach and GM Art Ross bought his rights from Minneapolis despite never having seen him play.

IN A BRUINS UNIFORM AND BEYOND

Thompson wasted no time justifying Ross's faith. He blanked Pittsburgh in the 1928 season opener and started every game that year, allowing no more than three goals in any of them. He then turned away shot after shot in the playoffs. His sterling 0.6 goals against average against the Rangers and Canadiens brought Boston its first Stanley Cup crown. That certainly impressed his brother Paul, who was playing for Montreal (and became the first NHL player ever to score a goal on his brother on December 21, 1937). Thompson surrendered just 1.15 goals per game that year, which remains the second-lowest in league history.

He was just getting started. Thompson won his first of four Vezina Trophies in 1930 by again leading the league by yielding 2.19 goals per game—rules changes created to boost scoring prevented him from matching his statistics of the previous season. But he became stingier as time marched on. He posted an under two goals against average in four of the next eight years, pacing the NHL three more times during that stretch and earning four All-Star nods.

Thompson developed a rivalry with Canadiens counterpart George Hainsworth, who captured three consecutive Vezina Trophies before he arrived on the scene and began to hog them. Hainsworth outdueled Thompson in the 1930 finals and went on to win two more. Both goaltenders reached the Hall of Fame.

In an era when goaltenders were expected to play every game, Thompson did not let his team down. He started all 48 each year aside from when he missed five during the 1931–32 season. He remained on top of his game until the Bruins traded him to Detroit in November 1938. Thompson finished his Boston career with 252 wins, a record that stood until broken by Tuukka Rask in 2019.

HIS GREATEST GAME

Granted, it was a defeat. Thompson blanked Toronto in the last game of the 1933 playoffs through regulation and *five overtimes*. Neither team had scored. Bruins coach Art Ross and Maple Leafs counterpart Conn

Smythe asked NHL President Frank Calder to halt the proceedings but were turned down. Boston star Eddie Shore then lost the puck to Ken Doraty, who raced toward Thompson on a breakaway and scored in the sixth overtime to doom the Bruins. It is still considered his finest performance.

SIDE STORY

Thompson was known to swear quite a bit. Junior hockey player Guilford Brett, whom he scouted in 1945, recalled Thompson screaming at him for considering post-secondary education rather than forging a hockey career immediately. "I'm used to bad language," Brett said. "It wasn't uncommon for me to hear vulgarity. But [Thompson] was unbelievable. He said, 'What do you mean you want to go to school? Get out of here! I don't want to talk to you if you don't want to play hockey and get your teeth knocked out.' . . . That was Tiny Thompson. That was the character he was."[1]

WHAT THOMPSON SAID

"Just about everyone I played against in those days was bigger than me so they nicknamed me 'Tiny,' although I wasn't crazy about it. I guess alongside them, I looked tiny."[2]

WHAT WAS SAID ABOUT THOMPSON

"He's a guy who I always thought didn't get the credit he deserved. He was a really good goalie." —Hockey historian Bob Duff[3]

CHAPTER 50

Robert Grove

"Lefty"

Robert Moses "Lefty" Grove. Jefferson R. Burdick Collection,
Metropolitan Museum of Art. Donated to the public domain

ESSENTIALS
Sport: Baseball

Born: March 6, 1900

Died: May 22, 1975

Years Active: 1925–1941

Years with Boston: 1934–1941

Position: Starting pitcher

KNOW THE CAREER NUMBERS
300–141 Win–loss record

3.06 ERA

2,266 Strikeouts

8.8 Hits per nine innings pitched

1.278 WHIP

9 ERA titles

113.3 WAR

6 All-Star appearances

2 World Series championships

WHY GROVE IS NO. 50
The man with the uninspiring, unimaginative nickname "Lefty" certainly would have been ranked far higher had he not played the majority of his career for the Philadelphia Athletics. He was limited to eight seasons with Boston, the last two after he had hit 40 and had decidedly faded. He remained arguably the best pitcher in the sport the previous five years, leading the American League in ERA four times despite having lost the overpowering stuff that resulted in seven consecutive strikeout titles with the A's.

Baseball had changed by the time he arrived with the Sox. The dead-ball era was long gone. Hitters were riding on Babe Ruth's coat-tails and blasting far more home runs. Batting averages of .350 and better had become common. Grove remained just as effective as he had been in Philadelphia into his late 30s. Nearly 100 years later—and given Sandy Koufax's comparatively short peak—Grove is still arguably the finest left-hander in baseball history. Modern analytics agree. He paced every pitcher in WAR eight times, including three with Boston. His .680 career winning percentage is the best among 300-game winners. He helped the Sox finally emerge from the dark ages—the worst era in franchise history.

ALL ABOUT GROVE BEFORE BOSTON

Grove was born at the turn of the 20th century in the mining town of Lonaconing, Maryland. But he had no intention of becoming a miner. While his father and older brothers toiled in the mines, he quit after two weeks. He worked instead in various jobs such as spinning spools to make silk thread, glass blowing, and railroad worker laying rails and driving spikes.

Like many boys in struggling communities in his era he required a bit of ingenuity to play baseball. He placed cork stoppers in wool socks and wrapped them in back tape and hit them with a picket fence. His enabler became general store owner Dick Stakem, who invited the 17-year-old Grove to play in games played on a local field resting between a forest and train tracks. He never pitched until age 19. In his first game he struck out 15 batters in just seven innings. Soon thereafter he fanned 18 in a no-hitter.

His talent piqued the interest of Bill Louden, who managed the Martinsburg, West Virginia, team in the Class C Blue Ridge League. He was offered $125 a month, far more than Grove's father and siblings earned. He traversed through the mountains on a train and reached his destination to launch his professional career. He performed well enough to impress Double-A Baltimore Orioles owner Jack Dunn, who had gained notoriety several years earlier for selling Babe Ruth to the Red Sox. He bought Grove from the Martinsburg team for about $3,000.

Soon he blossomed into a consistent winner and strikeout machine. He compiled a 108-36 record and 1,108 strikeouts over five minor league seasons and eventually overcame his wildness. He pitched with a cockiness that remained with him throughout his career. He even exclaimed to Ruth before a series of exhibitions "I'm not afraid of you" and proceeded to fan him nine times in 11 at-bats.[1]

The asking price skyrocketed. The Dodgers and Cubs both bid Dunn $100,000 for Grove. But Dunn had an ace in the hole—old buddy Connie Mack. The A's owner and manager offered $600 more—higher than the amount the Yankees paid for Ruth—so off he went to Philadelphia.

At first, the sale backfired. Grove continued to strike out batters—he even led the AL with 116 as a rookie. But he walked batters at a record rate. "Catching him was like catching bullets from a rifleman with bad aim," offered Hall of Fame catcher Mickey Cochrane years later. Grove worked on his control in the offseason and returned with it. He led the league in ERA and strikeouts the following year while limiting his walks significantly.

He was on his way. Grove never again walked more than 83 in a season. He won at least 20 games seven consecutive years, peaking by winning 28 games and saving nine more in 1930 and posting an incredible 31–4 record and career-best 2.06 ERA in 1931 to earn AL MVP honors. He was the first pitcher since Walter Johnson to earn that award.

Grove was the ace of a staff that helped Philadelphia rise above Ruth and the Yankees to dominate the American League. He was used as both a starter and reliever in World Series triumphs in 1929 and 1930 and in a Fall Classic defeat in 1931. He allowed just three earned runs in 25 1/3 innings in the two championship runs. He beat St. Louis twice in both 1930 and 1931.

His days in the World Series spotlight were soon over. The Great Depression had become quite depressing for Mack, who needed the money when attendance dropped precipitously in the early 1930s. In 1934 he sold Grove to Boston, which was trying to rebuild.

IN A RED SOX UNIFORM AND BEYOND
Whispers that Grove was on the decline that began when he occasionally struggled down the stretch in 1933 grew louder when a sore arm resulted in a terrible first season in Boston. His ERA doubled to 6.50 as

the fingers of blame pointed at him for the failure of the team to live up to expectations.

Grove was forced to change his approach. He could no longer blow batters away with his fastball so he focused on his curve and throwing quality strikes. He realized that he had been throwing his curveball too fast, which did not allow enough time for it to break. There was not enough velocity difference to fool hitters. His metamorphosis gave his career a new life at age 35. He won 20 games in 1935 and the first of four ERA titles with the Red Sox.

His problem in Boston was not performance. It was his disrespect for manager Joe Cronin. Grove often disagreed with strategy and how he was handled. He had not only played a role in attendance that more than doubled after he arrived in Boston but also much stronger teams. His Red Sox finished second in both 1938 and 1939 greatly because he was a winner. Grove not only led the league in ERA again in both years but managed a 29–8 record combined.

He had nearly achieved it all as he hit 40. His last task was to reach 300 career victories, and he did that quietly in the midst of one of the most exciting seasons in baseball history as Williams was in the process of batting .406 and Joe DiMaggio had broken the all-time record by hitting safely in 56 consecutive games. Grove finally won his 300th in an albeit shaky complete game 10–6 defeat of Cleveland on July 25. He pitched horribly through August, then announced his retirement four months later. It was not big news. The Japanese attack on Pearl Harbor had overshadowed everything else. He spent some of his retirement back in Lonaconing coaching kids.

HIS GREATEST GAME

Grove was one of many Hall of Fame pitchers who never threw a no-hitter but he led the league with six shutouts in 1936. Among them was an Opening Day two-hitter against the Yankees. Both were Lou Gehrig singles in an 8–0 Boston victory.

SIDE STORY

Legendary Athletics manager Connie Mack had a big influence on Grove both personally and professionally. His advice to the southpaw to move some of his savings out of the bank helped Grove survive the 1929 stock market crash. He spent $5,700 to build Lefty's Place in his hometown of Lonaconing. The establishment featured three bowling alleys, a pool table, and a counter filled with goodies such as cigars, candy, and soda.

WHAT GROVE SAID

"I always loved the game. I loved the smell of the grass, the crack of the bat, the roar of the crowd. It was like magic to me."[2]

WHAT WAS SAID ABOUT GROVE

"When planes take off from a ship, they say they catapult. That's what his fastball did halfway to the plate. He threw just plain fastballs—he didn't need anything else." —Yankees shortstop Frank Crosetti[3]

Honorable Mentions

Baseball

Wally Berger (OF)

Mookie Betts (OF)

Rafael Devers (3B)

Fred Lynn (OF)

Johnny Pesky (SS)

Rico Petrocelli (SS, 3B)

Manny Ramirez (OF)

Babe Ruth (SP, OF)

Chris Sale (SP)

Warren Spahn (SP)

Luis Tiant (SP)

"Smoky" Joe Wood (SP)

Basketball

Ray Allen (SG)

Jaylen Brown (SF)

Kevin Garnett (PF)

Dennis Johnson (PG, SG)

Ed Macauley (C)

Cedric Maxwell (SF)

Rajon Rondo (PG)

FOOTBALL

Bruce Armstrong (OT)

Tedy Bruschi (LB)

Ben Coates (TE)

Sam Cunningham (FB)

Julian Edelman (WR)

Steve Grogan (QB)

Logan Mankins (OG)

Stanley Morgan (WR)

Vince Wilfork (DT)

HOCKEY

Frank Brimsek (G)

Wayne Cashman (LW)

Zdeno Chara (D)

Dit Clapper (RW, D)

Bill Cowley (C)

Woody Dumart (LW)

Rick Middleton (RW)

Brad Park (D)

David Pastrnak (RW)

Tuukka Rask (G)

Best from Boston (35-mile radius)

1. Rocky Marciano (Boxing)
Born in Brockton
Marciano is rarely ranked the greatest heavyweight of all time but, hey, you can't do any better than undefeated with 43 knockouts in 49 fights. Marciano was no Muhammad Ali in elusiveness but he could brawl with the best of them, even beating the great Joe Louis along the way. He used his strength and endurance to wear down opponents and set them up for the killer blow.

2. Patrick Ewing (Basketball)
Born in Cambridge
Granted, Ewing starred for the rival Knicks but his consistent offensive production and defensive stinginess earned that team its last trip to the NBA Finals (through 2023) and himself a place in the Hall of Fame. Ewing finished among the top 5 in MVP voting five times. He averaged at least 20 points per game 11 years in a row and double-figure rebounds nine consecutive seasons. He ended his career with a fine .504 shooting percentage.

3. Tom Glavine (Baseball)
Born in Billerica
One of the finest left-handers in baseball history, Glavine anchored along with Greg Maddux and John Smoltz the incredible rotation that

routinely won division titles and a World Series championship in 1995. A five-time 20-game winner, he concluded his career with 305 victories and two Cy Young awards. He was also voted onto 10 National League All-Star teams.

4. PIE TRAYNOR (BASEBALL)
Born in Framingham

Traynor never displayed anything close to Ruthian power in the post-dead ball era but his consistent production made him a sure-fire Hall of Famer. He recorded seven plus-100 RBI seasons and a career .320 batting average as a Pittsburgh Pirates star throughout the 1920s. He used his speed as one of the premier triple hitters of his generation, reaching double figures in that category in 10 of 11 seasons during his prime and leading the league with 19 in 1923.

5. HOWIE LONG (FOOTBALL)
Born in Somerville

One of the most feared pass-rushing defensive ends in NFL history, Long earned eight Pro Bowl selections and led the Raiders to a Super Bowl championship in 1983. Long registered 35 sacks over three years from 1983 to 1985 and was a first-team All-Pro in the last two of those seasons. He was named to the 1980s All-Decade Team and landed in the Pro Football Hall of Fame.

6. JOHNNY KELLEY (TRACK AND FIELD)
Born in Medford

Kelley remains one of the premier marathon runners of all time. He was voted "Runner of the Century" by *Runner's World* in 1999. He won the Boston Marathon in 1935 and 1945 but finished second seven times and completed the event an incredible 58 times, often placing in the top 10. Kelley was honored as the first road runner in the National Track and Field Hall of Fame, even participating with three US Olympic teams.

7. MICKEY COCHRANE (BASEBALL)
Born in Bridgewater

One of the finest all-around catchers ever won two American League MVP awards, one with the dominant Philadelphia Athletics teams managed by Connie Mack in the late 1920s and early 1930s, then in his first season with Detroit in 1934. He was such a feared hitter—he batted over .300 in nine of his 13 seasons—that he twice drew over 100 walks a season and concluded his amazing career with a .419 on-base percentage.

8. ALY RAISMAN (GYMNASTICS)
Born in Needham

One of the greatest American gymnasts ever on one of the greatest teams in Olympic history, Raisman was the best of the best in the 2012 Summer Games in London. She won individual gold in the floor exercise after winning the same event at the World Championships in Tokyo the previous year. She took silver in the floor exercise and the all-around in the 2016 Olympics.

9. TENLEY ALBRIGHT (FIGURE SKATING)
Born in Newton

This amazing, trailblazing woman became a surgeon after dominating on the ice. She won gold at the 1956 Winter Olympics four years after taking silver. In between she took the 1953 and 1955 World Championship and North American Championship. She eventually earned a spot in the National Women's Hall of Fame.

10. BILL LAIMBEER (BASKETBALL)
Born in Boston

One of the most physical and feared players in the sport, he was among the faces of the bruising Detroit teams in the 1980s. Laimbeer helped the Pistons win two NBA championships with his consistent scoring, rebounding, and defense. He was always available. Laimbeer played in nearly every game for a decade despite the bumps and bruises associated with his rough style on the court. He earned three All-Star nods during his 15-year career.

11. TONY CONIGLIARO (BASEBALL)
Born in Revere

Conigliaro had it all. He was talented, handsome, and the ultimate hometown hero. He seemed destined for the Hall of Fame after his promotion to the Red Sox in 1964 at age 19 and leading the American League in home runs the following season. But his career and life took a violent and tragic turn when he was struck in the eye by a Jack Hamilton fastball in 1967. He recovered enough to post big numbers in 1969 and 1970, but deteriorating eyesight severely shortened his career and a heart attack killed him at age 45.

12. JEREMY ROENICK (HOCKEY)
Born in Boston

Roenick was among the most prolific American-borns in NHL history. He averaged more than 100 points over a four-season period with Chicago in the early 1990s and continued to light the lamp or help a teammate do it after moving to Phoenix and playing for the Coyotes at the end of the decade.

13. JOHN L. SULLIVAN (BOXING)
Born in Boston

One of the first stars of his sport bridged the bare-knuckles and gloved eras. He was the last recognized heavyweight champion of the former and the first of the latter. Sullivan lost just one of his 44 fights and finished his storied career with 34 knockouts.

14. KELLY AMONTE HILLER (LACROSSE)
Born in Hingham

Hiller was among the greatest women's lacrosse players ever. She twice earned Player of the Year honors in the early 1990s at the University of Maryland and helped that team win successive NCAA crowns. She played for the US National Team for nearly a decade before landing a coaching job at Northwestern and guiding that team to seven national championships.

15. Keith Tkachuk (Hockey)

Born in Melrose

Tkachuk was a power forward who played with power. He bullied his way to become the fifth-leading American-born scorer in NHL history during a career that spanned from 1991 to 2010. The two-time All-Star played with four different teams, mostly with Winnipeg, Phoenix, and St. Louis. He was the first American to lead the league in goals scored in 1997 with 52 and tallied more than 70 points in seven different seasons.

NOTES

CHAPTER 1: BILL RUSSELL

1. Divij Kulkarni, "Wilt Chamberlain once explained why Bill Russell is the GOAT center over him," Fadeaway World, September 16, 2023, https://fadeawayworld.net/wilt-chamberlain-explained-bill-russell-goat-center.

2. *New York Times*, "Among pro athletes, Bill Russell was a pioneering activist," July 31, 2022, https://www.nytimes.com/2022/07/31/sports/basketball/bill-russell-activism.html.

3. AZ quotes, Bill Russell, https://www.azquotes.com/quote/644541.

4. Kurt Helin, "Others in praise of Bill Russell," NBC Sports, February 16, 2011, https://www.nbcsports.com/nba/news/others-in-praise-of-bill-russell.

CHAPTER 2: TOM BRADY

1. Chris Bengel, "Tom Brady explains why he still gets 'fired up' over NFL draft scouting report from 2000," CBS Sports, March 1, 2021, https://www.cbssports.com/nfl/news/tom-brady-explains-why-he-still-gets-fired-up-over-nfl-draft-scouting-report-from-2000/#:~:text=Brady%20tweeted%20that%20the%20infamous,more%20than%20two%20decades%20later.&text=The%20scouting%20report%20reads%20as,and%20gets%20knocked%20down%20easily.%22.

2. Associated Press, "Brady leads biggest comeback, Patriots win 34–28 in OT," https://www.espn.com/nfl/recap/_/gameId/400927752.

3. Brainy Quote, https://www.brainyquote.com/quotes/tom_brady_179849.

4. https://www.nfl.com/news/sidelines/taking-on-tom-brady-nfl-defenders-coaches-share-what-it-s-like-to-face-the-g-o-a

CHAPTER 3: BOBBY ORR

1. Jack Olsen, "Sportsman of the Year: Bobby Orr," *Sports Illustrated*, December 21, 1970, https://vault.si.com/vault/1970/12/21/sportsman-of-the-year-bobby-orr.

2. Bobby Orr Hall of Fame, https://bobbyorrhalloffame.com/inductee/bobby-orr/.

3. Brainy Quote, https://www.brainyquote.com/quotes/bobby_orr_586312.

4. Olsen, "Sportsman of the Year: Bobby Orr."

CHAPTER 4: TED WILLIAMS

1. Josh Jackson, "Williams, Padres, give San Diego thrill in 30s," MLB.com, March 13, 2017. https://www.milb.com/milb/news/boston-red-sox-legend-ted-williams-was-a-rookie-with-hometown-san-diego-padres-in-pacific-coast-league/c-215058460.

2. JFK Presidential Library and Museum, "The immortal life of Ted Williams," December 8, 2013, https://www.jfklibrary.org/events-and-awards/forums/past-forums/transcripts/the-immortal-life-of-ted-williams.

3. Bill Pennington, "Ted Williams' .406 is more than a number," *New York Times*, September 17, 2011, https://www.nytimes.com/2011/09/18/sports/baseball/ted-williamss-406-average-is-more-than-a-number.html.

4. Brainy Quote, https://www.brainyquote.com/quotes/ted_williams_140000.

CHAPTER 5: LARRY BIRD

1. Jayson Jenks, "You wouldn't believe what he said: The greatest trash talker ever, Larry Bird," *The Athletic*, April 29, 2020, https://www.nytimes.com/athletic/1725703/2020/04/09/you-wouldnt-believe-what-he-said-the-greatest-trash-talker-ever-larry-bird/.

2. Ibid.

3. Joe Kozlowski, "Larry Bird reveals that a piece of his legendary trash talk was a 'joke'," *Newsweek*, February 21, 2024, https://www.newsweek.com/larry-bird-reveals-legendary-three-point-contest-trash-talk-was-joke-1871672.

CHAPTER 6: RAY BOURQUE

1. Frank Lidz, "Bulwark of the Bruins," *Sports Illustrated*, March 9, 1987, https://vault.si.com/vault/1987/03/09/bulwark-of-the-bruins-bostons-ray-bourque-might-resemble-linus-at-home-but-on-the-ice-he-could-be-the-best-defenseman-in-the-nhl.

2. Ibid.

3. Ibid.

CHAPTER 7: CARL YASTRZEMSKI

1. Walter Bingham, "'In left field for Boston.'" *Sports Illustrated*, April 3, 1961, https://vault.si.com/vault/1961/04/03/in-left-field-for-boston.

2. SABR, Carl Yastrzemski bio, https://sabr.org/bioproj/person/Carl-Yastrzemski/.

3. David Schoenfield, "'Ball Four' still an American classic," ESPN, December 4, 2013, https://www.espn.com/blog/sweetspot/post/_/id/42739/ball-four-still-an-american-classic.

4. AZ Quotes, Carl Yastrzemski, https://www.azquotes.com/author/16036-Carl_Yastrzemski.

5. Bob Carter, "Yaz lifted Sox," ESPN Classic, https://www.espn.com/classic/biography/s/Yastrzemski_Carl.html.

CHAPTER 8: BOB COUSY

1. Julian Eschenbach, "'Am I supposed to win or please the local yokels?' Red Auerbach on his decision to overlook Bob Cousy in the 1950 draft," Basketball Network, November 12, 2023, https://www.basketballnetwork.net/old-school/red-auerbach-on-his-decision-to-overlook-local-favorite-bob-cousy-in-1950-draft.

2. NBA.com, Legend profile: Bob Cousy, https://www.nba.com/news/history-nba-legend-bob-cousy.

3. Ibid.

4. AZ Quotes, Bob Cousy, https://www.azquotes.com/author/23272-Bob_Cousy.

5. Herbert Warren Wind, "Visitors from far away," *Sports Illustrated*, January 9, 1956, https://vault.si.com/vault/1956/01/09/bob-cousy-basketballs-creative-genius.

CHAPTER 9: JOHN HANNAH

1. Paul Zimmerman, "John Hannah doesn't fiddle around," *Sports Illustrated*, August 3, 1981, https://vault.si.com/vault/1981/08/03/john-hannah-doesnt-fiddle-around-at-least-not-on-the-football-field-where-says-the-author-his-brains-brawn-and-speed-have-made-him-the-top-offensive-lineman-in-nfl-history.

2. Ibid.

3. Ibid.

4. Mark Inabinett, "The 'biggest lesson' John Hannah learned from Bear Bryant," Alabama.com, July 18, 2021, https://www.al.com/sports/2021/07/the-biggest-lesson-that-john-hannah-learned-from-bear-bryant.html.

5. Paul Zimmerman, "John Hannah doesn't fiddle around," *Sports Illustrated*, August 3, 1981, https://vault.si.com/vault/1981/08/03/john-hannah-doesnt-fiddle-around-at-least-not-on-the-football-field-where-says-the-author-his-brains-brawn-and-speed-have-made-him-the-top-offensive-lineman-in-nfl-history.

CHAPTER 10: JOHN HAVLICEK

1. Harvey Araton, "John Havlicek, a dynamo of two eras of Celtics glory, dies at 79," *New York Times*, April 25, 2019, https://www.nytimes.com/2019/04/25/sports/basketball/john-havlicek-dead-boston-celtics-hall-of-famer.html#:~:text=In%20an%20interview%2C%20Ryan%2C%20Havlicek's,historical%20measure%20when%20compared%20to.

2. Ibid.

3. Brainy Quote, John Havlicek, https://www.brainyquote.com/quotes/john_havlicek_1214076.

4. John Underwood, "The green running machine," *Sports Illustrated*, October 28, 1974, https://vault.si.com/vault/1974/10/28/the-green-running-machine.

Chapter 11: Phil Esposito

1. Jack Olsen, "Oh brother! A pair to watch," *Sports Illustrated*, March 29, 1971, https://vault.si.com/vault/1971/03/29/oh-brother-a-pair-to-watch.

2. Ibid.

Chapter 12: David Ortiz

1. ESPBN.com, "What makes David Ortiz a Hall of Famer? Stories from those who know him best," July 24, 2022, https://www.espn.com/mlb/story/_/id /33138746/what-makes-david-ortiz-hall-famer-stories-know-best.

2. Chris Greenberg, "Red Sox ceremony: Boston honors victims, police; David Ortiz says, 'This is our f-ing city,'" *Huffington Post*, April 20, 2013, https://www .huffpost.com/entry/red-sox-ceremony-david-ortiz-boston_n_3123316.

3. Piet Levy, Lainey Seyler, JR Radcliffe, and Kendra Meinert, "26 famous fans of the Green Bay Packers, from Harry Styles to Simone Biles to Lil Wayne," *Milwaukee Journal Sentinel*, September 13, 2018, http://www.jsonline.com/story /entertainment/2018/09/13/green-bay-packers-17-biggest-celebrity-fans-justin -timberlake-lil-wayne-ellen-degeneres-harry-styles/1259418002/.

Chapter 13: Paul Pierce

1. Paulpierce.net, http://www.paulpierce.net/biography/.

2. Virgil Villanueva, "Al Harrington on his iconic trash talk exchange with Paul Pierce," Basketball Network, October 26, 2023, https://www.basketballnetwork.net /old-school/al-harrington-on-his-iconic-trash-talk-exchange-with-paul-pierce.

3. Brainy Quote, Paul Pierce, https://www.brainyquote.com/quotes/paul_pierce _861503.

4. S. L. Price, "The truth revealed," *Sports Illustrated*, December 8, 2008, https:// vault.si.com/vault/2008/12/08/the-truth-revealed.

Chapter 14: Bobby Doerr

1. Cynthia J. Wilber, *For the Love of the Game* (New York: William Morrow, 1992), 117.

2. Steve Buckley, "The Silent Captain Still," *Boston Herald*, May 22, 2005.

3. Brad Horn, "Bobby Doerr reflects on a life in baseball," Baseball Hall of Fame, https://baseballhall.org/discover-more/stories/baseball-history/the-captain-speaks.

4. IMDB Quotes, Bobby Doerr, https://m.imdb.com/name/nm1208352 /quotes/.

5. Richard Goldstein, "Bobby Doerr, 99, Red Sox Hall of Fame second baseman, is dead," *New York Times*, November 14, 2017, https://www.nytimes.com/2017/11 /14/obituaries/bobby-doerr-dead-red-sox.html.

CHAPTER 15: ANDRE TIPPETT

1. Mentor Motivation, "Zero to hero: The extraordinary life of pro football's karate master Andre Tippett," MAIA, January 4, 2019, https://www.maiahub.com /blog/zero-to-hero-the-extraordinary-life-of-pro-football-s-karate-master-andre -tippett.

2. Molly Parr, "Four questions with Andre Tippett, former Patriots linebacker," *Jewish Boston*, July 16, 2012, https://www.jewishboston.com/read/four-questions -with-andre-tippett-former-patriots-linebacker/.

3. Josh Weir, "Andre Tippett: One of NFL's most feared linebackers," *State Journal-Register*, July 30, 2008, https://www.sj-r.com/story/news/2008/07/30/andre -tippett-one-nfl-s/46801267007/.

4. Pro Football Hall of Fame: Notes and quotes, Andre Tippett, https://www .profootballhof.com/news/2005/01/news-andre-tippett-notes-and-quotes/.

CHAPTER 16: PATRICE BERGERON

1. Ryan Dixon, "But wait, there's more," Sportsnet, https://www.sportsnet.ca /hockey/nhl/big-read-bruins-star-bergeron-still-underappreciated/.

2. Steve Hopkins, "Boston Bruins 4th annual Pucks and Paddles raises %150,000," Table Tennis for You, March 8, 2023, https://butterflyonline.com /boston-bruins-4th-annual-pucks-and-paddles-raises-150000/.

3. Ryan Dixon, "But wait, there's more," Sportsnet, https://www.sportsnet.ca /hockey/nhl/big-read-bruins-star-bergeron-still-underappreciated/.

CHAPTER 17: PEDRO MARTINEZ

1. Mike Lupica, "'Peak Pedro' most dominant in '99? Try history," MLB.com, April 30, 2020, https://www.mlb.com/news/pedro-martinez-most-dominant -pitcher-at-peak.

CHAPTER 18: KEVIN MCHALE

1. Mike Thomas, "How good was Kevin McHale? Charles Barkley weighed in on the Boston Celtics legend: I'd rather face Larry Bird," SportsCasting, May 30, 2022, https://www.sportscasting.com/how-good-was-kevin-mchale-charles-barkley -weighed-in-on-the-boston-celtics-star-id-rather-face-larry-bird/.

2. Decide.com, Today in TV history, https://decider.com/2016/11/07/today-in -tv-history-cheers-kevin-mchale/.

3. https://www.nba.com/news/history-nba-legend-kevin-mchale.

4. Mike Thomas, "How good was Kevin McHale? Charles Barkley weighed in on the Boston Celtics legend: I'd rather face Larry Bird," SportsCasting, May 30, 2022, https://www.sportscasting.com/how-good-was-kevin-mchale-charles-barkley-weighed-in-on-the-boston-celtics-star-id-rather-face-larry-bird/.

CHAPTER 19: WADE BOGGS

1. American Masters, Wade Boggs, https://www.pbs.org/wnet/americanmasters/archive/interview/wade-boggs/.

2. Marc Topkin, "Appreciating Wade," *Tampa Bay Times*, January 5, 2005, https://www.tampabay.com/archive/2005/01/05/appreciating-wade/.

CHAPTER 20: EDDIE SHORE

1. Canadian history EHX, Eddie Shore, https://canadaehx.com/2020/12/27/eddie-shore/.

2. Stan Fischler, "If it was staggering, it had to be Eddie," *Sports Illustrated*, March 13, 1967, https://vault.si.com/vault/1967/03/13/if-it-was-staggering-it-had-to-be-eddie#:~:text=Between%201926%20and%201942%20Shore,other%20man%20in%20the%20game.

3. Ibid.

CHAPTER 21: CY YOUNG

1. *Detroit Tribune*, quoted in "Cy Young's Life Is Simple Story," *Pittsburgh Weekly Gazette*, December 27, 1904, p. 7.

2. Baseball Almanac quotes, https://www.baseball-almanac.com/quotes/quoyung.shtml.

3. Bill Nowlin and David Southwick, "Cy Young," SABR, https://sabr.org/bioproj/person/Cy-Young/.

CHAPTER 22: ROBERT PARISH

1. Justin Quinn, "Celtics legend Robert Parish on why he preferred playing for Boston over Bulls," Yahoo.com, December 7, 2023, https://sports.yahoo.com/celtics-legend-robert-parish-why-110037996.html.

2. Greg Keraghosian, "The blockbuster Warriors draft deal that created a dynasty—for the other team," SFGate, November 12, 2020, https://www.sfgate.com/warriors/article/joe-barry-carroll-draft-Warriors-celtics-trade-15723442.php.

3. Brainy Quote, Robert Parish, https://www.brainyquote.com/quotes/robert_parish_1097759.

4. NBA.com, "NBA legend Robert Parish," https://www.N.com/news/history-nba-legend-robert-parish.

CHAPTER 23: JIM RICE

1. Boston Baseball History, "New! Jim Rice looks back on his Hall of Fame career," https://bostonbaseballhistory.com/new-jim-rice-looks-back-on-his-hall-of -fame-career/.

2. NESN, "Transcript: Jim Rice's Hall of Fame induction speech," https://nesn .com/2009/07/transcript-jim-rices-hall-of-fame-induction-speech/.

3. Boston Baseball History, "New! Jim Rice looks back on his Hall of Fame career," https://bostonbaseballhistory.com/new-jim-rice-looks-back-on-his-hall-of -fame-career/

CHAPTER 24: ROB GRONKOWSKI

1. Michael Rosenberg, "What makes Gronk as great as he is? Even he doesn't know the answer," *Sports Illustrated*, January 28, 2015, https://www.si.com/nfl/2015 /01/29/super-bowl-xlix-rob-gronkowski-patriots-seahawks.

2. Jenna West, "Tampa Zoo names baby rhino after Rob Gronkowski," SI.com, October 24, 2020, https://www.si.com/nfl/2020/10/24/tampa-zoo-names-baby -rhino-after-rob-gronkowski.

3. Michael Rosenberg, "What makes Gronk as great as he is? Even he doesn't know the answer," *Sports Illustrated*, January 28, 2015, https://www.si.com/nfl/2015 /01/29/super-bowl-xlix-rob-gronkowski-patriots-seahawks.

CHAPTER 25: JOHNNY BUCYK

1. Stu Hackel, "Johnny Bucyk: 100 Greatest NHL players," NHL.com, January 1, 2017, https://www.nhl.com/news/johnny-bucyk-100-greatest-nhl-hockey-players -284246332.

2. Ibid.

3. Ibid.

CHAPTER 26: DAVE COWENS

1. Amino Apps, Dave Cowens, https://aminoapps.com/c/basketz/page/item/ dave-cowens/D86z_8PKTNIxwrq7VjJ8YqeGj6lrWXZxMzz.

2. NBA.com, "Legends profile: Dave Cowens," https://www.nba.com/news/ history-nba-legend-dave-cowens.

CHAPTER 27: JAYSON TATUM

1. Oliver Fox, "The quiet, overwhelming greatness of Jayson Tatum," Celtics Blog, February 17, 2024, https://www.celticsblog.com/2024/2/17/24074355/the -quiet-overwhelming-greatness-of-jayson-tatum.

2. Shane Garry Acedera, "Paul Pierce says Jayson Tatum is the best American player," Basketball Network, November 22, 2023, https://www.basketballnetwork .net/latest-news/paul-pierce-says-jayson-tatum-is-the-best-american-player.

CHAPTER 28: DWIGHT EVANS

1. Boston Baseball History, "Dwight 'Dewey' Evans remembers 1975," https:// bostonbaseballhistory.com/new-dwight-dewey-evans-remembers-1975-2/#:~:text =What%20message%20does%20Dwight%20Evans,are%20great%2C%E2%80%9D %20he%20replies.

2. Howard, "Does he belong in the Hall of Fame: Dwight Evans," Baseball Past and Present, https://baseballpastandpresent.com/mlb/belong-hall-fame-dwight -evans/.

CHAPTER 29: TY LAW

1. Dennis Waszak, "Law was guided by dreams," *Amarillo Globe-News*, August 1, 2019, https://www.amarillo.com/story/sports/nfl/2019/08/01/law-was-guided-by -dreams/4558491007/.

2. Ibid.

3. Ibid.

4. Ibid.

CHAPTER 30: CAM NEELY

1. Michael Blinn, "For Cam Neely. Comics Come Home event is more than a fundraiser," SI.com, September 21, 2017, https://www.si.com/nhl/2017/09/21/cam -neely-comics-come-home-dennis-leary-lenny-clarke.

2. CBS Boston, "Neely: 'It was difficult to leave the way I did.'" June 16, 2010, https://www.cbsnews.com/boston/news/neely-it-was-difficult-to-leave-the-way-i -did/.

CHAPTER 31: SAM JONES

1. Boston Celtics history, "The purest shooter," https://bostoncelticshistory.com /item/the-purist-shooter/?postId=3595.

2. Michael D. McClellan, "Mr. Clutch: The Sam Jones interview," *Celtic Nation*, October 11, 2007, https://www.celtic-nation.com/interviews/sam_jones/sam_jones _page4.htm.

3. NBA.com, "NBA legend Sam Jones," https://www.nba.com/news/history -nba-legend-sam-jones.

4. Matt Schudel, "Sam Jones, Hall of Fame shooting star of Boston Celtics dynasty, dies at 88," *Washington Post*, January 1, 2022, https://www.washingtonpost .com/obituaries/2022/01/01/boston-celtics-sam-jones-dies/.

CHAPTER 32: RICHARD SEYMOUR

1. Bernd Buchmasser, "Why Patriots legend Richard Seymour was selected to the Pro Football Hall of Fame," SB Nation, February 11, 2022, https://www.patspulpit.com/2022/2/11/22928789/why-patriots-richard-seymour-was-selected-to-pro-football-hall-of-fame.

2. Steve Doerschuk, "Tom Brady was Bill Belichick's best player: Was Richard Seymour Belichick's best defender?" *Canton Repository*, August 3, 2022, https://www.cantonrep.com/story/sports/pro/pro-football-hof/2022/08/03/richard-seymour-pro-football-hall-fame-class-2022-patriots-super-bowl-champions-bill-belichick/7662590001/.

3. John Breech, "Former Patriots star goes out on brutal hand in 2023 World Series of Poker after outlasting 9,700 other players," CBS Sports, July 13, 2023, https://www.cbssports.com/nfl/news/former-patriots-star-goes-out-on-brutal-hand-in-2023-world-series-of-poker-after-outlasting-9700-players/amp/.

4. Josh Weir, "'Overwhelmed . . . with humility.' Selfless star Richard Seymour deflects Hall of Fame moment," *Canton Repository*, August 6, 2022, https://www.cantonrep.com/story/sports/pro/pro-football-hof/2022/08/06/pro-football-hall-of-fame-enshrinement-richard-seymour-speech-new-england-patriots-raiders/65393651007/.

5. Bernd Buchmasser, "Patriots owner Robert Kraft: 'I couldn't be happier' for Richard Seymour making the Pro Football Hall of Fame," SB Nation, February 11, 2022, https://www.patspulpit.com/2022/2/11/22928783/patriots-owner-robert-kraft-reacts-richard-seymour-selected-pro-football-hall-of-fame.

CHAPTER 33: BILL SHARMAN

1. Dan Pattison, "Where are they now? Bill Sharman," *Deseret News*, April 8, 2001, https://www.deseret.com/2001/4/8/19579703/where-are-they-now-bill-sharman/.

2. AZ Quotes, Bill Sharman, https://www.azquotes.com/quote/912226.

3. David Wharton and Jerry Crowe, "Bill Sharman dies at 87: Basketball legend and former Lakes coach," *Los Angeles Times*, October 25, 2013, https://www.latimes.com/local/obituaries/la-me-bill-sharman-20131026-story.html.

CHAPTER 34: MILT SCHMIDT

1. Ken Campbell, "Milt Schmidt was a gentleman off the ice, relentless on it," *The Hockey News*, January 4, 2017, https://thehockeynews.com/news/milt-schmidt-was-a-gentleman-off-the-ice-relentless-on-it.

2. Associated Press, "Milt Schmidt, who was NHL's oldest living player, dies at 98," Syracuse.com, January 5, 2017, https://www.syracuse.com/sports/2017/01/milt_schmidt_who_was_nhls_oldest_living_player_passes_at_age_98.html.

3. NHL.com, "Milt Schmidt: 100 greatest NHL players, https://www.nhl.com /news/milt-schmidt-100-greatest-nhl-hockey-players-284175404.

CHAPTER 35: JIMMIE FOXX
1. Sudlersville Museum, "Jimmie Foxx statue," https://www.sudlersvillemuseum .org/foxx-statue.html.
2. Jimmie Foxx quotes, http://www.cmgww.com/baseball/foxx/quotes/index.htm.

CHAPTER 36: WES WELKER
1. Wayback Machine, "Cherokee Nation supports new Jack Brown Center, honors citizens," https://web.archive.org/web/20160831125014/http://www.cherokee .org/News/Stories/33323.aspx.

CHAPTER 37: ROGER CLEMENS
1. Devin Gordon, "The amazin' true story of Piazza, Clemens and the broken bat," SI.com, March 5, 2021, https://www.si.com/mlb/2021/03/05/piazza-clemens -and-the-broken-bat-daily-cover.
2. Brainy Quote, Roger Clemens, https://www.brainyquote.com/quotes/roger _clemens_480932.
3. Evan Grossman, "Rays heap praise on Clemens," *New York Post*, June 19, 2003, https://nypost.com/2003/06/19/rays-heap-praise-on-clemens/.

CHAPTER 38: JOSEPH WHITE
1. Bryan Marquard, "JoJo White, 71, former Celtics star," *Boston Globe*, January 17, 2018, https://c.o0bg.com/metro/2018/01/17/white-former-celtics-all-star-dies /24a544PhQxu8ZgM32eKdEO/story.html.
2. Celtic Nation blog, JoJo White interview, https://www.celtic-nation.com/blog /2018/12/22/the-jo-jo-white-interview/.
3. From Way Downtown, "On the bounce with JoJo White, 1975," May 14, 2023, https://from-way-downtown.com/2023/05/14/on-the-bounce-with-jo-jo-white-1975/.
4. Ibid.

CHAPTER 39: DUSTIN PEDROIA
1. John Perrotto, "Injury cost Dustin Pedroia any shot at Hall of Fame," Forbes .com, February 2, 2021, https://www.forbes.com/sites/johnperrotto/2021/02/01 /injury-cost-dustin-pedroia-any-shot-at-hall-of-fame/?sh=30bef066619d.
2. NESN, "'Laser show' leads list of top 10 Dustin Pedroia quotes," July 21, 2010, https://nesn.com/2010/07/laser-show-leads-list-of-top-10-dustin-pedroia -quotes/#:~:text=It%20might%20have%20cost%20him,to%20be%20a%20miniature %20badass.%E2%80%9D

3. Joon Lee, "Boston Red Sox's Dustin Pedroia announces retirement from MLB," ESPN, February 1, 2021, https://www.espn.com/mlb/story/_/id/30816259 /boston-red-sox-dustin-pedroia-announces-retirement-mlb.

Chapter 40: Gino Cappelletti

1. Sam Westmoreland, "Ron Santo and the 50 most beloved announcers in sports history," *Bleacher Report*, December 3, 2010, https://bleacherreport.com/articles /533564-ron-santo-and-the-50-most-beloved-announcers-in-sports-history.

2. WBZ News, "Patriots pioneer Gino Cappelletti on 'romance with football.'" January 23, 2018, https://www.cbsnews.com/boston/news/gino-cappelletti-patriots -super-bowl-minnesota/.

3. Edwin Shrake, "Boston Patriots," *Sports Illustrated*, September 13, 1965, https://vault.si.com/vault/1965/09/13/boston-patriots.

Chapter 41: Tris Speaker

1. Bookey.app, "30 best Tris Speaker quotes with images," https://www.bookey .app/quote-author/tris-speaker.

2. Don Jensen, "Tris Speaker," SABR, https://sabr.org/bioproj/person/Tris -Speaker/.

Chapter 42: Brad Marchand

1. Michael Farber, "The little ball of hate," *Sports Illustrated*, February 20, 2012. https://vault.si.com/vault/2012/02/20/the-little-ball-of-hate/.

2. Kevin Koczwara, "Brad Marchand was ready for the captain's C," *GQ Sports*, November 27, 2023, https://www.gq.com/story/brad-marchand-interview.

3. Willy Palov, "Wayne Gretzky heaps praise on Brad Marchand: 'His leadership is untouched,'" *PNI Atlantic News*, April 30, 2024, https://www.saltwire.com /atlantic-canada/sports/wayne-gretzky-heaps-praise-on-brad-marchand-his-leadership-is-untouched-100961079/#:~:text=%22So%20to%20me%2C %20that's%20the,the%20butt%20to%20play%20against.

Chapter 43: Charles Nichols

1. John Thorn, "Kid Nichols, in his own words," Our Game, July 10, 2012, https://ourgame.mlblogs.com/kid-nichols-in-his-own-words-c06896ab5f71.

2. Ibid.

Chapter 44: Tom Heinsohn

1. Celtics Nation, "The Tom Heinsohn interview," https://www.celtic-nation .com/blog/2018/10/23/the-tom-heinsohn-interview/.

2. Ibid.

3. Chris Forsberg, "Tommy Heinsohn 'symbolizes' the great Celtics dynasty," NBC Sports Boston, November 12, 2020, https://www.nbcsportsboston.com /nba/boston-celtics/cousy-tommy-heinsohn-symbolizes-the-great-celtics-dynasty /165930/.

CHAPTER 45: CARLTON FISK

1. *Associated Press*, "Left-field foul pole in Fenway officially renamed 'Fisk pole,'" June 14, 2005, https://www.spokesman.com/stories/2005/jun/14/left-field-foul -pole-in-fenway-officially-renamed/.

2. Roger Angell, *Season Ticket* (Boston: Houghton Mifflin Company, 1988), 40.

CHAPTER 46: MIKE HAYNES

1. Steve Buckley, "NFL 100: Mike Haynes wanted to be a receiver. He turned into one of the greatest cornerbacks ever," *The Athletic*, July 19, 2021, https://the-athletic.com/2707613/2021/07/19/nfl-100-at-no-79-mike-haynes-wanted-to-be -receiver-he-turned-into-one-of-greatest-cornerbacks-ever/.

2. Pro Football Hall of Fame. Mike Haynes, https://www.profootballhof.com /players/mike-haynes/.

3. Joe Horrigan, "Mike Haynes: Hall of Fame defender," Pro Football Researchers, 1997, https://profootballresearchers.org/archives/Website_Files/Coffin_Corner/19 -02-690.pdf.

CHAPTER 47: DREW BLEDSOE

1. Devon Clements, "Drew Bledsoe says it took 'quite a while' for him to wear Super Bowl 36 ring," SI.com, February 11, 2020, https://www.si.com/nfl/patriots /news/bledsoe-took-while-to-wear-36-ring.

2. Jeff Howe, "Patriots notebook: Drew Bledsoe honored to be named honorary captain," *Boston Herald*, January 20, 2018, https://www.bostonherald.com/2018/01 /20/patriots-notebook-drew-bledsoe-happy-to-be-named-honorary-captain/.

CHAPTER 48: NOMAR GARCIAPARRA

1. Brainy Quote, Nomar Garciaparra, https://www.brainyquote.com/quotes /nomar_garciaparra_427278.

2. Claire Smith, "Baseball; Garciaparra is named top rookie in landslide," *New York Times*, November 4, 1997, https://www.nytimes.com/1997/11/04/sports /baseball-garciaparra-is-named-top-rookie-in-landslide.html.

CHAPTER 49: CECIL THOMPSON

1. Greg Nesteroff, "Tiny Thompson and Sandon," *The Kutne Reader*, March 5, 2021, https://www.kutnereader.com/post/tiny-thompson-and-sandon.

2. Ibid.

3. Ken Campbell, "Top 100 goalies: No. 21—Tiny Thompson," *The Hockey News*, November 9, 2018, https://thehockeynews.com/all-access/top-100-goalies -no-21-tiny-thompson.

CHAPTER 50: ROBERT GROVE

1. Jim Kaplan, "Lefty Grove," SABR, https://sabr.org/bioproj/person/Lefty -Grove/.

2. Bookey.app. Lefty Grove quote, https://www.bookey.app/quote-author/lefty -grove.

3. Ibid.